KT-407-441

Cardiff Libraries
www.cardiff.gov.uk/libraries

Llyfrgelloedd Caerdydd
www.caerdydd.gov.uk/llyfrgelloedd

CAERDYDD

ACC. No: 05098264

ULTIMATE TRAVELIST

THE 500 BEST PLACES ON THE PLANET... RANKED

Introduction

We've all got a list of places that we want to see for ourselves: places friends have enthused about after a holiday, places we've read about, dreamed about. This is our list. It's the 500 most thrilling, memorable, downright interesting places on this planet – and what's more we've ranked them in order of their brilliance. These are the places that we think you should experience; there are sights that will humble you, amaze you and surprise you. They'll provoke thoughts, emotions or just an urgent need to tell someone about them.

So, how did we do it? The longlist was compiled from every highlight in every Lonely Planet guidebook. Every attraction and sight that had caught our authors' attention over the years was included. This list of thousands of places was whittled down until we had a shortlist. Then we asked everybody in the Lonely Planet community to vote on their 20 top sights. With a bit of mathematical alchemy, which weighted results in favour of sights that had consistently high votes, rather than lots of low votes, we ended up with a score for each entry in our top 500 places to see. It was very close throughout, with the exception of our leading sight, which, with a score of 10,162, was in a class of its own.

Each entry gives a taste of what makes that place worthy of a spot in this book, and the See It! section is a starting point for planning a trip – you can turn to our guidebooks and lonelyplanet.com for more detailed directions on how to visit every attraction in the top 500.

This is Lonely Planet's Ultimate Travelist.
We hope that it will inspire many more travel wishlists of your own.

01—99 Contents

page

10	Temples of Angkor
14	Great Barrier Reef
17	Machu Picchu
18	Great Wall of China
18	Taj Mahal
21	Grand Canyon National Park
22	Colosseum
23	Iguazú Falls
24	Alhambra
27	Aya Sofya
28	Fez Medina
28	Twelve Apostles
31	Petra
32	Tikal
34	British Museum
35	Sagrada Familia
36	Fiordland National Park
38	Santorini
39	Galapagos Islands
41	Museum of Old and New Art
42	Yosemite National Park
43	Dubrovnik Old City Walls
44	Salar de Uyuni
47	Bagan
48	Pyramids of Giza
48	Piazza San Marco
48	Victoria Falls
48	Acropolis
50	Chateau De Versailles
51	Djemaa El-Fna
53	Hanoi Old Quarter
54	Cradle Mountain
55	Uluru

page

56	Charles Bridge
58	Abel Tasman National Park
59	Lake District National Park
60	The Louvre
60	Torres del Paine
61	Lake Baikal
61	Eiffel Tower
62	Pompeii
63	Habana Vieja
64	Table Mountain
64	Prague's Old Town Square
65	Serengeti National Park
66	Hermitage
67	Bay of Kotor
68	Jaisalmer
70	Ngorongoro Crater
70	Hiroshima Peace Memorial Park
71	Pantheon
71	Tate Modern
72	Naqsh-e Jahan
73	Tiger Leaping Gorge
73	Notre Dame
74	Kakadu National Park
74	Sydney Opera House
74	Edinburgh Castle
74	Anne Frank Huis
76	Jökulsárlón
77	Yellowstone National Park
78	Stonehenge
78	Berlin Wall
79	Isle of Skye
80	Halong Bay
82	Duomo Santa Maria di Fiore

page

83	Cappadocia
83	Ko Tao
84	Palenque
86	Ilulissat Kangerlua
88	Mt Sinai
88	Pão de Açúcar
89	Mezquita
90	Lalibela
91	Arashiyama's Bamboo Grove
91	Lake Bled
92	Redwood National Park
93	Chichén Itzá
93	Masai Mara National Reserve
94	Metropolitan Museum of Art
95	Franz Josef & Fox Glacier
95	Valley of the Kings
96	Hoi An Old Town
97	Monument Valley
97	St Peter's Basilica
98	Dome of the Rock
98	Red Square
99	Forbidden City
99	The Uffizi
99	Everest Base Camp
100	Shwedagon Paya
101	Pyramids of Teotihuacán
101	Blue Lagoon
101	Lake Wanaka
102	Abu Simbel
102	Cimetière Du Père Lachaise
103	Big Sur
103	Matterhorn
104	Gamla Stan

100–199

page

107	Okavango Delta
108	Golden Gate Bridge
108	Dashashwamedh Ghat
109	Giant's Causeway
109	Auschwitz-Birkenau
110	Parque Nacional Corcovado
110	Niagara Falls
111	Potala Palace
112	Bora Bora
112	Empire State Building
113	Budapest's Thermal Baths
114	Topkapi Palace
114	Tallinn Old Town
114	Stari Most
115	Ayuthaya
116	Vatican Museums
116	Anakena Beach
116	The Peak
117	St Paul's Cathedral
117	Meteora
118	Confucius Temple
118	Copper Canyon
118	Cerro Fitz Roy
118	Aiguille du Midi
120	Bryggen
121	Stewart Island
122	Durbar Square
122	Bazaruto Archipelago
122	Prinsengracht Canal
122	Plitvice Lakes National Park
124	Bay of Islands
125	The Pantanal
125	Daibutsu (Great Buddha) of Nara
126	National Museum of Anthropology

page

127	Skara Brae
128	Geirangerfjord
128	Tayrona National Park
129	Choquequirao
129	Ephesus
130	Kruger National Park
131	Tulum
131	Tsukiji Market
132	Sintra
133	Carcassonne Walled City
134	Statue of Liberty & Ellis Island
134	Vatnajökull National Park
135	Blue Mosque
136	Gion District
136	Grand Buddha, Lèshān
136	ATM Cave
137	Haida Gwaii
137	Bairro of Ribeira
138	Kōya-san
138	Mt Etna
138	Eiger
139	Walt Disney World
139	Chernobyl
140	Shibuya Crossing
140	Valle de Viñales
141	Schloss Neuschwanstein
142	Terracotta Warriors
143	Shackleton's Hut
143	Icehotel
144	Moraine Lake
144	Roman Baths
145	Chobe National Park
145	Inle Lake

page

145	Mt Kinabalu
146	Phong Nha-Ke Bang National Park
146	Royal Mile
146	Cristo Redentor
146	National Mall
148	Prague Castle
148	Ghana's Slave Forts
148	Brussels' Grand Place
149	Kinkaku-ji
150	Gullfoss
151	Rocky Mountain National Park
151	Egyptian Museum
151	Gorges du Verdon
152	Amber Fort
152	Snowdonia
153	Volcanoes National Park
154	Xochimilco
154	Glencoe
154	Mont Blanc
155	Karnak
155	Gardens by the Bay
155	iSimangaliso Wetland Park
156	York Minster
156	Van Gogh Museum
156	Sigiriya Rock
157	Meenakshi Amman Temple
158	Tbilisi Old Town
158	Changdeokgung Palace
158	The DMZ
159	Bodhnath Stupa
159	Rynek Główny
159	Mògāo Caves
159	Wat Phou

200–299

page

162	Island of Gorée
162	Mont St-Michel
163	Blue Mountains National Park
164	Mozambique Island
164	Erg Chebbi Dunes
165	Historic Centre of San Gimignano
166	Vasamuseet
166	Portmeirion
166	Times Square
167	Bacuit Archipelago
168	Robben Island
168	Borgarfjörður Eystri & Seyðisfjörður
168	Sossusvlei
169	Wieliczka Salt Mine
169	Parque Nacional Nahuel Huapi
169	Jellyfish Lake
170	Vigelandsparken
170	Summer Palace
171	Old Québec City
171	Canterbury Cathedral
171	Carthage
172	Reichstag
173	Virupaksha Temple
174	Malecón
174	Brú na Bóinne
174	Museo del Prado
175	Lago de Atitlán
175	Gunung Leuser National Park
175	Alcatraz
176	Piazza del Campo
177	Postojna Cave
177	Rila Monastery
177	The Bund
178	Rijksmuseum

page

179	Pont du Gard
179	Real Alcázar
179	Singapore Zoo
180	Wadi Rum
180	Luxor Temple
181	Natural History Museum
181	Old Delhi
181	Cinque Terre
183	Borobudur
184	Bosque Nuboso Monteverde
184	Parque Nacional Manuel Antonio
185	Milan's Duomo
185	Burj Khalifa
185	Djenné Mosque
186	Naoshima
186	Tajik National Park
186	Silfra
186	Bwindi Impenetrable National Park
187	La Citadelle la Ferrière
187	Gallipoli Cemeteries
188	Davit Gareja
188	Rhodes Old Town
188	Church of the Holy Sepulchre
189	Registan
190	Itsukushima-Jinja gate
190	Lincoln Memorial
191	Château de Chenonceau
191	South Luangwa National Park
192	Valle de la Luna
192	National September 11 Museum & Memorial
193	Glaciar Perito Moreno
193	Ningaloo Marine Park
193	Lóngjï Rice Terraces

page

194	Mt McKinley
194	Athabasca Glacier
194	Timgad Ruins
195	Selous Game Reserve
195	Volcán Arenal
195	Asa Wright Nature Centre
196	Parque Nacional de los Picos de Europa
198	Angel Falls
199	Yakushima
199	Whakarewarewa
199	Memento Park
200	Death Valley National Park
202	Ko Phi-Phi
202	Waitomo Caves
203	Eden Project
203	Kizhi Pogost
204	Mt Kailash
205	Rainbow Reef
206	Te Papa Tongarewa
206	Ross Ice Shelf
207	Ras al-Jinz
207	Anse Vata
207	Kilwa Kisiwani
208	Socotra Island
208	Old Dhaka
208	Underwater Sculpture Park
209	Pulau Sipadan
209	St Davids Cathedral
210	Dead Sea
210	Mt Kilimanjaro
211	Cologne Cathedral
211	Drakensburg Amphitheatre
211	Parque Nacional Cotopaxi

300–399

page		page		page	
214	Chatuchak Weekend Market	230	Jokhang Temple	245	Glover's Reef
214	Parque Nacional Tortuguero	230	Kigali Memorial Centre	245	Meeting of the Waters
215	Parc National d'Andringitra	231	Lisbon's Alfama	246	Baalbek
215	Capri	232	Museo Del Oro	247	Museu Picasso
216	Bamburgh Castle	232	MuseumsQuartier	247	Mosteiro Dos Jerónimos
216	Lake Geneva	233	798 Art District	247	Tintern Abbey
216	Cu Chi Tunnels	233	D-Day Beaches	248	Tōshō-gū Shrine
217	Art Institute of Chicago	233	Białowieża Forest	248	Pamukkale
218	Gros Piton	234	N Seoul Tower	248	Diocletian's Palace
219	Louisana Museum of Modern Art	234	Lake Manasarovar	249	Ruta de las Flores
219	Lower Zambezi National Park	234	Grossglockner Road	249	Cliffs of Moher
220	Temppeliaukio Kirkko	235	Pelourinho	249	Isla del Sol
220	Petronas Towers	235	Glacier Skywalk	250	Jesuit missions of Trinidad
221	Calakmul	235	Casino de Monte Carlo		and Jesus
221	Murchison Falls	236	Lahore Fort	250	Parque Nacional Dos Lençóis
222	Caernarfon Castle	236	İshak Paşa Palace		Maranhenses
222	Ben Nevis	236	Mo'orea	250	Polonnaruwa
222	Chitwan National Park	237	Snæfellsnes	251	Cathedral, Santiago de Compostela
223	Museo Guggenheim	238	Himeji Castle	251	Komodo National Park
224	Pulpit Rock	238	Sedlec Ossuary	252	Kelvingrove Art Gallery & Museum
224	Bay of Fundy	238	Aït Benhaddou	252	Copán
224	Reed Islands	239	Fatehpur Sikri	253	Hill of Crosses
225	Sheikh Zayed Grand Mosque	240	Blyde River Canyon	253	Wolf's Lair
225	Cape Cod National Seashore	240	Ancient Persepolis	255	Cartagena Old Town
225	Isla de Ometepe	240	Ao Phang-Nga	256	Tsarskoe Selo
226	Wat Pho	241	Geysir	256	Mt Rushmore
227	Golden Temple	241	Lake Malawi	257	Butrint
228	Central Kalahari Game Reserve	241	Teatre-Museu Dalí	257	Burgess Shale
228	Beit She'an	242	Karlštejn Castle	257	Loch Lomond
228	Majorelle Garden	242	Danube Delta	258	Blue Hole
229	Bioluminescent Bays	243	Blue Ridge Parkway	259	Thiksey Monastery
229	Tian Tan Buddha	244	Brecon Beacons	260	National Palace Museum
229	Makhtesh Ramon	244	Kalemegdan	261	Hadrian's wall
230	Grotte De Lascaux	244	Punakha Dzong	261	Galle Fort

400–500

page

264 Great Zimbabwe
264 Swayambhunath
264 Tuol Sleng and the Killing Fields
265 Standing Stones of Callanish
265 Avebury Stone Circle
266 Caracol
266 Malbork Castle
267 Temple of the Tooth
267 La Boca District
268 Heydar Aliyev Cultural Centre
268 Kashgar's Grand Bazaar
268 Bardo National Museum
269 Salzwelten
269 Khao Sok National Park
269 Mansudae Grand Monument
270 Etosha National Park
272 Port Arthur
272 Jungfraujoch
273 Phu Quoc Island
273 Melk Abbey
274 Nazca Lines
274 Cementerio de la Recoleta
274 Altun Ha
275 Khongoryn Els
276 Titanic Belfast
276 Zwinger
276 Skeleton Coast
277 Iona
277 Stirling Castle
278 Zócalo
278 Nyungwe Forest National Park
279 St Fagans National History Museum
279 Eisriesenwelt
279 Pafos Archaeological Site

page

280 Lavena Coastal Walk
280 Brandenburg Gate
280 Amboseli National Park
281 Ifugao (Banaue) Rice Terraces
281 Carpathian National Nature Park
281 Segovia's Acueducto
283 Ipanema beach
284 Matmata
284 Everglades National Park
285 Sea of Galilee
285 Ostrog Monastery
286 Kinderdijk Windmills
286 Church of Sveti Jovan Bigorksi
287 Hal Saflieni Hypogeum
287 Taipei 101
287 Si Phan Don
288 Church on the Spilled Blood
289 Archipiélago de San Blas
289 Kyevo-Pecherska Lavra
290 Horton Plains & World's End
290 Mt Roraima
290 Nizwa Fort
291 Bucovina Monasteries
292 L'Anse aux Meadows
292 Black Forest
292 Mt Fuji
293 The Mighty Volcano
293 Mt Kenya
294 Kalon Minaret
294 Trakai Castle
295 El-Jem
295 Schilthorn
297 Griffith Observatory
298 Tower of London

page

298 Trinity College
299 Capital Castles
299 Camp Nou
299 Panama Canal
300 Bay Islands
300 Monet's Garden
300 Grouse Mountain
301 Graceland
301 To Sua Ocean Trench
301 Plaza Mayor
303 Flanders Fields
304 Pol-e Khaju
304 Sanduny Baths
305 Cañón del Colca
306 Spiš Castle
306 Aletsch Glacier
306 Mt Ararat
307 Stingray City
307 Foteviken Viking
307 Wawel Castle
309 Rock-Hewn Churches of Tigray
309 Isla Mujeres
309 Fingal's Cave
309 Leaning Tower of Pisa
309 Orheiul Vechi
309 Musée Océanographique de Monaco
310 Oslo Opera House
311 Kolmanskop
312 Mutrah Souq
312 Rock of Cashel
313 Erdene Zuu Khiid
314 Grand Palace
316 Independence National Historic Park

01–99

01

Temples of Angkor

CAMBODIA // When all the votes were counted, the no.1 sight in the Ultimate Travelist was the undisputed champion by some margin: it won 36 percent more votes than the very closely fought second and third places. In electoral terms, this was a landslide. So, how did Angkor Wat do it?

As the world's greatest temple to the Hindu god Vishnu, Angkor Wat might seem a bit off the grid in Buddhist Cambodia, but this magnificent monument is the greatest treasure of a Hindu kingdom that once stretched as far as Burma, Laos and southern China. Even in a region as richly gifted with temples as Southeast Asia, Angkor is something out of the ordinary – a literal representation of heaven on earth, hewn from thousands of sandstone blocks and carved floor-to-ceiling with legends from the Ramayana, Mahabharata and Puranas.

Even better, Angkor Wat is the crowning glory in a complex of more than 1000 temples, shrines and tombs that forms a virtual city of spires in the jungles of northern Cambodia. International flights drop into ➲

**ANCIENT
TEMPLES**

↓

Borobudur, Java's
monumental series
of temples, ringed
by volcanoes, dates
back 1200 years.
Mesmerising.

👉 page 183

↓

In India's Karnataka
state, the ancient
city of Hampi,
strewn around with
giant boulders,
may only have one
temple, but what a
temple it is.

👉 page 173

↓

Construction be-
gan at Bagan in the
11th century, now
Myanmar's no.1
attraction returns
to life.

👉 page 47

nearby Siem Reap, so it would be hard to describe Angkor as 'undiscovered', yet every visitor who steps among the ruins, where tree roots tear through ancient walls and the heads of forgotten deities poke out from between the vines, feels like Indiana Jones, peeling back the foliage for the first time. Over Angkor's long centuries, the residents of this celestial city traded Hinduism for Buddhism, leaving many temples fusing mythologies. Few experiences can match arriving at the ruins of the Bayon at dawn and watching dozens of benevolent faces of the Avalokiteshvara, the Buddhist bodhisattva of compassion, appearing slowly out of the mist like heavenly apparitions. Indeed, Angkor offers so many hard-to-match experiences that many travellers spend weeks soaking up the glory of all the temples and ruins.

Angkor Wat itself is the undisputed highlight, a massive representation of Mt Meru, the mountain home of the gods of Hinduism, executed in stone blocks adorned with bas-reliefs of such delicacy and grace that they could almost have been carved in the presence of the divine. Travellers feel similar emotions when exploring the overgrown ruins of Ta Prohm, a 12th-century temple that was almost completely consumed by the jungle, left much as it was when European explorers first ventured to Angkor in the 17th century.

Away from this central hub are sacred pools and stone bridges that have hand-rails depicting demons holding monstrous serpents, as well as a panoply of crumbling temples, scattered over an area of more than 400 sq km. Some of these outlying groups have become must-see sights in their own right – the complex at Banteay Srei features some of the finest stone-carving at Angkor, and the artistry continues underwater at nearby Kbal Spean, the river of a thousand *linga* (Shiva symbols).

More than anything else, Angkor is a powerful reminder of the soaring ambitions of human creativity, the fundamental human need to leave something permanent behind, and the very Buddhist realisation that nothing material is eternal, and that given time, all will be reclaimed by the jungle. Angkor isn't just an interesting ruin – it's a spiritual epiphany in stone.

👉 **SEE IT ! *Stay in Siem Reap; zip to the temples by motorbike taxi or tuk-tuk. Book trips the night before for a dawn spectacular.***

Scenes from Angkor
Wat: left and previous
page, monks at Ta
Prohm temple; below,
an Apsara dancer.

02

Great Barrier Reef

OZ'S UNDERWATER WONDERLAND

AUSTRALIA // Second place in our list goes to a natural wonder stretching for more than 3000km up the northeastern coast of Australia. The Great Barrier Reef hardly needs an introduction. But here are some facts: this is the world's largest network of coral reefs, with 400 types of coral and 1500 species of fish. Some 30 kinds of whales, dolphins and porpoises have been spotted here, along with six species of sea turtles and 17 kinds of sea snake.

If that doesn't convince you to hop on a plane to Oz, there's this: the reef may not be around for much longer, at least in its present state of glory. Rising sea temperatures have been bleaching and killing the coral, and the trend shows no sign of stopping. But for now, the reef is a psychedelic underwater playground for divers and snorkellers. Even above the surface, and closer to the Queensland coast, this vital ecosystem enthrals all who visit, with abundant bird life and countless tropical islands and beaches.

☛ SEE IT ! *Major access points to the reef include the cities of Cairns, Port Douglas and Airlie Beach, all in Queensland.*

Glide through forests of waving anemones, swim alongside sea turtles and peer into the mouths of metre-long giant clams

Left, a traditionally dressed Peruvian woman. Below, a view of Machu Picchu, with llama.

Machu Picchu

03

RAMBLING RUINS

↓

Visitors can explore Sri Lanka's 12th-century garden city, Polonnaruwa, by bicycle, but mind the monkeys.

 page 250

↓

The expansive ruins of Baalbek in Lebanon were the Roman Empire's most ambitious construction project.

☛ page 246

↓

The sand-blown mining town of Kolmanskop in Namibia is now deserted, literally.

☛ page 311

INCAN ENIGMA

PERU // Just a handful of votes separates second and third spot in the Ultimate Travelist.

But they could not be more different... Gawping down at Machu Picchu from the Sun Gate after a lung-busting four-day hike along the Inca Trail is a rite of passage for travellers to Peru. But it's not the outrageously dramatic Andean setting, nor the way that the city clings to impossibly precipitous slopes that makes Machu Picchu so mind-blowing – it's the fact that no-one really knows what happened here. You've found a proper enigma. There are theories aplenty – from royal retreat and temple for virgins, through to alien landing pad – but they remain just that. Theories. Even Hiram Bingham, the American amateur-archaeologist who stumbled across the ruins in 1911 and spent years excavating them, didn't know what he was looking at. (Bingham died, claiming erroneously that he'd found a different site altogether – Vilcabamba, the fabled lost city of the Incas.) Today, you can wander wide-eyed around the mysterious mountain metropolis in a liberating knowledge vacuum, forming your own ideas. Be sure to climb Huayna Picchu, the Andean shard towering over the ruins, with its mettle-testing trail to the Temple of the Moon.

☛ SEE IT ! *Cuzco is the gateway to Machu Picchu. Take a train to Kilometre 88, then walk the 42km Camino Inca.*

Great Wall of China

04

WHAT A WALL!

CHINA // Every country has its must-see monument – in China, that monument covers most of the country. The Great Wall of China is not just one wall but an awe-inspiring maze of walls and fortifications stretching for an astonishing 8850km across the rugged landscape of the north of the country. Constructed in waves over more than a thousand years, the Great Wall ultimately failed in its objective of keeping the Mongol hordes out of China, but it became the defining symbol of the Ming Empire, the greatest power to rise in East Asia until the arrival of Chairman Mao.

It's a myth that you can see the Great Wall from space, but when confronted by the sight of this endless structure stretching off into infinite distance, it seems almost impossible that this wouldn't be true. A few rugged souls trek the entire length of the wall, but even if you pick just one section, you'll be humbled by its aura of indestructibility. Which part you choose to explore depends on whether you're after imperial grandeur (near Beijing), military precision (in Gansu) or timeless desolation (in Inner Mongolia).

 SEE IT ! *The most accessible sections are close to Beijing: Badaling for the touristy reconstructed version, or Jiankou and Huanghuacheng for unrestored atmosphere.*

UNFORGETTABLE MEMORIALS

↓

The Kigali Memorial Centre honours the dead of Rwanda's 1994 genocide, when up to a million people were killed in a matter of months.
 page 230

↓

The twin pools of Manhattan's National September 11 Memorial sit within the footprint of the Twin Towers.
 page 192

↓

White gravestones and – in spring – red poppies cover the WWI battlegrounds of Flanders.
page 302

Taj Mahal

05

MAGNIFICENT MUGHAL MASTERPIECE

INDIA // How do you achieve architectural perfection? Start with acres of shimmering white marble. Add a few thousand semi-precious stones, carved and inlaid in intricate Islamic patterns. Take a sublime setting by a sacred river, in jewel-like formal gardens. Apply a little perfect symmetry, and tie up the whole package in an outlandish story of timeless love. And there you have the Taj Mahal.

Built by the Mughal Emperor Shah Jahan as a mausoleum for his favourite wife, Mumtaz Mahal, the Taj has been attracting travellers to India for centuries. Ironically, the emperor spent his final years incarcerated in Agra Fort by his ambitious son, with just a view of the Taj to remind him of everything he had lost.

Despite the incredible multitudes of visitors it draws, the Taj Mahal still presents a misty window through time. The ghosts of Mughal India wander the gleaming marble courtyards, drifting like shadows under archways and floating behind latticework screens. There's no other building in India that so perfectly encapsulates the attitudes and atmosphere of its era.

 SEE IT ! *Dusty, noisy Agra is the main base for Taj visits – and for rampant touts and souvenir vendors; to escape the crowds arrive when the gates open at dawn.*

Scenes from the Taj Mahal, best viewed in dawn's soft light.

Rafting trips on the Grand Canyon can take from one day, with commercial outfitters, or up to a month if self-guided; permit required.

Grand Canyon National Park

USA // Stand before this vast rent in the earth's crust and you're looking down at two-billion years of geologic time. That fact does something funny to the human brain. Lit by flaming sunsets, filled with billowing seas of fog and iced with crystal dustings of snow, the mile-deep, 277-mile-long Grand Canyon is nature's cathedral. You'll feel tiny yet soaring, awed yet peaceful, capable of poetry yet totally tongue-tied. As the explorer John Wesley Powell once said, 'The wonders of the Grand Canyon cannot be adequately represented in symbols of speech, nor by speech itself.' But we had to try anyway. Come here to hike, to raft the wild Colorado River, to spot condors, black bears and elk, or simply to marvel.

☛ SEE IT ! *Most visitors access the canyon from the South Rim, about 75 miles north of Flagstaff, Arizona. The North Rim is more remote, with fewer services.*

Colosseum

BLOODY ROMANS

ITALY // There's nothing like a feisty Roman monument to rev up your inner historian, and the Colosseum performs brilliantly. A monument to raw, merciless power, this massive 50,000-seat amphitheatre is the most thrilling of Rome's ancient sights. Gladiators met here in mortal combat, and condemned prisoners fought off wild beasts in front of baying, bloodthirsty crowds. Two millennia on, the hold it exerts over anyone who steps foot inside is as powerful as ever.

The Colosseum really is colossal and it is this that first impresses (although the amphitheatre was named not after its size but after a nearby statue of Nero, the Colosso di Nerone). Simply navigating the 80 entrance arches through which the audience entered and could be seated within minutes is a complicated affair – imagine the other 49,999 spectators who, in Roman times, would have been jockeying simultaneously for a spot alongside you and the mind boggles. Magistrates and senior officials sat in the lowest tier nearest the action, wealthy citizens sat in the middle tier, and the plebs on the highest tier. Women, being even more 2nd-class citizens than the plebs, were relegated to straining their necks to watch from the cheapest sections on the top tier.

Despite the gruesome shows that went on here, there's no denying the majesty and grace of the arena. Less glam is what went on backstage: guided tours (a must) take the historically curious into the subterranean guts of the Colosseum where the full grunge, gore and filth of Roman gladiator combats come uncomfortably to life. Known as the hypogeum, this underground labyrinth of corridors, animal cages and ramps beneath the arena floor is vast and complex. Chuck in the bestial noise, stench, chaos of wounded men and dead or injured animals and you realise how gut-wrenching and bloody those Roman performances were.

👉 SEE IT ! *The Colosseum is a 20-minute walk from Rome's Stazione Termini. Buy tickets online to avoid queuing.*

Below, Rome's Colosseum, which dates from 70AD, is Europe's highest entry in the Ultimate Travelist.

08

Iguazú Falls

**Thunderous
white-water thrills**

↓

BRAZIL–ARGENTINA
// The Guaraní
name for the point
where Río Iguazu
plummets over a
plateau just before
its confluence with
the Río Paraná is a
great understate-
ment: Big Water.
Big? These falls are
mind-bogglingly
mighty: tourist
boats that ply the
foaming plunge
pools below look
like matchsticks.
Boardwalks also
get you thrillingly
close. The whole
thing is glimpsed
through a stretch
of subtropical
rainforest forming
a 55,000-hectare
national park re-
plete with wildlife,
including jaguars.

☛ SEE IT ! *Most
visitors go to both
sides of the falls.*

Alhambra

The Palace of the Alhambra against a backdrop of the Alpujarras mountains.

SPAIN'S MOORISH MASTERPIECE

09

SPAIN // The palace complex of Granada's Alhambra is one of the most extraordinary structures on the planet, perhaps the most refined example of Islamic art anywhere in the world, and the most enduring symbol of 800 years of enlightened Moorish rule in medieval Spain. From afar, Alhambra's fortress towers dominate the Granada skyline, the sheer red walls rising from woods of cypress and elm, set against a backdrop of the Sierra Nevada's snow-capped peaks. Inside is a network of lavishly decorated palaces and irrigated gardens, which are the source of scores of legends and fantasies.

It's the combination of intricate detail and epic scale that gives Alhambra its breathtaking appeal. The perfectly proportioned Generalife gardens vividly evoke the Moorish vision of heaven, while the creations at Alhambra's heart are beautiful beyond belief. The many rooms of the Palacios Nazaríes, the central palace complex, are the pinnacle of Alhambra's design, a harmonious synthesis of space, light, shade, water and greenery that sought to conjure up an earthly paradise for the rulers who dwelt here. Expanses of tile, *muqarnas* (honeycomb) vaulting and stucco work adorn the walls, while the Patio de los Leones is a masterpiece of Islamic geometric design. Put simply, this is Spain's most beautiful monument.

SEE IT ! *Catch a train here, stay in Albayzín just across the valley and explore Granada on foot. Book Alhambra tickets online and well in advance.*

Aya Sofya

A FUSION OF FAITHS

SPIRITUAL SIGHTS

↓

London's great survivor, **St Paul's Cathedral**, retains its presence, despite the fast-growing skyscrapers around it.

 page 117

↓

The world's most famous pilgrimage, the Way of St James, winds up at the Cathedral of **Santiago de Compostela.**

☞ page 251

↓

Dashashwamedh **Ghat** in Varanasi, India is hazy with Hindu funeral pyres, as the Ganges flows on by.

☞ page 108

Istanbul, TURKEY // Church, mosque and museum in one, Aya Sofya is a structure unlike any other on the planet – defying easy categorisation just as it defied the rules of architecture when it was built almost 1500 years ago. The man behind it all was Byzantine Emperor Justinian I: he demanded a cathedral to eclipse the wonders of Byzantium's sister city, Rome, and moreover, one that would mimic the majesty of the heavens on earth. He got his wish, and Aya Sofya still dominates the skyline in modern-day Istanbul. It is a huge, almost cosmic space, with a sense of vastness unmatched in its ancient era. Inside, the building reveals her treasures in stages: firstly, soaring columns borrowed from ancient Greek and Roman cities; secondly, lofty galleries adorned with glittering mosaics. Then, the grand finale: the famous dome, teetering high over the smooth marble below. Looking up at the dome, it's worth remembering that its form was meant to imitate the vault of heaven (it's perhaps best not to remember that it's also collapsed once or twice over the years).

Almost as extraordinary as the building itself is its history – few structures have undergone as many career changes as Aya Sofya. After being looted during the Crusades, it was converted into a mosque after the Ottoman capture of Istanbul in 1453.

Four giant minarets remain as a testament to this, and remarkably, new mosques around Istanbul (including the famous Blue Mosque) took their cue from its design. In 1935, Aya Sofya was deconsecrated and designated a museum, yet stepping inside remains a spiritual experience – be it watching the evening light sparkle on a gold-leaf fresco, or seeing Christian artwork and Islamic calligraphy side by side. Like the beautiful city in which it stands, Aya Sofya represents a unique crossroads of continents and faiths.

☞ **SEE IT !** *Aya Sofya opens all year, arrive at 9am to beat the crowds. Also visit Aya Irini, a smaller Byzantine church nearby.*

Below, the Aya Sofya stands close to the Bosphorus waterway between Europe and Asia. Left, the interior of the Aya Sofya, with its Islamic details.

In 1935, Aya Sofya was deconsecrated and designated a museum, yet stepping inside remains a spiritual experience

Fez Medina

11

LABYRINTHINE MILLENNIA-OLD MALL

MOROCCO // Now, was it right? Or left? The camel head hanging glumly above the butcher's shop provides no advice at all (except, perhaps, become vegetarian). You'd swear that little slipper stall seems a bit familiar, but then one pile of bright babouches looks an awful lot like another... You plunge, hanging this way, then that, veering past the vat of boiling snails and the teetering pile of terracotta tagines, narrowly avoiding a man and his mule, and not really avoiding the steaming pile that the mule left behind... Argh, another crossroads! Another turn, another twist and, yes! Oh. Hello Mr Camel, we meet again. Fès el-Bali, the medieval heart of Morocco's 3rd-largest city, is less medina, more architectural spaghetti. There are in the region of 9400 alleyways, comprising some 14,000 buildings, housing around 160,000 people, in this tangled, unmappable labyrinth that dates back more than 1000 years. Mosques, medressas, restored riads, townhouse dars, silversmiths, copper-merchants, tourist-tat touts, leather tanners, real guides, faux guides and every other type of soul seem squeezed in tight. You can't begin to get to know the place – but that is part of the frenzied fun. Steel yourself with a sweet mint tea and just dive right in.

☛ SEE IT ! *Only official guides are permitted to show tourists around Fès el-Bali; watch out for touts and 'faux' guides.*

12

Twelve Apostles
Sea spires

↓

AUSTRALIA // How did a group of sea stacks feature so high in our list? There aren't even 12 of them; just seven or eight are visible from the roadside viewing platform.

The answer lies in where the 12 Apostles stand: on the Great Ocean Road, one of the world's must-do drives, which hugs Victoria's southwest coast. This limestone coast, pummelled by the Southern Ocean, is a scenic treat, especially for passengers. At about the four-hour mark from Melbourne, you'll meet the Apostles; stop, take the photo, then turn around and explore the Great Otway National Park on your return trip. The Apostles are the cherry on what is a very tasty cake.

☛ SEE IT ! *The Apostles are about a four-hour drive from Melbourne. Stay in Apollo Bay.*

An aerial view of the 12 Apostles, formed by the erosion of Victoria's south coast.

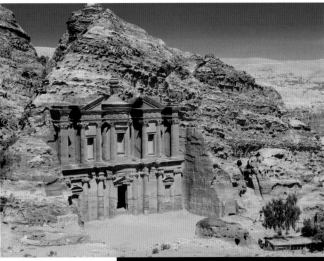

Left, the Monastery, Petra's largest monument. Right, a glimpse of the Treasury between the sandstone walls.

STARS OF THE SCREEN

↓

Martini-fuelled gambler James Bond was a regular at Monte Carlo's Casino, trying his luck there in *Never Say Never Again* and *Goldeneye*.

 page 235

↓

If you dream of being chased by a big, floating white ball, go to Portmeirion in Wales, setting for the 1960s TV series *The Prisoner*.

 page 166

↓

In a country far, far away (OK, Tunisia) is Luke Skywalker's home village, Mat-mata, where *Star Wars* fans can stay overnight.

page 284

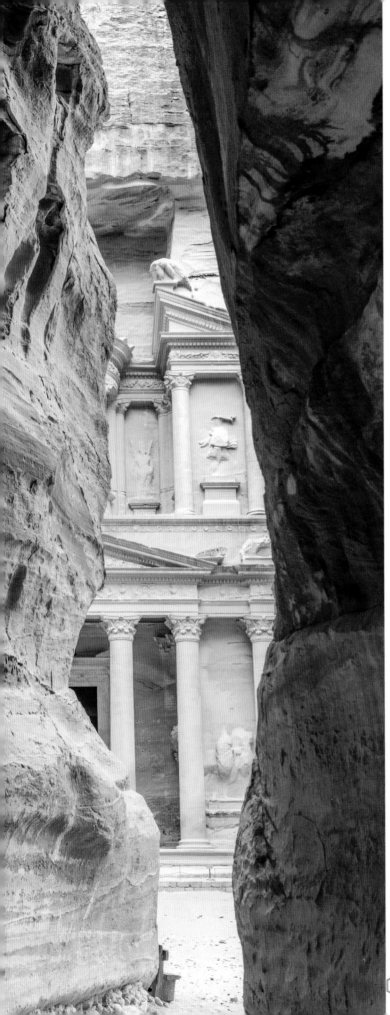

Petra

BETTER THAN INDIANA JONES

13

JORDAN // If we're honest, most people's mental image of Petra is of Indiana Jones – riding through a narrow canyon, marvelling at the rose-red facade of the Treasury, stepping inside and discovering the Holy Grail. In fact, if you step inside the Treasury all you'll find is a bare room rather lacking in holy grails. But in other respects the reality is as extraordinary as Hollywood fiction. Everyone can experience the drama of the Siq – the chasm from which the Treasury emerges – but unlike Indy, you can also explore the ruins beyond; the High Place of Sacrifice, the Monastery and countless tombs.

Johann Ludwig Burckhardt, a Swiss adventurer, first heard rumours of a lost city hidden in these canyons in the 19th century. What he discovered was the two-millennia old 'lost' city of the Nabataeans – a trading people whose routes extended across Arabia. Ever since, millions have followed him to Petra. But it's still just about possible to get away from the crowds – linger until closing time to find yourself alone in a corner of the city, treading stony pathways with only the ghosts of the past for company.

☛ SEE IT ! *Don't loiter in the Treasury on arrival, take a long morning hike to the Monastery, which is busier in the afternoon.*

Tikal

14

WALK IN ANCIENT MAJESTY

GUATEMALA // Mexico might have the most well-known Mayan sites, but it's Guatemala that grabs a place in the top 20. Filled with palpable notes of jungle, earth and stone, the air of Tikal feels suitably timeless. Twelve hundred years ago, you'd be walking through a bustling Mayan metropolis. Today, you're greeted by haunted jungle ambience: wind through vines, animal cries and the occasional cacophony of squawks emitted by the birds that now call the formerly great city home.

Tikal is Guatemala's most significant Mayan ruin site, and although archaeologists say it once rivalled Rome in size, population and political clout, less than 10% of its buildings have been excavated. The rest of the city remains beneath a thousand years of dense jungle that has claimed the entirety of the once-mighty empire. The park itself spreads over 26 sq km, making multiday explorations worth your while. Some visitors stay in Flores or El Remate, but overnighting in the park offers the chance to see the sun rise from atop an ancient, majestic temple. Spending the evening within earshot of the howler monkeys whose mating growls fill the night is another benefit of in-park accommodation. That, and sleeping in the shadow of ancient history.

☞ SEE IT ! *Tikal, 65km from Flores, is one of Guatemala's more accessible Maya sites. You can do a day trip from Belize if you rush.*

British Museum

15

ENGLAND // When Sir Hans Sloane first put his personal collection of treasures and curiosities on display, he probably had no idea what he was creating. Fast forward 260 years and the British Museum has evolved into perhaps the great treasure house of Europe. Indeed, many of Europe's – and indeed the world's – greatest treasures have ended up in its hallowed halls, a periodic bone of contention for the nations where those treasures originated.

Visiting the British Museum is a pilgrimage for fans of antiquity. Among its collection are such iconic heirlooms as the Rosetta Stone (the key to the translation of Egyptian hieroglyphs) and the Elgin Marbles (which once graced the Parthenon), alongside an astonishing collection of mummies and sarcophagi that would put ancient Thebes to shame.

Almost as impressive is the building – a grand Greek Revival temple to treasure, hiding an unexpected Norman Foster canopy over its vast central courtyard. Our personal top picks? The Mildenhall Treasure, an astonishing collection of Roman silver found hidden in a farmer's cupboard, and the Lewis Chessmen, allegedly unearthed by a cow on the Scottish island of Lewis.

☛ SEE IT ! *The British Museum is a short walk from Holborn Tube; free tours are led by guides who are experts on the collection.*

Left, the interior of the British Museum with its Norman Foster-designed dome. Below, Antoni Gaudí's Sagrada Familia, still under construction.

Sagrada Familia

SPAIN // Barcelona is home to many Gaudí architectural marvels, but the Sagrada Familia is our pick of the bunch, cranes or no cranes. Surely the world's most stunning building site, this iconic Modernista master-piece is still a work in progress close to 100 years after Gaudí's death, with architects now working from his original ideas.

The massive scale of the Gothic-style cathedral alone inspires long periods of standing in the surrounding streets with a craned neck as you gaze up admiringly at the 18 towers piercing the sky. But it's the decorative details, particularly the Passion and Nativity facades, where hours can be whiled away just absorbing the work and its symbolism. Although the exterior is captivat-ing, the interior is something else – this is one vision for which the adjective 'awe-inspiring' is entirely warranted. Once inside, visitors are struck by the unconventional architectural angles where columns arch towards the ceil-ing and light filters through rich and intricate stained-glass windows to give the effect of a forest. The completion date for Sagrada Familia is still unknown but estimates range from the 2020s to 2040s.

☞ SEE IT ! *The Sagrada Familia is in the centre of Barcelona. A guided tour is highly recommended to gain a deeper understanding of the site.*

Below, a giant sculpture of a takahē bird stands in the town of Te Anau. Right, sightseeing ships on Milford Sound.

Fiordland National Park

17

EPIC WORLD HERITAGE WILDERNESS

NATIONAL PARKS TO EXPLORE

↓

Meet mountain gorillas in Rwanda's **Volcanoes National Park**, where 10 family groups survive on steep, forested slopes.

 page 153

↓

Escape the crowds and bed down in a yurt in the **Tajik National Park**, laid out over the Pamir mountains in Tajikistan.

 page 186

↓

Dragons roam **Komodo National Park**, across Indonesian islands. If 3m-long lizards don't appeal, the scuba diving will.

 page 251

NEW ZEALAND // Second only to the Grand Canyon in the Ultimate list of national parks, Fiordland covers a mountainous corner of the South Island. Along with three neighbouring national parks, it forms the vast Te Wāhipounamu Southwest New Zealand World Heritage Area, gazetted by Unesco for its unique natural features.

The scale of this wilderness is mind-blowing enough, but its primeval atmosphere seals the deal. Fiordland is an almost untouched part of Gondwanaland, the supercontinent from which New Zealand was cast adrift 85 million years ago. It is a landscape of jagged peaks, glacial valleys, pristine lakes and sheer fjords. Ancient forests drip green and twitch with such birds as kiwi and takahe.

Fiordland's remoteness and rugged terrain mean most of it remains untouched, but there are still plenty of ways in. Three Great Walks – the Milford, Kepler and Routeburn – offer hikes into sublime wilderness with the bonus of overnighting in classic 'tramping' huts. Cruising and kayaking are also treats, particularly in Milford and Doubtful Sounds, where waterfalls tumble into seas bound by vertiginous mountains. Visiting Fiordland is like travelling back to a time before humans.

☞ SEE IT ! *The best base for adventure is Te Anau, two hours' drive south of Queenstown, which has good domestic air links.*

18

Santorini
Black-eyed beauty

↓

GREECE // Lying in the embrace of the Aegean, none of the coquettish Cyclades islands lack pulling power, but one offers a bit more. Santorini is the group's indie kid. Being the tip of a volcanic caldera has bequeathed it a unique look. Why settle for golden sands when you can have red and black beaches, backed by 300m multicoloured cliffs? Beyond the beaches, explore the Minoan site of Akrotiri and the hilltop village of Oia.

☞ **SEE IT !** *The ferry from Piraeus, Athens takes five to nine hours. Visit in spring and autumn to avoid crowds.*

Galapagos Islands

WHERE THE WILD THINGS ARE

ECUADOR // Nowhere else on earth does the animal kingdom turn the tables on humanity quite like on the Galapagos Islands. Afloat in the Pacific Ocean, 1000km from mainland Ecuador, it's a place where visitors can often feel more like the exhibit than the observer.

Blue-footed boobies stake nesting grounds in the middle of walking tracks, Galapagos sea lions lounge about on town seats, and frigate birds slipstream boats as they cruise between the archipelago's 17 islands. Step around any animal here and it invariably looks back at you with naive curiosity, as if it knows that you're strictly here on its terms.

Charles Darwin famously sailed through the archipelago in 1835, musing on the origin of species. Almost 200 years on, the animal life on the World Heritage–listed islands continues to astound and confound: birds with blue feet? Yellow lizards? Birds that take flight by falling off cliffs? Every animal here seems to come with a built-in party trick.

Rivalling only the Great Barrier Reef (p14) as a living location in this list, the Galapagos is the full wildlife wonder, yielding little even to the reef in underwater experiences. Roll overboard and you're in danger of bumping into a turtle, or encountering a sea lion that's keen to play around you. Hammerhead and reef sharks glide through the depths, and dolphins escort boats, leaping through their bow waves.

On the land there's a remarkable contrast. Each island is the tip of an underwater volcano – those in the west are still active – and the harsh, black surfaces look deceptively lifeless… until the ground itself seems to move. It's arguably the greatest wildlife show on the planet.

👉 SEE IT ! *The Galapagos are reached by air from Guayaquil, Ecuador. Seas are at their calmest from around January–May.*

Below, a marine iguana, indigenous to the Galapagos islands. The reptiles forage in the sea.

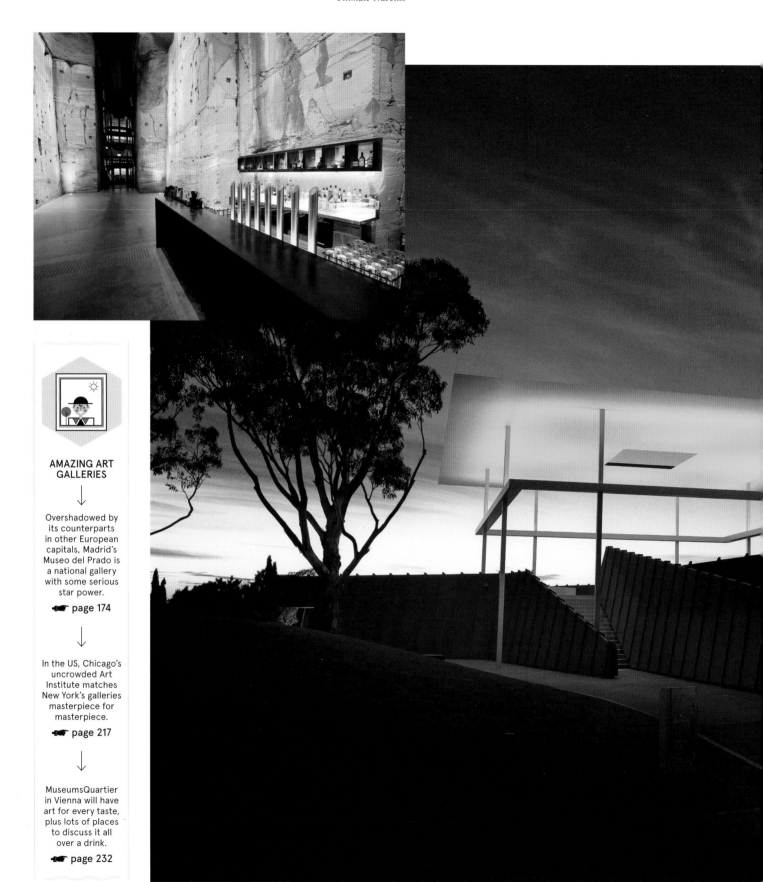

AMAZING ART GALLERIES

↓

Overshadowed by its counterparts in other European capitals, Madrid's Museo del Prado is a national gallery with some serious star power.

👉 page 174

↓

In the US, Chicago's uncrowded Art Institute matches New York's galleries masterpiece for masterpiece.

👉 page 217

↓

MuseumsQuartier in Vienna will have art for every taste, plus lots of places to discuss it all over a drink.

👉 page 232

Museum of Old & New Art

20

From the left, the subterranean bar; James Turrell's installation for stargazing, Amarna, at MONA; the interior and exterior of the gallery.

AUSTRALIA // At how many art galleries can you see wild dolphins playing in the surrounding water as you arrive by motor launch? Our highest ranking modern art gallery – beating New York's MoMA and London's Tate Modern – has an enviable location on the River Derwent, just upriver from Tasmania's still-quaint capital, Hobart.

When mathematically-gifted millionaire gambler David Walsh resolved to give something back to the city where he grew up, nobody predicted quite what he would start. In 1995 he bought a peninsula of land just outside Hobart. On it he built first a winery, Moorilla, then a brewery. And ten years later he commissioned the Museum of Old and New Art from architect Nonda Katsalidis. His engineers delved down, excavating 60,000 tonnes of earth. Walsh filled the subsequent cavern with items that had caught his eye over years of collecting – and he possesses a very eclectic eye, placing Stone Age arrow heads and Roman coins next to the most avant-garde of artworks. Outside, ambitious installations are surrounded by what must be the world's most naturally beautiful setting for any art gallery. It's this package – amazing architecture, provocative art, great food and wine, that justifies MONA's top 20 place here.

☛ **SEE IT ! *MONA can be reached by boat, bicycle or bus from Hobart. Take a flight to the city from most other Australian cities.***

Yosemite National Park

21

ROCKIN' IT

USA // Could Yosemite National Park be the world's most enduring rock star? It's a place where countless waterfalls burst out of the mountains, giant sequoias scratch at the sky, and bears roam the expanses (and often the camping grounds). But it's the rocks that are Yosemite's undisputed royalty.

Everywhere you look, sheer granite domes bubble up from the land. Half Dome hovers like a vast rock wave about to break over Yosemite Valley, and the ominous sentinel of El Capitan guards the entrance to the valley.

On Yosemite's rocks, some of the world's most epic climbing stories have been painstakingly carved. The first ascent of El Cap's legendary Nose, once considered unclimbable, took 47 days. In 2008, Alex Honnold famously scampered up Half Dome without ropes, and in 2015, Tommy Caldwell and Kevin Jorgeson spent 18 days (after years of practice) nutting out the puzzle of El Cap's Dawn Wall, a feat many consider the most difficult rock climb ever attempted.

Come to watch the waterfalls or come to watch the climbers, but prepare to stand and be awed.

☞ SEE IT ! *San Francisco is the nearest major airport. Yosemite's waterfalls are at their thunderous best around May and June.*

Below, Yosemite Falls seen from across the Merced River. Right, decor in a local bar.

22

Dubrovnik Old City Walls
Battlement beauty

↓

CROATIA // As the setting for King's Landing in *Game of Thrones,* Dubrovnik's fortifications are often splattered with stage blood. Should the camera ever pan back, you'd witness a headland jutting into the blue Adriatic, towers rising over masts of anchored ships and green Dalmatian islands. Explore Europe's most handsome ramparts – built from the 12th to 17th centuries and never breached – on the circular walking route.

☛ SEE IT ! *Get the best views before the daily cruise ships arrive.*

23

Salar de Uyuni

SALT OF THE EARTH

BOLIVIA // Licking the walls is strictly prohibited in the Palacio de Sal. Constructed from salt, the hotel wouldn't survive long if everyone got inquisitive with their tongues, and besides, it's bad for your heart – so you'll have to trust us. Walls, floors, ceilings, furniture, even the sculptures – all salt. Over a million blocks of the stuff. And the view – that's all salt too. Welcome to Bolivia's Salar de Uyuni, the planet's biggest salt lake. For 10,582 sq km there's virtually nothing to see here – not even a horizon – but you've never seen anything half as surreal as this, especially if you score a tour when there's a layer of water on the surface, transforming the floor into a mirror and convincing your frontal cortex that you're travelling through the middle of the sky. It's a sensation-bending, brain-melting experience, and it's a relief to focus on something real when you finally reach one of the lake's few features that isn't a mirage, such as Isla Incahuasi or Isla del Pescado, both populated by giant phallic-shaped cacti.

🠶 SEE IT ! *Salar de Uyuni is 350km south of La Paz. Arrange a tour by 4WD – or, even better, by bicycle – leaving from Uyuni.*

<u>Surface water transforms the floor into a mirror, convincing your frontal cortex that you're travelling through the sky</u>

Left, praying at the Ananda Pahto temple at Bagan. Below, exploring the complex by horse-and-cart.

Bagan

24

THE JEWEL IN MYANMAR'S CROWN

BIG BUDDHAS

↓

There are many big Buddhas in Japan but the Daibutsu of Nara, a 16m bronze statue, is arguably the most impressive.

☛ page 125

↓

But even he's dwarfed by the Grand Buddha carved into a mountain at Lèshān, whose toes alone are 8m long.

☛ page 136

↓

The Reclining Buddha at Wat Pho, Thailand, stretches out for 46m, and shines with gold leaf; the blingiest Buddha here.

☛ page 226

MYANMAR (BURMA) // Some places earn a position on this list through their incomprehensible scale, others through dazzling ornateness. But Bagan is an exception: emphatically winning at both. A religious site to be mentioned in the same breath as Machu Picchu (p16) or Angkor (p10), Bagan is a complex of Buddhist pagodas – a whopping 2200 of them on the banks of the Irrawaddy River.

Largely constructed between the 11th and 13th centuries by a dynasty of zealous temple-building kings, the pagodas come in all shapes, sizes and colours. Some, such as the Shwezigon pagoda, sparkle an ethereal gold in the sunset, whereas others such as the Ananda Temple are home to tall, serene Buddha statues. A few, the Shwesandaw pagoda for instance, have terraces with views over all Bagan – a vista of temples interspersed with shady copses and verdant farmland. And then there are innumerable others almost invisible among the undergrowth: places that go days without hearing the footfall of visitors. As Myanmar's tourism industry slowly gathers momentum, there's no time like the present to visit Bagan. But know that it would take many weeks to see everything, and a lifetime to fully understand it.

☛ SEE IT ! *Bagan covers about 40 sq miles, so you'll need private transport to get around – consider renting a bike.*

25 Pyramids of Giza

THE ANCIENT WONDER

EGYPT // Khufu is probably spinning in his tomb to find the Pyramids just scraping into the Top 25. Why aren't the Pyramids closer to the top? After all, they're the world's oldest tourist attraction, and remain truly awe-inspiring. The Great Pyramid of Giza clocked a 3800-year stint as the world's tallest building, while just down the road is the Sphinx, one of the oldest and largest statues in the world.

The answer might lie in those same sands of time. Found on the edge of sprawling Cairo, the Pyramids remain a magnet for would-be guides and hawkers. Plenty of world-class sights make a better fist of explaining and showcasing the wonders on offer. Perhaps, above all, the pyramids are too familiar to top this list. None of that really matters, though. The Pyramids will be here when you and I and this list are gone, and crowds will still be flocking to see them.

SEE IT ! *The closest metro station is Giza, 10km away. Most visitors arrive by private vehicle, taxi or tour.*

26 Piazza San Marco

ATTITUDE & AMBIENCE

Venice, ITALY // Don't worry – the waiter in Caffè Florian has seen you. He'll just take his sweet time preening himself before letting you order a staggeringly overpriced coffee. Think about it this way: you're in Italy's oldest cafe, in Europe's most famous public space – sitting pretty, where much-fêted members of the Old World aristocracy and literati once flounced during their Grand Tour. Napoleon called the Piazza the 'drawing room of Europe' when he invaded in 1797, and even the Little Corporal was probably left waiting for his Venetian tea. It's pointless staring impatiently at that famous clock tower. The *camerieri* (waiters) rush for no-one, which gives you time to drink in your surrounds and contemplate the historical shenanigans that the square has witnessed over the past millennia, through the Middle Ages and Renaissance period, to now – the age of the disgruntled tourist.

SEE IT ! *Travel to Venice by train. From Stazione Santa Lucia, follow the flock to the Piazza.*

27 Victoria Falls

THUNDERING WATERS

ZIMBABWE/ZAMBIA // With all due respect to other waterfalls, this is more than just a load of tumbling water. That's not to say the falls aren't spectacular. Whether viewed from the Zimbabwe or Zambia side, this relentless wave is an ear-assaulting, drenching flood of one remarkable view after another. That's if you come in the dry season: in the wet your visit will be even wetter and louder.

What distinguishes Mosi-Oa-Tunya (The Smoke That Thunders) is the wealth of wonderful activities on offer once you've seen the falls. Wildlife flocks to the Zambezi River and elephant, rhino and buffalo are among the big-ticket draws. Thrill-seekers will find bungee jumping, white-water rafting and seemingly perilous swims as ways to get the blood pumping. Lastly, the Victoria Falls Bridge offers arguably the world's most spectacular border crossing by road or rail.

SEE IT ! *Livingstone in Zambia has grown fast over recent years, but the Zimbabwe side is closer to the action.*

28 Acropolis

GREEK CLASSIC

Athens, GREECE // Considering it's been variously attacked, plundered, sacked, placed under siege and set ablaze by the Goths, Herulians, Persians, Venetians and Romans – not to mention vandalic restorers and a rapacious army of tourists – it's a wonder there's anything left of the Acropolis to gape at. But there is. Loads. When you walk amid the ruins of the Parthenon (one of three temples dating from the 5th century BC), the Odeon of Athens and Theatre of Dionysus, you don't need a Tardis to travel through time. And, unlike other antiquities in this illustrious list - yes, that's you Machu Picchu (p16) and Stonehenge (p78) – we know exactly what happened on the rock that towers over Athens, right back to the late Bronze Age, thanks to Homer and later scribes.

SEE IT ! *Entry to the site is €12, but it's free on the first Sunday of the winter months. View the Acropolis from afar at night to see it bathed in gold.*

Chateau de Versailles

29

FRANCE'S GRANDEST CHATEAU

FRANCE // How many abodes in the world have 700 rooms, 2153 windows, 67 staircases, 800 hectares of garden, 2100 statues and sculptures, and enough paintings to pave an 11km road? That's right, France's first entry in the Ultimate Travelist isn't the Eiffel Tower, it's the ultimate crash pad: the Chateau de Versailles. And what is possibly even more mesmerising than this building's extreme size is the ostentatious opulence that pervades every last brick and baroque, egg-and-dart carved cornice.

French 'Sun King' Louis XIV transformed his father's humble hunting lodge southwest of Paris into a monumental palace to house his 6000 sycophantic courtiers in the 17th century. It was the kingdom's political capital and seat of the royal court from 1682 until the French Revolution in 1789. Today a Unesco World Heritage site, the royal residence is a glittering evocation of French royal history and the conspiring, romancing, plotting, intrigue and back-stabbing drama that went on behind royal doors. Ogle at your reflection a dozen times in the shimmering Hall of Mirrors, imagine the queen giving birth in front of an audience in her bedchamber, watch fountains dance in the gardens, see horses prance in the stables, and congratulate yourself on making it to the ball.

🐾 **SEE IT !** *The RER C5 runs from Paris' Left Bank RER stations to Versailles-Chateau Rive Gauche. Buy tickets online.*

Left, the Hall of Mirrors in the Palace of Versailles. Below, scenes from Djemaa El-Fna.

SQUARES TO SEE

↓

Fortify yourself with *moules marinière* and strong Belgian beer before setting off into Brussels' Grand Place.

 PAGE 148

↓

More chilled out is Trinidad's colonial Plaza Mayor, where the Caribbean pace of life is slow and graceful, like the dancers that emerge at dusk.

PAGE 301

↓

Mexico City's vast Zócalo inspires awe and even a bit of footsoreness. Get here in an iconic VW Beetle cab.

 PAGE 278

Djemaa el-Fna

30

WHERE STREET THEATRE THRIVES

MOROCCO // Chaotic and enchanting in equal measures, Djemaa el-Fna is the vibrant heart of Marrakesh. This main square is a hub of hoopla, *halqa* (street theatre) and *hikayat* (oral storytelling) that has been thriving since medieval times. During the day, soothsayers and snake-charmers patrol the pavement along with a ragtag assortment of hawkers, henna tattoo artists and rather dubious dentists. Once the sun sets, the square transforms into a mashup of music and mayhem that is part circus and bawdy vaudeville act, and part open-air concert.

The original activity here was of a more gruesome nature. During the 11th century, this was Marrakesh's public executions site, which explains the square's name: 'assembly of the dead'. From these macabre beginnings, the Djemaa evolved into an entertainment centre and evenings here are now fuelled by food stalls offering tajines and snail broth, while acrobats, storytellers, musicians and weird and wonderful slapstick acts perform for milling crowds. Unesco proclaimed the Djemaa a 'Masterpiece of World Heritage' in 2001. Weave through the tutu-clad monkeys and cross-dressing belly dancers to search out a storyteller telling a tale or a Gnaoua musician hypnotising a huddle of spectators, and you'll understand why.

☛ SEE IT ! *For the full experience, arrive at sunset and spend the evening sampling the shows.*

Left, and below, street scenes from Hanoi: a street seller and a calligrapher.

Hanoi Old Quarter

31

MULTICULTURAL MELTING POT

OLD QUARTERS

↓

The blueprint of Gamla Stan dates from the Middle Ages. Its cobbled lanes are surrounded by the waters of the Swedish capital.

 page 104

↓

Tbilisi's Old Town is impossibly charming but if its buildings look on the verge of collapse, that's because they are.

 page 158

↓

On the Greek island of Rhodes this Old Town and port is a mongrel of medieval and classical architecture.

page 188

VIETNAM // Hanoi's Old Quarter is the complete Indochine package – a little bit French, a little bit Communist and a whole lot Vietnamese. In this neighbourhood, French colonial mansions rub chopsticks with frenetic Southeast Asian street markets and cool cafes where teenage metallers rock out to wailing guitars. Sprawling north from Hoan Kiem Lake, the Old Quarter is Hanoi's cosmopolitan heart and it's difficult not to fall in love with its unbridled exuberance and its brash joie de vivre.

Shop-houses in the Old Quarter are stacked up crazily like boxes in a warehouse, and storefronts spill out into the street in flowing reams of rainbow-coloured silk, leaving just enough room for a constant stream of weaving motorcycles and wandering streetfood vendors in conical straw hats. Dotted among the chaos are historic treasures – the One Pillar Pagoda, the Temple of Literature – and some truly spectacular places to munch on everything from *pho* (soup) to French baguettes.

Sure it's commercial – as Hanoi's main retail district that's rather the point – but it's also exactly what you'd hope to find in a bustling Asian metropolis.

SEE IT ! *There are frequent daily flights to Hanoi from Ho Chi Minh City; its best budget digs are near Hoan Kiem Lake.*

Cradle Mountain

32

NATURAL TASMANIAN SPLENDOUR

AUSTRALIA // Often abbreviated, Cradle Mountain–Lake St Clair National Park lies in the northwest of Tasmania, Australia's captivating island, which is to say that it's a long way from the rest of the world. Make the trip, however, and you'll encounter Australia's quirky wildlife – wombats, wallabies and Tasmanian devils if you're very lucky – and pristine natural scenery. Pack walking boots (and waterproofs) because this is hiking country, whether you do some of the many day walks or take on the Overland Track, a six-day trek from Cradle Valley to Lake St Clair across alpine heaths and buttongrass-filled valleys. Tree lovers will be in raptures thanks to the varied ecosystems that include old-growth rainforest, deciduous beech and lofty King Billy pines. The park, all 168,000 hectares of it, is a World Heritage area thanks to its biodiversity.

One early fan was Austrian immigrant Gustav Weindorfer, who built a chalet, christened Waldheim, and campaigned for the preservation of the region. Today, Waldheim has been joined by several comfortable lodges; after a hard day's hiking around icy lakes, overlooked by the distinctive fin of Mt Ossa (at 1617m, Tasmania's highest peak), kicking back to watch an impossible number of stars in the night sky with a glass of Tasmanian wine in your hand is one of the world's unforgettable experiences.

☛ SEE IT ! *The closest airport, Launceston, is a two-hour drive away. You'll need to take a ferry or flight from the mainland.*

Left, snowgum trees near Lake St Clair. Below, Uluru framed by gumtrees in the Outback.

NATURAL WONDERS

↓

Of the five major waterfalls in the Ultimate Travelist, the highest is Angel Falls in Venezuela, which plunges more than 900m.

 page 198

↓

Twice as deep as the Grand Canyon, Peru's vertiginous Cañón del Colca is home to soaring condors and a rich cultural history.

 page 305

↓

The Blue Hole, off Belize's coast is a massive plunge pool, created when an underwater cave roof collapsed.

page 258

Uluru

33

KALEIDOSCOPIC DESERT SKYSCRAPER

AUSTRALIA // For a whopping great stationary rock, Uluru has an uncanny ability to sneak up on people – even those who have spent hours driving through the desert specifically to see it (which is the best way to visit – though it's possible to fly in, with the bonus of an aerial view of the place).

Suddenly, boo! There it is, leaping up from the otherwise feature-free horizon. The profile is familiar, but the colour always surprises. For the full effect, wait until early morning. In the bone-chilling pre-dawn desert gloom, pick a spot and get a fix on the sacred silhouetted monolith. Have your camera ready – like a sniper with the safety catch off – because, when the sun leaps out from behind the dunes, an extraordinary but brief lightshow begins. Uluru blushes royally. A revolving palette of earthy tones washes across its face – an autumnal spectrum that rushes from red to gold, through 50 shades of brown. Afterwards, explore this continent-defining behemoth boulder up close, discovering myriad features including pools, waterfalls, sacred sites and an ancient indigenous classroom, complete with old lessons painted on the walls.

SEE IT ! *It's a 4½-hour drive from Alice Springs. Respect the Anangu people's wishes and don't climb on it. Walk the base instead.*

Charles Bridge

34

BRIDGE ACROSS TIME

CZECH REPUBLIC // If Charles Bridge was still the city's main artery, Prague would have gone purple and died years ago. Fortunately, there are now alternative ways across the Vltava River into the celebrated City of a Hundred Spires, and the iconic thoroughfare is pedestrianised. Elbowing through the throng of tourists that congeals on the bridge by 9am, you won't need reminding that this structure is all about large numbers. The bridge is 520m-long, has 16 arches and 30 baroque statues, but perhaps the most important number relates to the foundation stone, laid by Charles IV in 1357, on 9 July at 5.31am. Exactly. The Holy Roman Emperor, a numerologist, allegedly selected this precise moment because it forms a numerical bridge, or scale: 1 3 5 7 9 7 5 3 1.

The bridge has survived numerous floods and wars, and boasts many magnetic charms. Visit at dawn to dodge crowds, explore the stonework and enjoy views up and down the river, but keep an eye on the Bradáč (Bearded Man), a stone head at the Staré Město end. Traditionally, when the river rose above the Bradáč, locals legged it into the hills.

☛ SEE IT ! *View the bridge from a different angle during a boat trip along the Vltava.*

Abel Tasman National Park

35

NEW ZEALAND // This country's national parks can be hard work sometimes: arduous squelches through ankle-deep mud, frigid river crossings, gut-busting climbs over clagged-in mountain passes. Then it rains. Welcome to New Zealand.

But it needn't be this way. Near Nelson, at the top of South Island, Abel Tasman is a national park pleasuredome – a place where you can swim, sunbathe, kayak and kick back, enjoying all the fun of a beach-bum holiday. This is the country's smallest national park. It's also the sunniest and most popular, luring visitors with a seductive blend of golden beaches, sparkling seas, pretty coastal forest and sculpted granite cliffs.

There's no shame in simply admiring the view, but there's plenty to keep you active. The coastal track is Abel Tasman's cruisy multiday Great Walk with seaside campsites, communal huts and even luxury lodges. Day-trippers can hike shorter sections by hopping on and off water taxis. The ultimate adventure, however, is kayaking. Friendly waters and easy options make this an unforgettable way to explore Abel Tasman's hidden coves and cosy up to wildlife such as fur seals, penguins and dolphins.

SEE IT ! *The park is a year-round destination. It's an hour's drive west of Nelson, easily reached by domestic flights.*

Left, looking out on the Tasman Sea from the Abel Tasman National Park. Below, Buttermere in Cumbria's Lake District National Park.

Lake District National Park

36

ENGLAND // The Lake District contains England's highest mountain (Scafell Pike at 978m) and deepest and longest lakes (Wastwater and Windermere). None are global giants, but simple statistics don't do England's most famous outdoor destination justice. Seeing this landscape for the first time is wonderfully inspiring, partly because most visitors will feel they know it through the eyes of others: the Romantic poets swarmed here in the 19th century and defined the concept of sublime nature. More recently, Alfred Wainwright, whose illustrated midcentury hiking guides are still popular, was inspired here.

Walkers relish the demanding paths past the slate-capped fells, craggy peaks, tumbling waterfalls and shimmering lakes. You don't have to dust off your hiking boots, though: cruises on the lakes and visits to museums celebrating William Wordsworth and Beatrix Potter can be just as rewarding, while strolls around local towns and villages let you enjoy the panorama without getting drenched by the frequent rain. The Lake District also offers some wonderful food and drink, from Michelin-starred restaurants to small-batch ales. However you work up your thirst, England's wilderness will satisfy.

🖝 SEE IT ! *Keswick, Kendal, Windermere and Ambleside are the main bases. Trains stop at Oxenholme.*

37 Louvre

Paris, FRANCE // OK, so many of the millions who annually enter the Louvre immediately hunt down the *Mona Lisa* and *Venus de Milo*, then wander aimlessly – but the planet's most-visited museum is no two-hit wonder. This is a finely curated record of human endeavour and expression throughout time, housed in a 12th-century building that's as interesting as the exhibits. The glass pyramid was much criticised when installed, but the juxtaposition of ultra-modern architecture with the historic backdrop is a reflection of the eclectic selection of 35,000 objets d'art and international antiquities found within, and it's now a Parisian landmark. The Louvre's scale is a little intimidating. Imagine you're eating an elephant – tackle one section at a time, go for the juicy bits first (while your tastebuds and intellectual appetite are keenest) and don't attempt to finish it in one sitting.

SEE IT ! *Admission is free on the first Sunday of each month, but it gets packed as a result. Better to pay €16.*

38 Torres del Paine

HIKING-LOVERS' PARADISE

CHILE // Patagonia summons every iota of its fabled wilderness into one dramatic thrust of precipitous granite that sheers away above the wind-ravaged steppe in an outdoor-lovers' oasis of forest-cloaked mountains, lakes, plains and glacier. This 181,000-hectare Unesco Biosphere Reserve is as good as it sounds (and a good deal more remote) – small wonder many consider this South America's best hiking. A circuit right around the base of these 2800m-high jagged *torres* (towers) of rock is a week's worth of wild walking, and besides the rich mix of scenery you may glimpse rhea, Andean condors, guanacos and grey foxes. And rapidly changing weather systems ensure the view remains rivetingly kaleidoscopic wherever you wander.

SEE IT ! *Buses run to the park from Puerto Natales; if you plan on staying in the park's refugios (shelters) book ahead; if you don't get a reservation you'll have to camp.*

39 Lake Baikal

RUSSIA // Siberia is a profound place, and there's nowhere in its vast expanse deeper than Lake Baikal: literally. Plummeting 1642m from its azure waves (or, in winter, turquoise ice) to its almost unfathomable bottom, there's no lake deeper on the planet either. Of huge historical, cultural and spiritual significance – Russians call it 'the Sacred Sea' – the 30-million-year-old Baikal has an otherworldly air that's stirred and sustained nomadic tribes, Buddhists, Decembrists, artists and adventurers for centuries. The world's only exclusively freshwater seal, the nerpa, also calls Baikal home. Whether you swim in it, sail on it, swallow it (the waters are said to have magical properties), circumvent its southern tip by train, dogsled over it or just gawk at it from its 2000km of shoreline, you'll find 'the Pearl of Siberia' to be nature at her most sparkling.

SEE IT ! *Visit from Listvyanka via Irkutsk; Severobaikalsk (on the BAM railway) is best for trekking routes. Boats run in summer only.*

40 Eiffel Tower

Paris, FRANCE // How many world icons claim such an ungainly nickname as 'metal asparagus'? And who in their right mind would have any desire to climb such an eyesore? That, *ma chère*, is the beauty of Paris – a European capital that sends romantic shivers down spines and commands incessant admiration with its architectural grandeur, artistic pedigree and unfaltering style. Its biggest drawcard is La Tour Eiffel, the world's most coquettish tourist attraction. Round a corner, the wrought-iron spire pops provocatively into view, cross the boulevard, it's gone: spotting the Eiffel Tower from wherever you are in the city becomes an obsession for visitors to Paris – until there is nothing for it but to touch, scale and experience this 324m-tall French flirt right up close. Monumental crowds only contribute to the sweet climax at the top: the whole of Paris laid out at your feet.

SEE IT ! *Count 720 steps to the 2nd floor, from where it is lift-only access to the top. To avoid queues, walk or buy lift tickets online.*

Pompeii

BEHOLD THE EARTH'S FURY

ITALY // The dark, looming cone of Mt Vesuvius seems awfully close indeed. As you wander the eerily well-preserved alleyways of this ancient city, you can't help but keep looking back to that volcano – all 1280-still-active-metres of it. Its last cataclysmic eruption occurred in AD 79. And they reckon Vesuvius is likely to have a really big blowout about every 2000 years... Do the math. It certainly adds a frisson to exploring Pompeii, the unlucky spot that suffered the brunt of Vesuvius' incendiary ire back in the 1st century.

Pompeii itself is a marvel. The city was probably founded in the 7th century BC, and became a fashionable holiday spot on the Bay of Naples. When the volcano went boom, thousands perished, and Pompeii was entombed under a layer of *lapilli* (burning pumice stone) for over a millennia – a moment-in-time capsule of Roman life, albeit buried in horrific circumstances.

The city spanned 66 hectares; not all of it has been uncovered, and not all that has been uncovered can be seen in one visit. There are a million other tourists – most flocking to snigger at the rude frescoes in the Roman brothel – but also enough intriguing side streets to enable the curious to get away from the crowds. But where to

Above, frescoes of Roman residents and, right, the Forum at Pompeii.

start? There's the wide, pillared forum where you can almost still hear traders selling and philosophers philosophising. There are fat-stoned roads, gouged with the ruts of cartwheels past. There's an impressive amphitheatre, 150 years older than the Colosseum, making it the earliest surviving amphitheatre in the world. There are villas and frescoes and temples and a spa. And, most macabre of all, there are the plaster casts of cowering and desperate people, made from the ghostly shadows their corpses left behind.

☛ SEE IT ! *Pompeii is a 30- to 40-minute train ride from Naples and Sorrento; the site entrance is 50m from the station.*

42

Habana Vieja
Crumbling colonial splendour

↓

CUBA // Habana Vieja – old Havana – is the closest you can come to stepping into a sepia-tinted vintage photograph: stroll along cobbled streets, past pastel buildings and vintage cars. The atmospheric decay makes it a hit with photographers, but this is no mausoleum. Walk the alleys at night and see Cubanos dancing to the radio and playing dominos. With the opening of relations between Cuba and the US, modernisation will become rapid.

☛ SEE IT ! *Until direct travel from the US increases, book flights from Canada, Europe and Mexico.*

43 Table Mountain

TABLETOP CAPERS

SOUTH AFRICA // Other cities have signature buildings or manmade monuments, Cape Town has its own mountain. Watching clouds accumulate on Table Mountain's plateau, between Lion's Head and Devils Peak, and then spilling over its sides – a phenomenon known as the tablecloth effect – is a bankable travel moment. You can catch a cable car up, but it's better to earn the panorama across South Africa's most vibrant city towards the Cape of Good Hope. Various routes take you to vantage points. The classic climb follows Platteklip Gorge, in the footsteps of António de Saldanha, whose first recorded ascent was in 1503. To reach the top, aim for 1088m-high Maclear's Beacon, just above the Upper Cableway station. If your timing's right, join locals watching the moon rise above the Hottentots Holland Mountains, after hiking to the 669m-high Lion's Head.

☛ SEE IT ! *To experience Table Mountain a little differently, rent a mountain bike and go explore.*

44 Old Town Square

PRAGUE'S CLOCKWORK HEART

CZECH REPUBLIC // If you've ever wondered what it would be like to tumble into the pages of a Hans Christian Andersen fairy-tale, just step into Prague's Old Town Square. In this pedestrian-packed medieval market place, ornate frontages rise up on all sides like pieces of gingerbread and heels click on cobbles that have seen nearly a millennium of footfalls. As the setting for Prague's famous astronomical clock – a madcap creation from 1410 – the square is visited by almost everyone, but that doesn't diminish its sense of timeless wonder. There are busking jazz bands and concerts, political meetings and fashion shows, plus Christmas and Easter markets, all watched over by a brooding art nouveau statue of Jan Hus.

Climb the crude stone staircase that winds its way up the tower of the Old Town Hall and you'll be greeted by awesome views over a sea of terracotta rooftops, cobbled lanes and the needle spires of the Church of Our Lady before Týn.

☛ SEE IT ! *Old Town Square forms the cobbled heart of Staré Město (Old Town), a short stroll east from Charles Bridge and Vltava River.*

45

Serengeti National Park
The wildlife show

↓

TANZANIA // No other park in the world spawns such a magnificent wild-life spectacle. It starts on the plains of the Serengeti, where wildebeest are born between January and March. Together with their herds they number 1.5 million, and come late April they start 'The Great Migration' – a 3000km, eight-month round trip to the Masai Mara. Watching it all from the sidelines are some of Africa's greatest safari species: lion, elephant, rhino, giraffe and buffalo.

🐾 SEE IT ! *Fly into Kilimanjaro Airport; it is then a short hop by light aircraft.*

Hermitage

46

St Petersburg, RUSSIA // One of the oldest and most comprehensive museums in the world, the Hermitage is a superlative-defying assemblage of priceless artistic masterpieces and architectural marvels. Originally commissioned by Catherine the Great (a self-confessed art 'glutton') in 1764 to store her private collection, the museum now lays claim to a staggering three million items.

Housed in the gilded-green Winter Palace and five adjoining riverside buildings – all of them imposing and imperious – the Hermitage's labyrinthine halls and rarefied rooms teem with treasures spanning the ages. Under the museum's roofs are everything from Egyptian antiquities to contemporary installations and more Old Masters, Impressionists, post-Impressionists, Fabergé eggs and invaluable icons than you can shake a paintbrush at. It's easy to feel overwhelmed by the range and richness of this unmissable St Petersburg landmark, stretching sumptuously along the banks of the River Neva: it's been estimated that to view every display for one minute at the Hermitage would take 11 years. A bit of forward planning will save you sore feet, not to mention your sanity.

☞ SEE IT ! *To beat the long queues, buy your tickets online, or see if the courtyard ticket machines are working.*

FANTASTIC FJORDS & LOCHS

↓

Geirangerfjord is the archetypal Norwegian fjord and the most popular in that country. Other fjords are available.

☞ page 128

↓

On the opposite side of the world, New Zealand's Fiordland is similarly high profile. Milford and Doubtful Sounds are the star attractions.

☞ page 36

↓

On a slightly smaller scale are Scottish lochs. Some are open to the sea but the largest freshwater loch is Loch Lomond.

☞ page 257

Left, an interior view of the Hermitage. Below, scenes from Kotor.

Bay of Kotor

47

SEASIDE MOUNTAIN MAJESTY

MONTENEGRO // Geologists may quibble over whether the Bay of Kotor is the only fjord on the Mediterranean, but with a landscape this charismatic, who really cares what you call it. In the many twists and turns of the bay, rugged mountains of lavender-grey scree tumble down to a coastal fringe of olive and pomegranate trees above a limpid opal sea. Whether you are kayaking around rocky coves, sailing across to islands topped with monasteries or trekking into the craggy hinterland, you will be far too captivated by your surroundings to worry about how to classify it.

In fact, the bay does an excellent job of presenting all of the highlights of the Mediterranean in one neat package, fusing baroque architecture, Napoleonic history and Slavic bravado. The historic walled city of Kotor offers cafe culture, neat cobbled alleyways and Venetian loggia; Risan is home to Roman mosaics; and Perast is just one of numerous seaside hamlets fragrant with wild fig. The bay gets crowded with the yachting set during summer months, but you can escape on a mountain bike into the brooding hills, trip up to lofty Lovcen National Park or seek complete serenity in the 12th-century Cathedral of St Tryphon.

☞ SEE IT ! *Kotor town is a perfect base for exploring the bay, or make a day trip from Dubrovnik just across the Croatian border.*

Below, the walled desert fort of Jaisalmer. Right, the intricately carved Patwon Ki haveli, characteristic of Jaisalmer's architecture.

48
Jaisalmer

FABULOUS FORTS

↓

The marvellous and little-known Cita-delle de la Ferriere sternly looks out over Haiti, which perhaps explains its secret status.

 page 187

↓

On Sri Lanka's south coast, Galle Fort is a colonial construction built by the Portuguese, then managed by the Dutch before being taken over by the British.

 page 261

↓

Enter a world of sultans and desert derring-do in Oman's Nizwa Fort, west of Muscat.

page 290

LEAVE OTHER DESERT FORTS IN THE SHADE

INDIA // When the magnificent desert fortress of Jaisalmer finally fell to invading armies, its female inhabitants committed mass suicide while its warriors rode out to certain death; anything was better than the dishonour of being captured as a slave. So sure, the Rajputs of Jaisalmer were certainly a proud people, but when you look at their glorious sandstone city, you'll realise they had a lot to be proud of.

Even after four centuries, their honey-coloured fortress still rises from the sandy plains like a mirage, encircled by 99 mighty bastions. Inside, the beautiful structure is a crazed tangle of tiny lines, complete with graceful *havelis* (merchants' houses) and ancient temples that almost collapse under the weight of all the carvings and statuary. No place more successfully evokes the romance of Rajasthan.

Tourism is big business for the desert city, but somehow, as the first light illuminates streets that perfectly match the tones of the surrounding desert, it doesn't matter. To visit Jaisalmer is to step into an *Arabian Nights* fantasy made real, in a giant sandcastle seemingly carved out of the desert itself. Powerful stuff!

☛ SEE IT ! *The fragile fort is the heart of Jaisalmer but, for conservation reasons, most people stay in the surrounding bazaars.*

49 Ngorongoro Crater

TANZANIA // The rim of the Ngorongoro Crater is not just one of the world's largest intact volcanic calderas, but a place where every arriving visitor faces a dilemma – should I stay, or should I go? Staying is tempting as the views into the crater become more and more spellbinding the longer one looks. The fertile floor far below, hemmed in by dramatic escarpments hundreds of metres tall, is decorated with swamps, forests, Lake Magadi and swathes of savannah grasses. The fact everyone eventually pulls themselves away reflects nothing negative about the view, but rather the sheer riches of what lies beneath.

The concentration of wildlife on the Ngorongoro Crater floor, particularly of lions and other large predators, is unparalleled anywhere else in Africa, and it remains one of the planet's very best places to see black rhino in the wild.

☞ SEE IT ! *Kilimanjaro Airport is the main gateway. Find morning peace on the crater floor by arriving early (sleep at a nearby lodge).*

50 Hiroshima Peace Memorial Park

JAPAN // What was once ground zero for the world's first nuclear attack is now a green expanse, home to numerous memorials – a peaceful place to wander and reflect. The ruins of the only structure to survive the bombing, Genbaku Dome, still stand as a blunt reminder of the devastation. The Pond of Peace is the park's central feature and leads to the cenotaph, a curved monument displaying all the names of known victims. Emotions run high on a visit here, but with sadness also comes hope in the human spirit. Nowhere is this more apparent than at the Children's Peace Monument, with its colourful paper cranes – symbolising happiness and longevity – inspired by Sadako Sasaki. Sadako was two years old when the bomb dropped and she developed leukaemia aged 11. When she died before reaching her goal to fold 1000 cranes, her classmates completed the rest.

☞ SEE IT ! *Hiroshima is a major stop on the Tokyo–Osaka–Hakata Shinkansen bullet-train line.*

51 Pantheon

ITALY // It seems almost implausible that the ornate pavilion dominating Rome's Piazza della Rotonda could have been in use for 2000 years, but it's true. The Pantheon was commissioned by Marcus Agrippa sometime during the reign of Augustus (27 BC – AD 14), and rebuilt by Hadrian around AD 126.

Neoclassical buildings elsewhere are mostly copies of this magnificent blueprint: the mighty portico with its forest of Corinthian columns, the gravity-defying unsupported dome, even the sign above the door, which here announces Agrippa's monument to the world.

Stepping inside is to step into ancient Rome; consider for a moment the oculus in the roof, which has been open to the sky for 20 centuries (discrete drains carry away the rainwater that falls inside the Pantheon). When in Rome, visit the Pantheon, if nothing else.

☛ SEE IT ! *The Pantheon graces the southern end of the Piazza della Rotonda, one of Rome's favourite spots for an alfresco dinner.*

52 Tate Modern

ENGLAND // Five-million eager sightseers every year can't be wrong. London's Tate Modern is the most-visited contemporary art gallery in the world for good reason. And it's not just the art, although that is a pretty hefty drawcard, comprising, as it does, works by Rothko, Matisse, Warhol, Pollock, Hirst et al. It's the industrial architecture of the 200m-long building itself, a former power station built in the 1940s. Or is it? Maybe it's the location, standing grandly by the River Thames on the South Bank. And there'll be a whole new reason by the close of 2016, when a swanky 11-storey extension opens on the south side, doubling the current display space. Join the devotees and decide what does it for you.

☛ SEE IT ! *The most scenic arrival? Tough decision: either walk across Millennium Bridge from St Paul's Cathedral or take the Tate-to-Tate boat from Tate Britain on Millbank.*

53

Naqsh-e Jahan
Persian perfection

↓

IRAN // At the heart of Esfahan, Iran's most captivating city, lies the mighty square of Naqsh-e Jahan. Built in 1602 as the centrepiece of Shah Abbas' new capital, the square was designed to contain the finest architectural jewels of the Safavid Empire. On the south side stands the Shah Mosque, a melange of domes and vaulted arches. On the eastern edge the Sheikh Lotfollah mosque is a rhapsody in blue majolica tiles, and on the western side resides the palace of Ali Qapu.

🐎 SEE IT !
See families picnic and promenade in the early evening.

55

54 Tiger Leaping Gorge

TRAILS CARVED THROUGH TIME

CHINA // The Grand Canyon (p20) might win all the popularity contests but Tiger Leaping Gorge is nature's prettiest poster boy. Picture snowcapped mountains rising on either side of a gorge so deep that you can be 2km above the river rushing across the rocks far below. Then imagine winding up and down trails that pass through tiny farming villages, where you can rest while enjoying views so glorious they defy superlatives. That just about sums up Tiger Leaping Gorge. Sure, its knee-wrecking switchbacks might make you whimper at times, but it's one of the deepest canyons in the world, it's China's unmissable trek and it's gorgeous every step of the way.

☛ SEE IT ! *The gorge carves its way through remote northwest Yúnnán, near the Unesco-listed town of Lìjiāng. In May and early June, the hills are afire with plant and flower life.*

55 Notre-Dame

HOLY HEART OF PARIS

FRANCE // In the centre of Paris, on Île de la Cité in the Seine, Notre-Dame isn't merely the most mind-melting example of French Gothic architecture around, it's the most storied church in Europe. The Third Crusade began here in 1185 (before the cathedral was finished); Joan of Arc's mum petitioned for her daughter's conviction to be overturned in 1455; statues were beheaded during the French revolution; numerous royal marriages, and dramatic deaths, took place under its roof; and the liberation of Paris from the Nazis began when the Resistance rang Notre-Dame's oldest bell. Contemplate this while climbing 400 spiral steps to the western facade, where La Ville Lumière glows in front and grimacing gargoyles stand behind, threatening to push you off, à la Quasimodo in Victor Hugo's Gothic classic.

☛ SEE IT ! *Entry to the cathedral is free.*

Kakadu National Park

TROPICAL TIMEWARP

AUSTRALIA // Some say Australia lacks history, but in Kakadu, 50,000 years of stories are constantly being told – you just have to listen. Australia's largest national park is as big as Wales or New Jersey State, sprawling across 20,000 fecund sq km from the estuaries of the Alligator Rivers to the escarpment border with Arnhem Land. In its warm, wet and wild embrace you can explore billabongs, plunge into pools beneath waterfalls and climb through time to meet the oldest surviving culture on earth. Bininj and Mungguy people have lived here for millennia. Proof? Check out ancient rock art at Ubirr and the Anbangbang Shelter drawings at Burrunggui. Then, pull on your adventure pants and let an indigenous guide lead you through a primordial-looking landscape where nature has run riot in the greenhouse-like Top End, supersizing everything – including the crocs.

☛ SEE IT ! *Kakadu's gateway town, Jaibaru, is three hours' drive to the east from Darwin.*

Sydney Opera House

SINGING SAILS

AUSTRALIA // Architecturally, the world's most recognisable opera house has been compared to everything from a peeled orange to mating turtles – but most descriptions involve sails. Which is apt, considering its magnificent view across Sydney's sensational harbour, from a peach of a position betwixt Circular Quay and the Botanical Gardens. The building's über-modern design sent some Sydneysiders and operatic folk apoplectic when architect Jørn Utzon got the gig and construction began in 1959. The disgruntled Dane ended up walking out on the unfinished project in 1966 (never to return). Now, along with its neighbour the Harbour Bridge (AKA the Big Coat Hanger), the Opera House essentially is Sydney – at least as far as snowglobes and postcards go. Although the internal acoustics have been criticised, it's a spectacular vision, particularly viewed from the water.

☛ SEE IT ! *The Opera House stages performances ranging from rock gigs to comedy, and even the occasional opera. Tours can be arranged.*

Edinburgh Castle

TALL, DARK AND HANDSOME CASTLE

SCOTLAND // Squint up at Edinburgh Castle and you'd swear it wasn't built, but grew. Lording over the Scottish capital, this stronghold seems to segue organically out of the volcanic plug below; it's hard to tell where nature ends and masonry begins. But built it was, strategically placed to defend against invading armies – and it's seen plenty of those. It's a steep, uneven haul from the castle entrance to the Portcullis Gate, past the Honours (Scotland's crown jewels) and Stewart-era Great Hall, up to 12th-century St Margaret's Chapel – Edinburgh's oldest building, perched right at the very top. The views, on a good day, are sweeping, revealing the Firth of Forth, Pentland Hills and, of course, the splendid city itself. However, the One O'Clock Gun – a WWII 25-pounder that booms at 1pm daily (bar Sundays) – will remind you of this mount's military, rather than scenic, purpose.

☛ SEE IT ! *The castle is open from 9.30am to 5pm (to 6pm April to September); last admission is an hour before closing.*

Anne Frank Huis

HAUNTING HISTORY

Amsterdam, NETHERLANDS // Will it haunt you? Yes. Is it worth it? Absolutely, and one million visitors a year surely agree. The story of how Anne Frank and her family hid from the Nazis for several years before being mysteriously betrayed and sent to their deaths is legendary. Her diary, began on her 13th birthday in 1942, captured hearts and minds throughout the world, and a visit to this house in Amsterdam, now a museum, is a powerful experience. Step through the revolving bookcase of the 'Secret Annex' and up the steep stairs into the living quarters. It was in this dark and airless space that the Franks lived in complete silence during the day. The claustrophobic rooms, their windows still covered with blackout screens, portray an all-too-real feel for Anne's life in hiding. And seeing her diary in the flesh – well, it's moving, plain and simple.

☛ SEE IT ! *Anne Frank Huis is in the Western Ring neighbourhood of Amsterdam. Pre-purchase tickets online to avoid queuing onsite.*

60

Jökulsárlón
Luminous iceberg lagoon

↓

ICELAND //
Jökulsárlón is one of Iceland's many natural wonders but it's the country's highest entry here. How did a 17-sq-km lagoon of icebergs beat waterfalls and volcanoes? Easy. On a sunny day, with a bowl of lobster soup in your hands to brace against the chill, sit beside this mesmerising place and watch. Hear icebergs calve off the Breiðamerkur-jökull glacier, clink against each other as they drift out to sea. There. A seal pops up. Another. The stillness is punctuated with their splashes.

🐦 SEE IT ! *Hire a car from Reykjavik and stop here on a loop of the Ring Rd.*

Yellowstone National Park

ONE STEAMING GREAT WILDERNESS

Wyoming, USA // This place stinks. And it has no manners at all. The rotten-egg whiff taunts your nostrils; your ears are assaulted by a vulgarity of belches, burps and farts. But then, what do you expect when you're exploring the largest geothermal area in the world? Fully half of the globe's entire collection of geysers, mud-pots, fumaroles and other such restless, pungent features are located right here.

First doesn't always mean best – but Yellowstone is in with a reasonable shout. It was the world's very first national park, designated in 1872. It's centred on a vast volcanic caldera, and within its 8983 sq km sit not only strange and steamy eructations but also mountain ranges, wildlife-roamed plains, a plethora of lakes and rivers, some petrified forest and the park's very own Grand Canyon. Given the sheer volume of all this natural beauty on display, putting up with a little sulphur-smelliness seems a small price to pay.

So there are 1200 geysers to watch – Old Faithful being the most famous. And there are hot springs to visit – from the bloodshot eyeball of Grand Prismatic to the travertine shelves at Mammoth. But the wildlife is perhaps the biggest draw. This is like North America's answer to an African safari: the

sweeping savannah of the wild west is busy with creatures, although here the Big Five are bison, bighorn sheep, elk, bear and wolf. Watching a huge herd of shaggy bison warming up by a thermal pool, getting stuck in a 'bear jam' because a grizzly has halted the traffic, or visiting in winter to spot wolf prints in the snow – all are quintessential Yellowstone experiences. Just never forget there's a super-volcano – one of the world's largest – bubbling away underneath, and overdue to blow...

☛ SEE IT ! *The roads between Yellowstone's north and northeast entrances are open all year; other roads have seasonal closures.*

Below, Yellowstone's bison herd is the largest on public land in the US. Above, the Grand Prismatic Spring, the largest hot spring in the US.

GEOTHERMAL WONDERS

↓

Beneath Iceland's surface boils a pressure cooker of heat and water, which frequently blasts into our world at Geysir; yes that's where the name comes from.

☛ page 241

↓

Meet Maori people at Rotorua in New Zealand, against a backdrop of bubbling mud and a sulphurous odour.

☛ page 199

↓

In Japan, at Yakushima and beyond, *onsen*, or hot springs, offer a steamy treat for visitors.

☛ page 199

62 Stonehenge

ENGLAND // Beholding the bewilderingly familiar outline of Stonehenge abruptly erupting from the skyline of Salisbury Plain is an utterly surreal sight – especially seen through a car windscreen while travelling along the A303. Ancient and modern Britain collide head-to-head here, and the result is glorious confusion. How did the sarsen slabs and great bluestone blocks get here, some all the way from Wales, 5000 years ago? Why are they arranged thus – is it a calendar, a cemetery, an ancient place of healing? And how the hell did Neolithic people erect and balance them like giant Jenga blocks? Archaeologists have driven themselves in stone circles trying to crack these conundrums for centuries – ponder the problem yourself while exploring the site and perusing the new visitors centre.

☞ SEE IT ! *Stonehenge is less than two hours' drive from London. Direct access to the stones is prohibited, except during solstices and equinoxes, when you'll have to elbow through hordes of druids.*

63 Berlin Wall

GERMANY // That the Berlin Wall makes it on to this list is more to do with what you can't see than what you can. Erected by the German Democratic Republic, little remains of the infamous fortification that encircled West Berlin from 1961 to 1989. Graffitied stubs rear up in places; information panels along its original route tell of lives lost and families sundered; a reconstructed Checkpoint Charlie – the most notorious of the border crossings – now sits lonely, mid-Friedrichstrasse, dwarfed by office blocks.

However, the wall's absence is as affecting as the fragments that still stand; a reminder that, in Berlin, history isn't something ignorable that happened centuries ago. The Berlin Wall Memorial on Bernauer Strasse shows how it worked: the wall wasn't just a concrete blockade, but layers of barriers, forming a 'death zone'. To appreciate the scale, walk the Mauerweg, a waymarked loop-trail following the wall's 155km-long former footprint.

☞ SEE IT ! *The Berlin Wall Memorial visitor centre is open Tuesday-Sunday, 10am-6pm; guided tours (in German) run Sundays at 3pm.*

64

Isle of Skye
Magical island

↓

SCOTLAND // The largest island in the Inner Hebrides, Skye has castles and crofts, granite-grey seas and crystalline fairy pools, heather moors and emerald glens. Climbers tackle the Cuillin, Skye's mountain range of jagged black peaks. Wildlife watchers spot sea eagles, dolphins and minke whales. When you're hungry, stop for fish and chips in the pretty town of Portree. The summer sun doesn't set until after 11pm, casting an otherworldly golden glow over this magical island.

☛ SEE IT ! *Skye is accessible from the mainland by bridge. Rent a car.*

Halong Bay

VIETNAM // Imagine 2000 or more islands rising from the emerald waters of the Gulf of Tonkin and you have a vision of breathtaking beauty. Halong translates as 'where the dragon descends into the sea', and legend claims the islands of Halong Bay in northeast Vietnam were created by a great dragon from the mountains. As it charged towards the coast, its flailing tail gouged out valleys and crevasses. When it finally plunged into the sea, the area filled with water, leaving only the pinnacles visible.

Designated a World Heritage site in 1994, this mystical landscape of limestone islets is often compared to Guilin in China or Krabi in southern Thailand. In reality, Halong Bay is more spectacular. The bay's immense number of islands are dotted with wind- and wave-eroded grottoes, and their sparsely forested slopes ring with birdsong. It's highly unlikely you'll have it all to yourself, but when the view's this good, who cares?

☛ SEE IT ! *Sprawling Halong City is the bay's main gateway. Most visitors sensibly opt for tours that include sleeping on a boat in the bay. Weather can be unpredictable; from January to March it is often cool and drizzly while tropical storms are most frequent between May and September.*

66

Duomo Santa Maria del Fiore
Renaissance revisited

↓

Florence, ITALY //
Get yourself on
the outside of
some biscotti and
a stiff latte before
ascending the
463 steps into the
cupola that crowns
Il Duomo di Firenze
– it's quite a climb.
But how often do
you find yourself
nose-to-nose with
centuries' old fres-
coes of the Last
Judgment? With
each step, remem-
ber you're inside
an architectural
wonder that was
hundreds of years
in the making, and
a highlight of the
Renaissance, in the
city of its genesis.
You can't hurry
genius.

☞ SEE IT !
*The church is open
all week, but the
cupola (dome) is
closed on Sundays.*

68

Ko Tao

THAILAND // Why Ko Tao over Thailand's other islands? The answer lies beneath the warm, calm waters that surround this beautiful droplet of land. Its trump card is easy-to-get-to, diverse diving right off its shores and the underwater spectacles have won over divers and snorkellers the world over. Cavort with sharks and rays in a playground of tangled neon coral, toast the day with sunset cocktails on a white beach, then get up and do it all over again the next day. But what makes Tao even more special is there's so much more to the place. Hikers and hermits can get lost in the dripping coastal jungles. And when you're Robinson Crusoe-ed out, hit the pumpin' bar scene that rages until dawn.

SEE IT ! *Reach Ko Tao, off Thailand's southeast coast, by boat via Ko Pha-Ngan or Ko Samui. The best dive sites are at offshore pinnacles within 20km of the island.*

67

Cappadocia

TURKEY // As if plucked from a whimsical fairy tale and set down upon the stark Anatolian plains, Turkey's Cappadocia is a geological oddity of honeycombed hills and towering boulders of otherworldly beauty. The fantastical topography is matched by the human history here. People have long utilised the region's soft stone, seeking shelter underground and leaving the countryside scattered with fascinating troglodyte-style architecture. The fresco-adorned rock-cut churches of Göreme Open-Air Museum and the subterranean refuges of Derinkuyu and Kaymaklı are the most famous sights, but the dusky-orange-and-cream rock valleys also offer unique hiking. Even if you just come to stare at the psychedelic lunar-scapes, be sure to bed down in one of Cappadocia's cave hotels for an experience in 21st-century cavern dwelling.

SEE IT ! *Cappadocia is served by flights and buses from Istanbul. Visit in spring to see wildflowers colourfully transform the valley.*

69

Palenque

PYRAMID PERFECTION

MEXICO // Spilling out of the jungles of Chiapas like the sun-bleached bones of a vanquished Mayan king, Palenque is the most atmospheric of the Mayan sites scattered across southern Mexico. It could be the fearful symmetry of the Temple of the Inscriptions, where an honour guard of servants was slaughtered to accompany king K'inich Janaab' Pakal into the afterlife. It could be the eerie skull carved into the aptly named Temple of the Skull, almost certainly the inspiration for the creepy rabbit in *Donnie Darko*. Or it could be the noises in the jungle, which sound as if nature is coming to take its temple back.

Palenque is accessed from a dusty pit-stop town, but the road to the ruins is lined with relaxing places to stay, from boutique hotels to backpacker cabins – perfect for kicking back for a few days after the rigours of hot and sticky road travel. Complete the Mayan trinity with a boat trip to Yaxchilán and a bike ride through the jungle to mural-filled Bonampak.

🕿 SEE IT ! *More atmospheric than Palenque town, charming El Panchán is the pick of the forest retreats en route to the ruins.*

Palenque is the most atmospheric of southern Mexico's Mayan sites

70

Ilulissat Kangerlua

BUS-SIZED 'BERGS FLOATING ON A BAY

GREENLAND // Welcome to the Greenland of your wildest travel fantasies. This astonishing 40km ice-fjord, packed with icebergs the size of apartment blocks or whole towns, is the island's greatest attraction. It's fed by Sermeq Kujalleq, a prolific hulking glacier that flows an average of 25m daily. A phenomenal 35 billion tonnes of icebergs pass through here each year. There's no sight more mesmerising than gazing upon these monsters and listening to the almighty thunderclap roars that they emit when they fissure or explode in the warmth of the summer sun.

Best of all, the whole spectacle can be seen without the expense and organisation of a boat or helicopter rental that's required to see other 'bergs and fjords around the world. Scattered at the mouth of the bay, the rainbow-hued houses of Ilulissat town are within rowing distance of the live show, which is easily accessible on a short hike from town – although you might prefer to watch the surreal treadmill of icebergs from one of the boat tours plying the bay.

SEE IT ! *Greenland's third-largest town, Ilulissat is a spectacular spot to base yourself; drink in views of the ice-fjord from its bars and restaurants.*

71 Mt Sinai

MOSES' SPECTACULAR MOUNT

EGYPT // The pre-dawn scramble from Elijah's Basin up a steep series of 750 rocky and uneven steps to the top of sacred Mt Sinai is a humbling experience. As the sun comes up to warm the small chapel and mosque at its peak, you'll witness the magnificent spectacle of light washing over the sea of surrounding mountaintops and plunging valleys. Such a sight inspires reverence, as it does for the Christian, Muslim and Jewish pilgrims who believe God delivered his Ten Commandments to Moses at Mt Sinai's summit. Down below, tucked into the mountain's base, is St Katherine's Monastery. Its sturdy Byzantine fortifications are placed over the spot where Moses is believed to have witnessed the burning bush.

🕭 SEE IT ! *Mt Sinai is on the Sinai Peninsula in Egypt. At the time of writing, the peninsula was an area of conflict and travel there was not recommended; check the latest situation before visiting.*

72 Pão de Açúcar

ON TOP OF THE WORLD

BRAZIL // From the peak of Pão de Açúcar (Sugarloaf Mountain), the city of Rio de Janeiro unfolds beneath you to reveal undulating green hills and golden beaches lapped by blue sea, with skyscrapers sprouting along the shore. Once you've seen the city from atop this absurd confection of a mountain, you're unlikely to look at Rio (or your own comparatively lacklustre city) in the same way again. The ride up is good fun: all-glass aerial trams whisk you up to the top in two stages. The adventurous can even rock-climb their way to the summit. And if the breathtaking heights unsteady you, what better way to regain your composure than by nursing a caipirinha or *cerveja* (beer) on the pinnacle of the world.

🕭 SEE IT ! *Sunset on a clear day is the most rewarding time to make the ascent. If you can, avoid between 10am and 11am, and 2pm to 3pm, which is when most tourist buses arrive.*

73

Mezquita
**Worlds collide
in Cordoba**

↓

SPAIN // Picture
endless interwoven
horseshoe arches,
skylit domes and
a glittering *mihrab*
(prayer niche) that
echoes *Arabian
Nights*. Add 50 or
so chapels, a 16th-
century cathedral
shoehorned in the
centre and a min-
aret secreted in
an ecclesiastical
bell tower, and
you have an idea
of Cordoba's
Mezquita. The
resulting clash of
Christian and
Islamic archi-
tecture is an oddity
that must be seen
to be believed.

☛ SEE IT !
*Cordoba lies
between Seville
and Granada in
Andalucía.*

74

Lalibela
Africa's subterranean city

↓

ETHIOPIA //
Across this list,
monuments have
been built by
stacking stone
on top of stone.
One exception is
Lalibela – Ethiopia's
foremost historical
site. The 11 mono-
lithic churches of
this holy city were
chiselled out of
bedrock in the 12th
and 13th centuries.
The city is a head-
quarters of the
Ethiopian Ortho-
dox Church – one
of Christianity's
oldest strands of,
going back to the
days of Solomon
and the Queen of
Sheba. Pilgrims
cross the country
to pray here.

☛ SEE IT ! *Watch
sunrise from the
hill overlooking
Bet Giyorgis,
Lalibela's most
famous church.*

Lake Bled

PICTURE-PERFECT LAKESIDE SETTING

SLOVENIA // Lake Bled is so cute you couldn't make it up. Start with crystal-clear blue water, add a tiny island, then top it with a pretty church and a dramatic cliffside castle. Now attach some Alpine peaks to the backdrop. *Voila*! It really is that lovely and don't we know it. The lake has a reputation for winning the crowds, starting with medieval pilgrims, who came to pray at the island church, and has drawn wealthy Europeans and royalty for centuries. It measures just 2km by 1.4km, and there's a beautiful 6km walk along its shore. Otherwise, hire a *pletna* (gondola), dive beneath the glass-like surface, cycle or simply snap countless photos.

☛ SEE IT ! *In summer, mild thermal springs warm the water to a swimmable 26°C.*

Arashiyama's Bamboo Grove

MAGICAL NATURE

Kyoto, JAPAN // As if Kyoto wasn't enough to make any self-respecting tourist weep for joy, Arashiyama's ethereal bamboo grove could be the most magical place in Japan. If you've seen *Crouching Tiger, Hidden Dragon*, you'll know what to expect. The visual effect of walking among the seemingly infinite stalks of bamboo is like entering another world – the thick green prongs seem to continue endlessly in every direction and there's a strange quality to the light. Ditch the camera, because there's a palpable presence to the place that is utterly impossible to capture in pictures. Instead, slowly traverse the single walkway as it flows gently uphill and contemplate nature as she puts her best foot forward. Drink it in, breathe out. Sigh.

☛ SEE IT ! *Arashiyama flanks Kyoto's western mountains and is packed with sights; dedicate at least half a day for exploration.*

Redwood National Park

NATURAL CALIFORNIAN CATHEDRALS

USA // There's a heavy stillness in the air here, and it positively hums with energy. Underfoot, layers and layers of leaves and needles slowly return to the earth; up above – a long, long way above – the zingy breezes from the Pacific caress the leaves of the forest canopy.

Close to California's border with Oregon, this national park is home to the largest trees on earth: the coast redwood. The conifers thrive in the cool foggy conditions, often growing more than 100m in height (to put that in perspective, the Statue of Liberty is 93m tall) and living for hundreds, occasionally more than a thousand years.

Finding yourself alone in a grove of these giants can be a spiritual experience. But the Redwood National Park isn't just about the redwoods; the park covers Pacific coastline, rivers and a variety of ecosystems. A pilgrimage to these trees most likely begins in San Francisco; driving north, the towns, such as Garberville, get smaller, the vibe wilder and flannel shirts more ubiquitous.

👉 SEE IT ! *From San Francisco take Hwy 1 north along the Pacific coast and then Hwy 101 beyond Eureka. It's a wonderful drive.*

78 Chichén Itzá

A NEW WONDER OF THE WORLD

MEXICO // Arguably the most famous Mayan ruin, Chichén Itzá is a victim of its own success. Sure, it's on every tour-bus itinerary and you're never going to have the place to yourself, but there's a reason why this site was declared one of the new Seven Wonders of the World – it is simply spectacular. From the imposing, monolithic El Castillo pyramid (where the shadow of the plumed serpent god Kukulcán creeps down the staircase at spring and autumn equinoxes) to the Sacred Cenote and curiously designed El Caracol, you don't have to be an archaeologist to have an amazing time here. Chichén Itzá might not have the setting of nearby Palenque (p84) or the magic of neighbouring Tikal (p32), but it deserves its place at the party.

📷 SEE IT ! *Chichén Itzá is two hours from Cancún on the Yucatán Peninsula. The heat, humidity and crowds can be fierce; try to explore the site either early in the morning or late in the afternoon.*

79 Masai Mara National Reserve

KILLER AFRICAN WILDLIFE

KENYA // It's a sad reality that, after visiting the Masai Mara, other wildlife parks can be a little underwhelming. For the Mara is where nature is at her most ferocious, extrovert and heroic. You may wake here to see a herd of elephants lumbering around your camp or glimpse a cheetah whooshing at speed though the grasses, scattering her prey. The Mara rises to every wildlife documentary expectation – it is a vast tract of savannah, dotted with shady umbrella acacias and divided by meandering rivers. Its openness makes wildlife-spotting easy. But even so, the trick is not to get hung up on chasing the big five – lions, elephant, buffalo, rhino and leopards. Instead, let the Mara's primeval performance play out before your eyes: be it a sighting as common as a zebra or as elusive as an endangered African wild dog. Sadly, as in much of the rest of Africa, the Masai Mara is suffering from serious depletion of many species. Visit now, before they are gone forever.

📷 SEE IT ! *Peak season in the Mara is July to October, during the wildebeest migration – prices often rocket during this period.*

80

Metropolitan Museum of Art

State of the art

↓

New York, USA //
The Met's ability to
thrill, confound,
and inspire has
made it one of the
most popular mu-
seums in the world.
Six million visitors a
year come to ogle
at its collection of
ancient Egyptian
art, European
and American
paintings, chiselled
ancient Greek
sculptures, African
and Oceanic
masks, and me-
dieval arms. It's a
self-contained cul-
tural city-state. To
top it off, there's
a rooftop garden
with sculptures
and sublime views
over Central Park.

☞ SEE IT ! *The
Met is on New
York City's Upper
East Side.*

81

82 Valley of the Kings

EGYPT // The Valley of the Kings inspired generations of treasure hunters, archaeologists and dreamers. It was in this isolated hollow that the great pharaohs constructed their princely tombs for hundreds of years. For centuries, the dead were watched over by the pyramid-shaped mountain peak of Al-Qurn (The Horn), entombed with their treasures. Tutankhamun was its most famous inhabitant. Now the golden goodies are in short supply, shipped off to museums the world over, but what remains is a succession of 63 magnificent royal tombs, some little more than a series of bare chambers, others lavishly decorated with ancient scriptures, paintings, statues and the odd sarcophagus. It's a history lesson so good it's worth braving the hordes of visitors attracted to this famed site. Take your imagination and follow in the footsteps of the gods.

🠖 SEE IT ! *The valley lies on the west bank of Luxor. Tombs are opened up on rotation, to aid preservation.*

81 Franz Josef & Fox Glacier

NEW ZEALAND // In Te Wāhipounamu, a Unesco World Heritage site sprawled across the ultra-dramatic west coast of New Zealand's South Island, two tongues of ice permanently point from the mouth of the mountains towards the Tasman Sea, as though the land is absorbed in a Māori haka. Franz Josef and Fox are twin glaciers, remarkable for many reasons – including their proximity to the sea and the speed they move – but, most importantly, because visitors can venture on to their frozen flanks to explore an incredible ice-scape. Walking trails take you close to both (especially Fox), but tours get you on to the ice itself. Options include glacier walking, ice climbing and heli-hiking trips to explore blue-tinted ice caves and seracs. Franz Josef offers the best conditions but Fox is more accessible, and the town of the same name has more alpine charm.

🠖 SEE IT ! *Glacier Country is a four- to five-hour drive from Queenstown (which is five hours from Christchurch).*

82

83

**Hoi An
Old Town**

Old-world charm

↓

VIETNAM // If Hoi An were in Europe, we'd be describing it as 'chocolate box'. Vietnam's most civilised town is both cosmopolitan and provincial but, above all, beautiful. Once an ancient port, it's now bursting with gourmet restaurants, hip bars and cafes, boutiques and tailors. Immerse yourself in history in the warren-like lanes of the Old Town and explore its incredible legacy of tottering Japanese merchant houses, Chinese temples and old-world tea warehouses.

☛ SEE IT ! *Hoi An is between Hanoi and Ho Chi Minh City. Its nearest major transport hub is Danang.*

84 Monument Valley

SANDSTONE FANTASYLAND

USA // Like a classic movie star, Monument Valley has a face known around the world. Her fiery red spindles, sheer-walled mesas and grand buttes have starred in many films and commercials, and have been featured in magazine ads. Monument Valley's epic beauty is heightened by the drab landscape surrounding it. One minute you're in the middle of sand, rocks and infinite sky, then suddenly you're transported to a fantasyland of crimson sandstone towers soaring up to 400m skywards. At one time, the valley was home to Ancestral Puebloans, who abruptly abandoned the site some 700 years ago. The Navajo people arrived a few centuries later, calling it Valley Between the Rocks, and they still inhabit the land.

☛ SEE IT ! *The most famous formations here are conveniently visible from the rough 27km dirt road that loops through Monument Valley Navajo Tribal Park. You can also explore the park by foot or even from the back of a horse.*

85 St Peter's Basilica

OPULENT PAPAL MONUMENT

Vatican City, ITALY // If ever a building could make you feel small and humble in the eyes of a god, this is surely it. St Peter's is huge. It is the largest church in Italy, not to mention the grandest and the wealthiest. Construction began in the 16th century, replacing a smaller basilica that had fallen into disrepair, built on the tomb of the saint. Now St Peter's rises on the west bank of the Tiber like a gargantuan wedding cake. Its ornate facade measures 116m wide and 53m high; its great double dome, an architectural tour de force designed by Michelangelo, soars 137m skywards.

The cavernous interior shows hardly more modesty, oozing marble, bling and effigies of popes, plus Michelangelo's moving Pietà. Incredibly, during papal mass, more than 15,000 worshippers can easily squeeze inside it.

☛ SEE IT ! *A ticket (free) is required to attend the General Papal Audience on Wednesday mornings. These are issued by the Prefecture of the Papal Household; see www.vaticanstate.va.*

87

Red Square

RUSSIA'S HEART & HISTORIC SOUL

RUSSIA // Red Square and the Kremlin remain the historical, geographic and spiritual heart of Moscow, as they have been for nearly 900 years, and it evokes an incredible sense of importance to stroll across the cobblestoned place where so much of Russian history has unfolded. The tall towers and imposing walls of the Kremlin citadel, the iconic onion domes of St Basil's Cathedral and the granite mausoleum of Vladimir Lenin are among the city's most beloved heritage sights. The square is crowded on all sides by architectural marvels; individually they are impressive, but the ensemble is electrifying. The surrounding streets of Kitay Gorod are crammed with churches and old architecture. This is the starting point for any visit to Moscow, or indeed Russia.

🢂 SEE IT ! *Red Square is well served by Moscow's metro lines, three of which converge here. Come at night to see the square empty of crowds and the buildings awash with lights.*

86

Dome of the Rock

PRECIOUS SYMBOL OF FAITH

ISRAEL // The first sight of Jerusalem's Dome of the Rock – its gold top shimmering above a turquoise-hued octagonal base – never fails to take the breath away. It's perhaps the enduring symbol of the city and undoubtedly one of the most photographed buildings on earth. It was constructed between AD 689 and 691 under the patronage of the Umayyad caliph Abd al-Malik.

As its name suggests, the dome covers a slab of stone that is sacred to both the Muslim and Jewish faiths. According to Jewish tradition, it was here that Abraham prepared to sacrifice his son. Islamic tradition has the Prophet Mohammed ascending to heaven from this spot. The *mihrab* (prayer niche) in the sanctuary is said to be the oldest in the Islamic world.

🢂 SEE IT ! *The best view, some say, is from the Mount of Olives, but don't miss the chance to see it up close by taking an early-morning walk up to the Temple Mount/Al-Haram ash-Sharif.*

88

Forbidden City

LEGENDARY DYNASTIC INTRIGUE

Běijīng, **CHINA** // So it's not a city and it's no longer forbidden, but that just makes it all the more mystifying. This enormous palace complex, the largest in the world and home to 24 Chinese emperors over 500 years, is the ultimate in dynastic grandeur, due to its vast halls and splendid gates. No other place in China has so much history, legend and imperial intrigue. Violent forces during Chairman Mao's Cultural Revolution wanted to ruin the place – thankfully it was spared.

☞ SEE IT ! *The Forbidden City is the historical centrepiece of Běijīng, the Chinese capital.*

89

The Uffizi

RENAISSANCE SUPERSTAR

ITALY // The collection at Florence's Uffizi Gallery spans the gamut of art history. But its heart and soul is the Renaissance collection – the Botticellis alone are unmatched and easily bag a place on the bucket list. As extraordinary as the Michelangelo, da Vinci, Raphael, Titian and Car avaggio paintings is the setting – a gargantuan riverside palace, built by the Medici family in the 1500s and linked to Palazzo Pitto on the other side of the Arno by the enigmatic Vasari Corridor.

☞ SEE IT ! *The Uffizi is an easy walk from Stazione di Santa Maria Novella, with rail links to Pisa airport. Book tickets online.*

90

Everest Base Camp

THE TOP OF THE WORLD

NEPAL // In 2015 an avalanche devastated Mt Everest's base camp. But it wasn't the first disaster to strike Everest and history suggests that people will be back to make the two-week trek through villages where people live among the biggest mountains on earth. Most trekkers remember the human views as much as the mountains': orange-robed boys playing football at Thyangboche monastery; porters carrying loads strung over their foreheads; old ladies drying yak dung for fuel.

☞ SEE IT ! *Base Camp itself is only there during the climbing season (April-June). Everest views are best September-November.*

91

Shwedagon Paya
All that glitters...

↓

MYANMAR // Visible from almost everywhere in Yangon, Myanmar's signature monument, a 99m-high *zedi* (stupa), is coated with 27 tons of gold and topped with an eye-popping 2000 carats of diamonds. What's amazing is that nobody carted off its treasures over 1400 tumultuous years of Burmese history. The zedi is the centre point of a complex of shrines, statues, stupas and pagodas. Worshippers leave lotus blooms, prayer flags, candles, fruit, and folded paper umbrellas to honour the Buddha.

🐌 SEE IT ! *Take one of the city's ancient car-taxis to the pagoda.*

92

The Pyramids of Teotihuacán

MEXICO // The Mayan ruins might be more famous but Teotihuacán, with its sprawling complex of pyramids, was Mexico's biggest ancient city and the heart of the country's largest pre-Hispanic empire. Centuries after its fall, Teotihuacán remained a pilgrimage site for Aztec royalty and it is still an important one to this day. Built almost 2000 years ago, it is as significant as the ruins of the Yucatán (Chichén Itzá) and Chiapas (Palenque).

SEE IT ! *The pyramids lie 50km northeast of Mexico City. Avoid 10am to 2pm, when crowds are thickest.*

93

Blue Lagoon

ICELAND // In a land of steaming springs that ooze with mineral deposits, the Blue Lagoon is the big cheese. This milky, teal-coloured spa lounges in a magnificent black lava field, fed by waters marinating at a perfect 38°C from a futuristic geothermal plant. Rolling clouds of steam, the feel of the water and people daubed in white silica mud make you feel as if you're on another planet. Commercial? Yes. Expensive? Yes. Worth it? Certainly.

SEE IT ! *The lagoon is 47km southwest of Reykjavík and is even closer to the airport. Bus services run year-round, as do tours.*

94

Lake Wanaka

NEW ZEALAND // Wanaka town is New Zealand's alternative adventure hub – a smaller, cuter Queenstown, with the volume knob tweaked. Sitting pretty on the waterfront at the lake's southern end, this is the gateway to the South Island's mighty Mt Aspiring and the snowsport centres of Treble Cone, Cardrona, Harris Mountains and Pisa Range. Off-piste pursuits include tramping, mountain biking, climbing, canyoning and kayaking.

SEE IT ! *Make the drive in via the dramatic Haast Pass to fully whet your appetite for adventure.*

95
Abu Simbel

EGYPT // Standing in the awesome presence of Abu Simbel, overlooking Lake Nasser, it's hard to imagine that these two imposing ancient temples are also a marvel of modern engineering. Carved out of the mountain on the west bank of the Nile between 1274 BC and 1244 BC, the four colossal statues of the pharaoh fronting the Great Temple of Ramses II stood sentinel over the road south for centuries, before being lost in the shifting desert-sands of time. Rediscovered in 1813, the great temple and its little brother, the Temple of Hathor, were ambitiously relocated, block by block, to their current site in the 1960s to protect them from the flooding of Lake Nasser. From here they keep watch over a new dominion.

 SEE IT ! *Abu Simbel sits in a small Nubian town near the Sudan border, a four-hour bus ride from Aswan and linked to Cairo by air.*

96
Cimetière Du Père Lachaise

FRANCE // Paris' largest cemetery is testament to the fact that its inhabitants are just as stylish below ground as above. Everyone who was once anyone is buried here, from Balzac to Chopin to Édith Piaf to Oscar Wilde. But the cemetery's biggest draw is still the grave of Jim Morrison, lead singer of The Doors, who overdosed in a Paris bathtub in 1971 at the age of 27. Today, fans still come to pour out a beer on his grave. Opened in 1804, Père Lachaise's 44 hectares of ornate graves and mausoleums now house more than one million bodies. The tree-lined, cobblestoned cemetery is rich in folklore and superstition – for example, rub the bronze crotch of journalist Victor Noir's grave statue and you'll be granted a husband within the year.

 SEE IT ! *Père Lachaise is in the 20th arrondissement. The closest metro stops are Père Lachaise and Gambetta.*

97 Big Sur

WILDERNESS UNPLUGGED

USA // Big Sur is more a state of mind than a place you can pinpoint on a map. There are no traffic lights, banks or strip malls, and when the sun goes down, the moon and the stars are the only street lights. Nestled up against mossy, mysterious-looking redwood forests, the rocky Big Sur coast is a secretive place in which hot springs, water-falls and beaches lay hidden. Its raw beauty and energy has long been a muse for creative types; in the 1950s and 1960s it became a retreat for artists and writers, including Henry Miller and beat generation visionaries. Today, Big Sur attracts self-proclaimed artists, new-age mystics, latter-day hippies and city slickers seeking to unplug and reflect more deeply on this emerald-green edge of the continent.

☞ SEE IT ! *Big Sur is shoehorned between California's Santa Lucia Range and the Pacific Ocean. Explore it by car, because you'll be itching to stop frequently.*

98 Matterhorn

THE ALPS' DARK, BROODING BEAUTY

SWITZERLAND // No other mountain has so much pulling power and natural magnetism, or inspires as much obsession as this charismatic peak. It is Europe's most photographed mountain and once you've spied this celebrity of the Alps, you too will be snapping it from every last angle. Some 3000 worshipful Alpinists summit its 4478m-high peak each year. You don't need to be superhuman to do it, but you do need to be a skilled climber and in top physical shape to make the ascent up sheer rock and ice. For non-climbers, a trip to the glitzy resort of Zermatt is an easy way to get up close. The Matterhorn Museum offers insight into the 19th-century mountaineers who pio-neered the climb and the plucky souls who didn't make it.

☞ SEE IT ! *Matterhorn towers above the town of Zermatt, a good base for skiing or hiking, in the Swiss Alps.*

99

Gamla Stan
Stockholm's time capsule

↓

SWEDEN //History oozes from the edifices in Stockholm's old town. Here, cobblestone streets wriggle past Renaissance churches, baroque palaces and medieval squares, while spice-coloured buildings frame cosy cafes. Founded in 1250, Gamla Stan's past has taken many dark twists and turns. It's been blackened by plague and famine, consumed by flame, and embattled by Danish and Swedish factions. Dominating the skyline, Storkyrkan is the old town's medieval cathedral.

☛ SEE IT !
Västerlånggatan is the area's nerve centre.

100—
199

100

Okavango Delta

Beware: hippopotamuses, arguably Africa's most dangerous mammal, inhabit the Okavango's larger channels.

WONDERFUL WATER WORLD

BOTSWANA // Surely the only reason that Okavango Delta is not higher on this list is because relatively few people make it here. Botswana likes its visitors rich and low in numbers, and the Okavango is also remote. This huge inland delta's annual flood attracts a wonderful concentration of the continent's big-ticket animals and seeing them here feels intimate and personal.

Statistics bear out the Okavango's sublime status. When rain falls in the Angolan Highlands it takes a month to reach the Okavango, deluging the area in a vast 11 cu kilometres of water.

All of which has the happy effect of ensuring everyone who makes it into the heart of the Okavango – by incredibly scenic flight, 4WD, traditional Mokoro canoe or on foot – feel as if it's one of the most special experiences they'll ever have, not just in southern Africa, but anywhere.

👉 SEE IT ! *Maun is the main entry point to Okavango. From here, the delta is a spectacular hop by plane, or a few hours' drive away, but fly if you can.*

Golden Gate Bridge

101

San Francisco, USA // There was something elegant and visionary about the art-deco design movement of the 1930s, and San Franciscans must be eternally grateful for their signature landmark. It's a good thing the navy didn't get its way about the bridge (officials preferred a hulking concrete span, painted with caution-yellow stripes). Happily, architects Gertrude and Irving Murrow and engineer Joseph B Strauss won the day. When completed in 1937, it was the longest suspension bridge in the world, stretching 1.6 miles.

So what makes this piece of design totty a must-see over, say, Sydney's Harbour Bridge, which didn't even make our Top 500? Perhaps it's the way gusts billow through the bridge cables on foggy days, when its two towers are shrouded in near zero visibility, or maybe it's the wild, green streak of Golden Gate Park that hugs it, where you'll find locals roller-discoing and bison racing towards the Pacific.

☛ SEE IT ! *Pedestrians and cyclists can cross the bridge on the east side. For the best perspective, try viewing it from below at Fort Point. On foggy days, head for the north-end lookout at Marin's Vista Point.*

102

102 Dashashwamedh Ghat

HOLIEST OF HOLY SITES

Varanasi, INDIA // The hiss and spit of a thousand orange embers aglow on the banks of the river, framed by a brooding night sky or bathed in the mellow light of dawn, is an ethereal experience. Varanasi's 80 or so smouldering ghats, with their Hindu cremation pyres, offer a window into another world, one absorbed by the rituals of death. It is here, on this long stretch of steps leading down to the waters of the Ganges River, that the holiest city of India is at its brilliant best and most spiritually enlightening. In the early hours of the morning, pilgrims come to perform *puja* (the act of worship)

to the rising sun; at sunset, the main *ganga aarti* (river worship ceremony) takes place at Dashashwamedh Ghat – Varanasi's liveliest and most colourful ghat. Fire offerings in the form of small *diya* (lamps), with candles and flowers, are floated down the river and flamboyant dance electrifies the gathering. Despite the touts, it's a moving place to linger.

☛ SEE IT ! *The holy city of Varanasi is in the north Indian state of Uttar Pradesh; overnight trains run from Delhi.*

103

103

Giant's Causeway

NORTHERN IRELAND // Perched on a basalt column, as waves wallop the coast, it's easy to imagine 52½ft-tall Fionn MacCumhal building this causeway across the sea to challenge Scottish giant Benandonner. Benandonner chickened out, but there's lots left to explore. In the visitors centre, geologists spout alternative theories about the rocks' origin but, either way, the Causeway coast is an evocative spot.

☛ SEE IT ! *The Causeway is about an hour's drive from Derry, and some 75 minutes from Belfast.*

104

Auschwitz-Birkenau

POLAND // More than a million Jews, as well as many Poles and Roma, were murdered here by the Nazis during WWII. Now it's a museum and memorial. Surviving prison blocks house exhibitions as shocking as they are informative. Nearby, Birkenau holds the remnants of the gas chamber; visit both to appreciate the full horror of the place. It's a powerful reminder of an ugly modern era that we must not forget.

☛ SEE IT ! *Auschwitz-Birkenau is in Oświęcim, Poland. The easiest jumping-off point is the historic city of Kraków.*

105

Parque Nacional Corcovado

COSTA RICA // Welcome to the jungle. Famously labelled by *National Geographic* as 'the most biologically intense place on earth', Costa Rica's greatest national park is enough to make any would-be Tarzan swoon. Muddy, muggy and intense, this is the last great original tract of tropical rainforest in Pacific Central America. The further into the jungle you go, the better it gets: the country's best wildlife-watching, most desolate beaches and most vivid journeys lie down Corcovado's seldom-trodden trails. It's home to Costa Rica's largest population of scarlet macaws, as well as countless other endangered species, including Baird's tapir, the giant anteater and the world's largest bird of prey, the harpy eagle. Hold on to your hat, because this park is the adventure of a lifetime.

🐾 SEE IT ! *Corcovado is on Costa Rica's remote southwest Península de Osa. Base yourself at Puerto Jiménez (better for independent travellers) or Bahía Drake (dotted with all-inclusive resorts).*

106

Niagara Falls

CANADA // Niagara might not be the tallest waterfall in the world, nor the widest, but it's undoubtedly the world's most well known and, in terms of sheer volume, there's nothing like it – more than a million bathtubs of water plummet downwards every second. The falls forms a natural rift between Ontario and New York State: on the US side, Bridal Veil Falls crash on to mammoth fallen rocks. On the Canadian side, the grander Horseshoe Falls plunge into the cloudy Maid of the Mist Pool. Niagara town itself might feel a little like an outdated amusement park, but that hardly diminishes the force of the current and the hypnotic mist that delights 12 million visitors a year.

🐾 SEE IT ! *Niagara Falls is two hours from Toronto, on Canada's east coast, or six hours from New York City. The prime falls-watching spot is Table Rock (Canadian side) – arrive early to beat the crowds.*

106

107 Potala Palace

PALATIAL, POIGNANT, PROFOUND

Lhasa, TIBET // As haunting as it is magnificent, Potala Palace is the largest monastery in the Tibetan Buddhist world, and one of the most recognisable buildings on the planet. Spread over thirteen floors, cascading down the face of Marpo Ri (Red Hill), the palace formed the spiritual heart of Tibet before the Cultural Revolution, and it still towers over downtown Lhasa. Today, the Potala lives on as a humbling, but empty, memorial - more sightseers than monks stalk its passageways and painted chapels, but the intricate, rainbow-coloured murals and gilded statues and stupas speak eloquently of a vanished era. Come to immerse yourself in Tibet's past.

SEE IT ! *The Potala looms over central Lhasa; make sure you are properly acclimatised before tackling the steep walk to the top.*

108

Bora Bora

DREAMLIKE LAGOON PARADISE

FRENCH POLYNESIA // If you arrive here by plane, the promise of a wonderland is instantly made good: a ring of sand-edged *motu* (islets) encircle a glinting turquoise lagoon around soaring rainforest-covered basaltic peaks. Bora Bora's famed over-water bungalows reach out like tentacles into the lagoon. This dreamlike vision has made Bora Bora a byword for honeymooners. But there's much more to do than clink glasses in a high-end hotel. Divers and snorkellers can luxuriate in the bath-warm waters, perhaps spotting a black-tipped shark or stingray among the glittering shoals of fish, and hiking or parasailing is also readily available. And paradise is much more accessible than you think: as well as five-star resorts, a handful of quaint *pensions* and affordable hotels beckon.

SEE IT ! *Bora Bora in French Polynesia is situated 270km northwest of Tahiti and can be reached by air or boat from there. June to October is the driest and most popular time to visit.*

109

Empire State Building

TALL STOREYS

New York, USA // This is America, and there are always options to upsize if you splash more cash, so you've a choice: be content with the killer view of the Big Apple from the open-air deck on the 86th floor of the Empire State, or make like King Kong and keep climbing to the top, where a smaller, enclosed space awaits on 102. Photographers and romantics prefer the tactile lower experience, where wind tickles skin and sounds of the sleepless city float ever-so faintly in the air, and this option leaves some coin for the New York Sky ride, a simulated aerial tour of the city voiced by Kevin Bacon. But this art deco skytickler has appeared in more movies than Bacon and every actor he's connected to within six degrees, and it's also the world's most famous building – so who wouldn't want to stand in its forehead?

SEE IT ! *Viewing platforms open 8am to 2am. Go very early or late to avoid horrendous queues.*

110 Budapest's Thermal Baths

CLEANLINESS IS NEXT TO...

HUNGARY // You've got to love a city where long, luxurious baths are a civic pastime. Here in Budapest, locals and visitors revel in the many public bathhouses, which range from 16th-century Turkish-style domed pools to Gilded Era palaces to modern spas. Choose a co-ed or single-sex (read: naked) spa, grab a towel, and prepare for a ritual soak lasting several hours. The lightly sulphur-scented waters are said to heal everything from arthritis to asthma. We can't vouch for that, but after several rounds of dunking yourself in pools of various temperatures, you'll certainly feel healthy. Add a massage – bathhouses

offer a variety of spa treatments, from Soviet-style baby-oil beatdowns to New Agey aromatherapy – and you'll leave floating on air. Budapest's bathing tradition goes back to the Celts, who named their settlement Ak-Ink, which means 'abundant waters'. The Romans later built bathhouses, as did the Ottomans and the Austro-Hungarians. So bathing here is as much about culture as cleanliness.

☛ SEE IT ! *There are 15 thermal baths in Budapest. Many are male- or female-only on alternate days.*

113

111

Topkapi Palace

OSTENTATIOUS OTTOMAN PALACE

TURKEY // Topkapı Palace and its park-like setting sprout out of Istanbul like a self-contained fairy-tale kingdom with more colourful stories than most of the world's museums put together. Libidinous sultans, ambitious courtiers, beautiful concubines and scheming eunuchs lived and worked here between the 15th and 19th centuries when it was the court of the Ottoman empire. Visiting the palace's pavilions, treasury and Harem offers a glimpse into their lives.

🖝 SEE IT ! *The Palace is in Sultanahmet, crammed with museums and ostentatious Byzantine and Ottoman monuments.*

112

Tallinn Old Town

MEDIEVAL JEWEL OF ESTONIA

ESTONIA // Picking your way along the narrow, cobbled streets of old Tallinn is like strolling into the 15th century – not least due to the tendency of local businesses to dress their staff up in peasant garb. You'll pass old merchant houses, hidden medieval courtyards, looming spires and winding staircases leading to sweeping views over the city. Its fairy-tale charms, two-tiered setting and impressive city walls have made it a favourite tourist trap, but it carries this burden well.

🖝 SEE IT ! *Tallinn is the capital of Estonia. In summer, cruise-ship crowds can swamp the Old Town, but they leave by 5pm.*

113

Stari Most

A BRIDGE FOR PEACE

BOSNIA–HERZEGOVINA // A magnificent 16th-century Ottoman bridge, spanning the turquoise currents of the Neretva River, Stari Most is a structure whose fortunes mirror those of its location. From 1992–95, Mostar was the frontline between opposing Bosniak and Croat forces: thousands died and the bridge was destroyed. Two decades on, Bosnia is once again peaceful, and the bridge was reconstructed to its original design in 2004. It serves as a powerful icon of recovery.

🖝 SEE IT ! *Watch the Mostar Diving Club jump 24m into the river below – a tradition dating to Ottoman times.*

114

Ayuthaya
Crumbling chedi complex

↓

THAILAND //
Despite once being one of the world's top capitals and a Siamese kingdom for 400 years, Ayuthaya is over-shadowed by its proximity to Angkor Wat. But it offers a glimpse into glories past and it's easy to imagine the ghosts of Eastern empire lurking among the once treasure-lad-en palace ruins, crumbling *chedi* (stupas) and head-less Buddha im-ages. At its zenith, 400 temples stood at its heart. In 1767 an invading Bur-mese army swept through. Today more than a dozen restored ruins can be found.

☛ SEE IT !
Ayuthaya, an hour north of Bangkok, is served by boat, bus and train.

115

Vatican Museums

FAMOUS FRESCOED CHAPEL

Rome, ITALY // Once you've faced the queues to gain an audience with Michelangelo's frescoes in the Sistine Chapel you can pinch yourself, because it was worth it. A kaleidoscopic barrage of colours and images, they are the grand finale of the Vatican Museums. This vast complex houses more masterpieces than many small countries, crowned by the frescoed Raphael Rooms and, beyond that, the chapel where millions come to gaze heavenwards at God pointing at Adam.

☛ SEE IT ! *Vatican City is in Rome. The Museums are wildly popular: beware ticket touts and buy in advance.*

116

Anakena Beach

SUNBATHING WITH STATUES

Easter Island, CHILE // OK, so no one comes to Easter Island just to catch some rays, but Anakena is a beach worth talking about. A proud line of seven *moai* – the island's famous statues – overlook Rapa Nui's only serious stretch of sand. They stand sentinel by the spot where legend suggests Hotu Matu'a, the Polynesian chief who first colonised the island, landed. Anakena is a wonderful place to finish a guided hike along the dramatic northern coast, and to contemplate the wonderful otherness of this place.

☛ SEE IT ! *Easter Island is a five-hour flight from Tahiti or Santiago de Chile.*

117

The Peak

KEEPING A COOL HEAD

Hong Kong, CHINA // Emerging from a tramcar at The Peak is like leaving a sauna, such is the relief from the humidity smothering Hong Kong city. The funicular has ferried people up here for 120 years, to escape the heat and gulp in the panorama. Watch black kites gliding on thermals while the metropolis below goes about its frenetic business. There are observation decks at Sky Terrace 428 and Peak Galleria. To fully absorb your surrounds, do the 3.5km Peak Circle Walk.

☛ SEE IT ! *Riding the Peak Tram on its vertiginous route past HK's mega modern skyscrapers is an experience in its own right.*

118 St Paul's Cathedral

London, ENGLAND // St Paul's has seen it all. Sir Christopher Wren's baroque cathedral was built after the Great Fire at the end of the 17th century, but there's been a church on this site since 604 AD. It survived Nazi bombing to become a symbol of British resistance, its great dome tall above the smoke of the Blitz.

Just wandering the soaring interior is an uplifting experience. Steps take you up to the Whispering Gallery, where, if you talk close to the wall, your words will carry the 32m to the opposite side. Staircases of stone and iron bring you to the Golden Gallery, which has wonderful views of London. The crypt has hundreds of memorials to historic figures including Wellington and Nelson. Wren's tomb bears a Latin inscription that simply and poignantly reads: 'If you seek his memorial, look about you.'

☛ SEE IT ! *Admission (unless you're visiting to worship) is £17 (£7.50 for children). There are regular tours (free with admission). The nearest tube station is St Paul's.*

119

118

119 Meteora

GREECE // A monk's life is not for everyone. Yet if you are cutting yourself off from worldly temptations it makes sense to do so somewhere that Mother Nature offers other consolations. So it is with the monasteries of Meteora (variously translated as 'suspended in the air' or 'in the heavens above'), set on giant bulbs of rock that burst forth from the fertile green plains of Thessaly. Built in the 16th century, there were originally 24 of these Greek Orthodox monasteries set on towering rocky outcrops. They were only accessible by rope ladders, so for the novices in residence there was little to do but contemplate the beauty of God's creation. For travellers arriving today, there are only six monasteries remaining but they are accessible via stairs. And in the hallowed halls overlooking the surrounding countryside you still get a feel for the rigours – and exaltation – of the monastic life.

☛ SEE IT ! *There's nowhere to stay in Meteora itself; make a day trip from nearby Kalambaka, which is fully equipped for travellers.*

120 Confucius Temple

LAVISH ALTAR TO A GREAT TEACHER

Qūfù, CHINA // Coming face to face with the 10 fearsome dragon-coiled columns of Dàchéng Hall, it's hard to imagine the humble beginnings of this expansive temple complex. Once Confucius' three-room house, the site was consecrated as a temple after his death in 478 BC. Now it's more museum than altar and could give Běijīng's Forbidden City a run for its money. Imperial gifts, ambitious expansions and lavish renovations in subsequent centuries meant that, by the 11th century, Confucius' once-simple abode had four courtyards and more than 300 rooms, enshrined within an imperial-palace-style wall. The heart of the complex is the huge yellow-eaved Dàchéng Hall, where streams of visitors come to pay their respects to a huge statue of the great man himself, resplendent on a throne.

SEE IT ! *Confucius Temple is in the ancient city of Qūfù, 3½ hours from Shànghǎi by train and a short plane hop from Běijīng.*

121 Copper Canyon

RIVER DEEP MOUNTAIN HIGH

MEXICO // Several canyons appear in the Ultimate Travelist but only one has its very own railway. This colossal series of creases in northwest Mexico – deeper in places than the Grand Canyon and covering four times as wide an area – features beautifully rugged landscapes, home to the Tarahumara people, famed for their long-distance, barefoot running. That's one way of exploring the place, but a better idea might be to take Chepe (the Ferrocaril Chihuahua-Pacifico, an amazing feat of engineering), the railway that skirts cliffsides and trundles through pine forests for 656km between the coast and Chihuahua. Break the journey at mountain towns such as Creel – close to rock formations, lakes and hot springs – or smaller villages such as Urique and Cerocahui to explore this adventurous region on horseback, mountain bike, or, near Divisadero, some of the world's longest zip-lines.

SEE IT ! *The port of Los Mochis is the departure point for Chepe, book a month ahead, by phone and email, for peak-season travel.*

123 Aiguille du Midi

360-DEGREE ALPS VIEW

FRANCE // A jagged finger of rock soaring above glaciers, snowfields and rocky crags, 8km from the hump of Mont Blanc, Aiguille du Midi (3842m) is a distinctive geographical beacon. If you can handle the altitude, the 360-degree views of the French, Swiss and Italian Alps from the summit are (quite literally) breathtaking. Year-round, you can float in a cable car from Chamonix to the Aiguille du Midi on the vertiginous Téléphérique de l'Aiguille du Midi. Unfortunately, the queues in summer slightly detract from the experience (we're talking two-hour waits). For that reason, it doesn't rank as highly as the striking jagged figure of remote Cerro Fitz Roy in Patagonia.

SEE IT ! *The Aiguille du Midi can be reached via the French resort town of Chamonix. Bring warm clothes with you, because even in summer the temperature at the top seldom rises above -10°C (in winter be prepared for -25°C).*

122 Cerro Fitz Roy

PATAGONIA'S PEAK OF FIRE

ARGENTINA // Toothy Cerro Fitz Roy looms over the Patagonian frontier town of El Chaltén with an ominous leer that thrills world-class climbers and, quite frankly, scares the rest of us. It dominates the northern section of Parque Nacional Los Glaciares and draws peak baggers for whom Fitz Roy is a milestone ascent notorious for brutal weather conditions. The base town of El Chaltén is named after Cerro Fitz Roy's Tehuelche name, meaning 'peak of fire' or 'smoking mountain' – an apt description of the cloud-enshrouded summit. When it's not cloaked in clouds, its snow-dusted crags are simply breathtaking and, thankfully, scaling it isn't the only way to enjoy this mountain. Beautiful hiking trails framed by Fitz Roy are surprisingly easy and accessible, and the best views are just a day's hike from town.

SEE IT ! *The gateway town of El Chaltén lies on the Argentinian-Chilean border in Patagonia. Avoid winter (from May to September), when facilities shut down.*

Bryggen

124

NORWAY // The fire-hued wooden wharf houses of Bergen's cutesy old town create a warm glow along Vågen harbourfront and a striking contrast to the cool blue fjord beyond. Bryggen might not have the grandeur of other historic centres such as Stockholm's Gamla Stan (p104) or Tallinn's Old Town (p114), but in our book its provincial feel simply adds to its charm. Salt-of-the-earth tradespeople were once the lifeblood of this town, which was an important hub in the Hanseatic League's trading empire from the 14th to 16th centuries. The atmosphere of an intimate waterfront community remains intact, and losing yourself among the wooden alleyways – now a haven for artists and craftspeople – is one of the greatest pleasures Norway has to offer. Repeatedly ravaged by fire, Bryggen's characteristic, often skewiff, wooden-gabled buildings have been rebuilt many times and what remains is a relic of a past life, its enchantment only slightly diminished by its inevitable popularity with cruise ships and tour buses.

☞ SEE IT ! *Surrounded by seven hills and seven fjords, Bergen lies in Norway's southwestern fjordlands.*

Stewart Island

125

HOME OF THE KIWI

NEW ZEALAND // Separated from the mainland by choppy Foveaux Strait, New Zealand's third island is way down south. It's a classic end-of-the-earth environment, where nature reigns and a handful of hardy humans fit in around it.

Rakiura National Park makes up 85 percent of the land, which ranges from long beaches and sheltered inlets to lush forest carpeted in ferns and moss. It's a pristine, remote world, and an internationally renowned bird haven. It's said that you can spot more species here than anywhere else in New Zealand.

This is the kingdom of the kiwi, New Zealand's endangered national icon. Numbering some 20,000, they outnumber locals by more than 50 to one, and are so relaxed they will head out before sundown despite being nocturnal and usually shy.

Wilderness walks are also a drawcard, particularly the Rakiura Track Great Walk and the epic North West Circuit, but don't expect to bump into too many people. For hustle and bustle you'll need to head to Oban's South Seas Hotel, the island's main meeting point and as salty a pub as you're ever likely to discover.

🐦 SEE IT ! *An hour's ferry ride from Invercargill, Stewart Island is best visited on a tour of Fiordland and the Southern Lakes.*

Left, Bergen's historic quarter. Below, a brown kiwi; the Stewart Island sub-species numbers around 20,000 and is active day and night.

126
Durbar Square

BEAUTIFUL, TIME-WARPED MUSEUM

Patan, NEPAL // With a swoon-worthy collection of Hindu temples and Newari palaces, it's little wonder many locals still call Patan by its original Sanskrit name of Lalitpur (City of Beauty). But the city took a terrible jolt in spring 2015 when a huge earthquake, centred on Kathmandu Valley, struck. The vision of loveliness that is the museum-like Durbar Square was severely damaged, with some of its multi-tiered temples collapsing. Restoration work is underway, and it is fervently hoped that the traditional timber and red brick buildings can be rebuilt and that once again visitors may join the locals hanging off the barrel-chested lions on the steps of the 16th-century Jagannarayan Temple to stare at the Royal Palace – because there is nowhere else in the world where time has stood quite so beautifully still.

🐟 SEE IT ! *Patan is now almost a suburb of Kathmandu and can be reached by bicycle, taxi, bus or even on foot from the capital.*

129
Plitvice Lakes National Park

STRIKING TURQUOISE WATER WORLD

CROATIA // A striking ribbon of crystal water and gushing waterfalls in the forested heart of continental Croatia, Plitvice Lakes National Park is excruciatingly scenic and has to be one of the most singular parks in the world. There are dozens of lakes here – from 4km-long Kozjak to reed-fringed ponds – all in surreal shades of turquoise that are a product of the karst terrain. Travertine expanses covered with mossy plants divide the lakes, while boardwalks allow you to step right over this exquisite water world, and trails lead deep into beech, spruce, fir and pine trees. Bears, wolves and deer roam around here, but perhaps you're more likely to catch a glimpse of a swooping hawk or the occasional black stork.

🐟 SEE IT ! *Plitvice is located in Croatia's Adriatic hinterland, a couple of hours from the capital Zagreb. Avoid July and August, when the volume of visitors can turn the walking tracks into a conga line.*

127
Bazaruto Archipelago

AQUATIC BEACH BONANZA

MOZAMBIQUE // There are almost as many shades of blue in the archipelago's waters as there are different aquatic species in its depths; given this island chain forms part of a bountiful 1400 sq km marine national park, that's saying something. Whether you travel here by air or sea, its splendour is apparent before you even set foot on shore.

Besides its aesthetic appeal and its exclusive nature (there are only a handful of upmarket lodges), what sets the Bazaruto Archipelago apart is its wildlife, both above and below the surface of the Indian Ocean. On the islands, there is abundant birdlife, several antelope species and Nile crocodiles in freshwater lakes. Divers and snorkellers explore rich coral reefs, observing dolphins, sea turtles, dugongs, manta rays, some 2000 varieties of fish and migrating humpback whales.

🐟 SEE IT ! *Fly into Vilankulu, from where you can arrange a boat, helicopter or plane transfer. Visit May to November.*

128
Prinsengracht Canal

PRINCELY WATERWAY PULSING WITH LIFE

Amsterdam, NETHERLANDS // Take to the water and you'll understand why Unesco named Amsterdam's waterways a World Heritage site. In a city that has more canals than Venice, you can learn a lot by following the flow of these important arteries, nowhere more so than on Prinsengracht (Prince's canal). Most people come here to visit Anne Frank's house and see the famous diary, but the canal is a fascinating sight in its own right as the centrepiece of one of Amsterdam's most gorgeous areas. It was carved out in the early 1600s, when a dramatic growth spurt catapulted Amsterdam to the third biggest city in the world. Prinsengracht is flanked by 17th-century merchants' houses and crammed with houseboats, so pull up a pew at one of the pavement cafes and watch the ebb and flow of city life from its banks.

🐟 SEE IT ! *Prinsengracht is part of Amsterdam's Western Canal Ring and best experienced by boat, bicycle or on foot.*

130

Bay of Islands
The life aquatic

↓

NEW ZEALAND //
While New Zealand's coast has no shortage of handsome nooks and crannies, the Bay of Islands tops the lot for its sheltered anchorage, kind climate and abundance of wildlife, onshore and off.

Maori were living in the Bay before Europeans sailed in and it's where the Treaty of Waitangi – the country's founding document – was signed. But it's natural beauty that makes the Bay of Islands so appealing, with 150 undeveloped islands sprinkled across hidden coves awash in shimmering turquoise waters.

🐦 SEE IT ! *The Bay of Islands is three hours' drive from Auckland. Russell is the best base.*

131 Pantanal

WONDROUS WILDLIFE-RICH WETLANDS

BRAZIL // Of all the natural wonders of South America, the Pantanal outdoes even the Amazon basin as the number one wildlife-watching locale. These twinkling blue-green tropical wetlands sprawl across 200,000-odd sq km: home to some 400 fish species, 1000-odd bird species, and an illustrious list of animal residents, including the capybara (the world's largest rodent), giant river otters, caimans, maned wolves, pumas, tapirs, anteaters, armadillos and the world's most flourishing jaguar population. In the dry season from July to November, a menagerie comprising all of the above descends upon the limited water resources in one of the most colourful concentrations of wildlife anywhere on the planet.

☛ SEE IT ! *Tours here mostly run from the cities of Campo Grande, to the southeast, Corumbá, to the west, and Cuiabá, to the north.*

132 Daibutsu (Great Buddha) of Nara

IMPRESSIVE BRONZE BEARER OF ENLIGHTENMENT

JAPAN // The world is brimful of statues of Buddha, but if you're going to see just one, the Daibutsu of Nara has to be it. Cocooned inside Tōdai-ji temple, the largest wooden building in the world, this image of the cosmic Buddha is one of the planet's largest bronze figures, towering more than 16m high. One can hardly believe it's a mere two-thirds of the size of the original, cast in 746 AD. Can you imagine the reverence it must have inspired? As you circle the statue towards the back, you'll see a wooden column with a hole through its base. Popular belief maintains those who can squeeze through the hole, exactly the same size as one of the Great Buddha's nostrils, are ensured of enlightenment. Isn't that reason enough to pay him a visit?

☛ SEE IT ! *Nara is located in the region of Kansai, about an hour by train from Kyoto and Osaka.*

133 National Museum of Anthropology

MEXICO // Do you know your Toltecs from your Zapotecs? Have you wondered what those basketball-style hoops were doing at Mayan ruins? Any visit to Mexico will prompt a lot of questions about its immensely rich layers of history and nowhere answers those questions quite as enthrallingly as the National Museum of Anthropology in Mexico City.

The ground floor of this modernist building, which was opened in the 1960s, houses relics from pre-Hispanic Mexico that illustrate the complexity of those ancient societies. Aztec gods and goddesses preside over beautiful carved jaguars, and a 3.5m-wide sculpture known as the

Sun Stone that was a cosmic calendar. Olmec icons and statues abound. And the models of vast Mayan cities help you picture life as it was then. It's a trusim to say that one visit isn't enough but wandering the huge number of pre-Hispanic exhibits here, it's clear that few museums in the world match the depth of the National Museum of Anthropology's collection.

☛ SEE IT ! *The museum is in the Bosque de Chapultepec, Mexico City's largest park; Auditorio is the closest of the metro stations. Explore the bohemian neighbourhood of Roma while you're in the area.*

134 Skara Brae

PREHISTORIC VILLAGE FROZEN IN TIME

SCOTLAND // When the Pyramids of Giza (p48) were just a glint in the pharaohs' eyes and Stonehenge (p78) had yet to be cleaved from rock, the village of Skara Brae in Orkney was already a bustling Stone Age centre. Buried in coastal sand dunes for centuries until an 1850 storm exposed the houses underneath, the site is so well preserved it can feel as though the inhabitants have just slipped out to go fishing. Even the stone furniture – beds, boxes and dressers – has survived the 5000 years since a community lived and breathed here. When visiting ancient sites, it can sometimes be difficult to feel the gulf of years or sense a connection with the people who built them, but Scotland's superb prehistoric remains have an immediate effect. Start with the excellent interactive exhibit, move on to a reconstructed house and then finish up at the excavation itself. This is the best window into Stone Age life that you'll ever see.

➤ SEE IT ! *Skara Brae is idyllically situated by a sandy bay approximately 13km north of Stromness on Orkney, an island in Scotland's Northern Isles chain.*

135

Geirangerfjord

ULTIMATE FJORD-MEANDERING FERRY RIDE

NORWAY // The 20km chug along Geirangerfjord must rank as the world's loveliest ferry journey. Long-abandoned farmsteads still cling to the fjord's near-sheer cliffs while ice-cold cascading waterfalls tumble, twist and gush down to emerald-green waters. The main ferry travels between Hellesylt and Geiranger village. If you start out from Hellesylt, docking in Geiranger can come as a shock to the system despite its fabulous location at the head of the fjord, as you mingle with the waves of people delivered by bus and ship. Every year, Geiranger wilts under the presence of over 600,000 visitors, and more than 150 cruise ships. No matter: out on the water it's total calm. Prime your camera, head for the open-air top deck and enjoy what's literally the only way to travel Geirangerfjord's secluded reaches.

☛ SEE IT ! *Geirangerfjord lies in Norway's Northern Fjords and is connected to Oslo, Trondheim and Bergen by daily direct bus.*

136

Tayrona National Park

CARIBBEAN CAMPING

COLOMBIA // This could be the first time that you'll hire a horse to get to a campsite. Reaching the park gate is easy, but finding the ultimate beach – nestled in a curve of the Caribbean, between the foothills of the Sierra Nevada de Santa Marta and the Colombian coast – takes a whole lot more commitment.

Once you've negotiated the jungle track, pitched your tent and strung up your hammock, it's time to kick back and chill out with a book and a *cerveza* (beer). Mind you, there is a sultry swathe of Caribbean coast to explore, spread across six sensational bays – Chengue, Gayraca, Cinto, Neguanje, Concha and Guachaquita – that all offer snorkelling and beachcombing. And there are persistent rumours of mysterious archaeological remains in the jungle... maybe that book can wait a while after all.

☛ SEE IT ! *Take a bus from Santa Marta to the park entrance. Cañaveral is the closest, but most expensive and busiest beach. For solitude, hire a horse and head to Cabo San Juan del Guia or Arrecifes.*

137 Choquequirao

THE UNTRAMMELLED INCA TRAIL

PERU // Imagine a Machu Picchu – meaning a spectacular Inca citadel perched on a mountain above the jungle – with no crowds. This is Choquequirao: a four-day out-and-back hike from the already remote outpost of Cachora, 60km and a world away from touristy Cuzco. Straddling a broccoli-green ridge at 3000m, the ruins mark the refuge of Manca Inca, on the run after he tried to retake Cuzco from the Spanish. Above is the famous truncated summit, a ceremonial plaza hewn out of the hill by indigenous tribes. Parts of the site still remain unexcavated, and a rarely-traipsed multiday trek on from here to Machu Picchu (p16) is also possible: a voyage into the pre-Columbian unknown, if ever there was one.

☛ SEE IT ! *Choquequirao is normally visited via a four-day hike, run by Cuzco tour agencies: the path there is not always obvious and it's better not to go solo.*

138 Ephesus

A GRECO-ROMAN WONDER IN TURKEY

TURKEY // Ephesus is one of the most phenomenal ancient sites in the world. It was once an important city for the Greeks, while the Romans made this great port the capital of Asia Minor. The Temple of Artemis here was the biggest ever built and became one of the Seven Wonders of the Ancient World.

Most of the ancient city has yet to be excavated, which makes you marvel at what still lies beneath the earth, because what's exposed is wonderfully impressive, from the towering columns of the Library of Celsus to the grand amphitheatre. A fascinating museum holds houses stacked on top of each other like Lego. The main route through Ephesus is packed with great buildings and holds gladiatorial re-enactments, but you can also explore the quieter, but still magnificently evocative corners of the site, or climb to the higher ground and admire this ruin's vast scope.

☛ SEE IT ! *Nearby Selçuk is the best base – arrive early or late in the day to avoid the heat and the worst of the crowds.*

139

Kruger National Park
Unique wildlife experience

↓

SOUTH AFRICA //
What makes Kruger stand out over other African game reserves? There are many things but the icing on the cake is its accessibility. Where else can you drive your hire car through the front gate, strike out on a bush walk and then trundle off on a mountain bike all in the same trip? Numbers and variety of species; staggering size; and the range of activities have made Kruger park famous, and this is arguably one of the greatest places on earth to watch wildlife.

☛ SEE IT ! *In the northeast of South Africa, Kruger has an airport. Wildlife viewing is best from June to September.*

140

140 Tulum

MAYA BEAUTY QUEEN

MEXICO // Your first glimpse of Tulum is postcard-perfect. Picture an impossibly jade-green sea lapping at an impossibly sugar-white swathe of beach, framing an impossibly classic-looking Maya temple clinging to a cliffside. Oh, and don't forget the palm trees. It can't possibly be real, you say. Thankfully for travellers, it is. And although the 13th-century *castillo* doesn't rank as highly as the more sophisticated ruins of nearby Chichén Itzá (p93) or Palenque (p84) for design and scale, it has won over many a visitor on looks alone. You can even swim in that sea. Tulum Pueblo, the town that has sprouted up around this magnificent confection of a ruin, isn't up to much but when the main attraction is this, well, attractive, who cares?

🕿 SEE IT ! *Tulum is on the Yucatán Peninsula, less than a two-hour drive from Cancun, Mexico's southernmost gateway city by air. Visit early morning or late afternoon to avoid the tour groups.*

141 Tsukiji Market

BEHIND-THE-SCENES TOKYO

Tokyo, JAPAN // It's only fitting that the world's sushi capital is home to the world's biggest seafood market. Just imagine the smell: an astounding 2000 tonnes of seafood splish-splashes through frenetic Tsukiji each day. You can see all manner of fascinating creatures being hawked, but it is the *maguro* (bluefin tuna) that has emerged as the star. Get down here at dawn and you can see these prized fish auctioned off to the highest bidder. The market is one of Tokyo's unique sights, and a rare peek into the working life of the city. Once you've seen enough, retreat from the fray and follow up with a sushi breakfast in the outer market, where hundreds of food stalls and restaurants serve up their catch.

🕿 SEE IT ! *Visitor numbers to the tuna auctions are restricted and places are allotted on a first-come, first-served basis. Would-be viewers begin pitching up around 3.30am; auctions start about 5am.*

142 Sintra

STUPENDOUSLY SILLY CASTLE CRAZINESS

PORTUGAL // If you're fond of castles, fairy tales, pastel colours, palaces and an abundance of wicked trashiness on top of a mountain, Unesco-listed Sintra is your dream come true. Start with a combined ticket for Palácio Nacional de Sintra, Castelos dos Mouros, Parque de Pena and Palácio Nacional da Pena: enough palace and castle action for one day. Spend an hour admiring the luxurious Palácio Nacional de Sintra and its opulent tiles. But don't get too carried away just yet. The 2km-walk up the steep, spiralling, cobblestoned hill to Castelo dos Mourous is not for everyone but is rewarding in its rainforesty

peacefulness, as are the views. But there's more. Trek through Parque de Pena to the summit, where you'll probably laugh and run to Palácio Nacional da Pena: an architectural frenzy of clashing colours, Gothic facades and domes – the summer house King Fernando II built. You're going to love him for it, bless his eccentric pastel-loving heart.

☛ SEE IT ! *Take a 30-minute train trip from Lisbon's Rossio station to Sintra. A combined bus-train ticket includes Sintra tourist buses; recommended if you're not a hiker.*

143 Carcassonne Walled City

FAIRY-TALE FRENCH CASTLE

FRANCE // The brooding walled city of Carcassonne has to be the most perfect vision of a medieval castle. Perched on a rocky hilltop and bristling with zigzag battlements, stout walls and witch's-hat turrets, from afar the fortified city looks like something out of a children's storybook. That first glimpse is enough to make your hair stand on end, and the mystical atmosphere is turned up a notch at night when the old city is illuminated and glowing. If La Cité was anywhere near as good inside the town walls, it would rank higher in this list. Sadly, tacky souvenir shops, cheap cafes and the summer tourist crush can sometimes leave the place feeling devoid of any magic and mystery. To properly savour the city, linger at dusk when the old town belongs to its 100 or so inhabitants and the handful of visitors who are staying within its ramparts.

👉 SEE IT ! *Carcassonne is in France's southern Languedoc region. A cruise along the Canal du Midi beneath Carcassonne's steely gaze can be a beautiful way to appreciate the architecture from afar, while surrounded by gorgeous French countryside.*

144

Statue of Liberty & Ellis Island

WELCOME TO AMERICA

USA // Peeking past the Lady of Liberty's crown at the vapour trails streaking New York's skyline, try imagining a time – before the age of airline travel took off – when the first glimpse of America that visitors and immigrants got as their ship arrived was this giant statue of Libertas, the Roman goddess of freedom. A gift to the US from France, she's looked over Upper New York Bay since 1886. Until 1916 you could climb her raised arm to the freedom flame, but that's off-limits now. While ruing this First-World problem, think of the thousands of Europeans fleeing poverty and persecution who were buoyed by the sight of this towering effigy, heavily pregnant with potent and positive symbolism. With luck, their optimism would survive health checks and interrogation at neighbouring Ellis Island. Picture the scene at the immigration post – crowded and chaotic – not altogether dissimilar to today.

☛ SEE IT ! *Ferries to the Statue of Liberty and Ellis Island depart from Battery Park. Plus you can view for free from Staten Island ferry.*

144

145

Vatnajökull National Park

FIRE-&-ICE MEGAPARK

ICELAND // If your inner explorer has ever dreamt of conquering the Arctic, you'll love Vatnajökull – a megapark of glacial ice and volcanic landscapes set up to protect the world's largest ice cap outside the poles. Formed by the merging of two parks in 2008, the reserve covers 14 percent of Iceland and is the largest national park in Europe. The Jökulsárgljúfur (northern) portion of it protects a unique subglacial eruptive ridge and 30km gorge; the southern part is anchored by Skaftafell, a wildly popular collection of peaks and glaciers. Although visitors flock here, so vast is the wilderness that there's always a trail to call your own. Head for brilliant blue-white Vatnajökull with its lurching tongues of ice, and strike out from there.

☛ SEE IT ! *Vatnajökull is some 200km northeast of Reykjavík. Accommodation near the park is scarce and hugely in demand in summer; factor this in if you want to explore properly.*

145

146

146 Blue Mosque

ISTANBUL'S SHOW-STOPPER

TURKEY // When you're up against Aya Sofya (p26), the greatest monument to Byzantine civilisation, you've really got to pull out all the stops. The architects and builders of Istanbul's Sultan Ahmed Mosque certainly did that, with six minarets, a vast main dome and an imposingly huge courtyard. In cladding its spectacular interior with İznik tiles, the builders gave it a nickname to resonate down the centuries. Sizing up the Blue Mosque for this list is tricky, as it is a sublime structure in a city stuffed with wonderful Islamic buildings and, as such, is just one of many must-sees Istanbul has to offer.

Its effect would certainly be all the greater were it not that most tourists visit it on the same day they enter Aya Sofya and stumble blinking back into daylight after experiencing the astonishing Basilica Cistern complex. But the Blue Mosque's existence and splendour inside and out is significant in telling a crucial part of Istanbul's story, and it's a simply incredible building.

☛ SEE IT ! *The mosque is the first great building of Istanbul visible on the approach from the airport. Tourists go in via a side entrance.*

147

Gion District

MEMORIES OF A GEISHA

Kyoto, JAPAN // The mysterious geisha could be forgiven for confining their appearances to best-selling novels. Yet you can see them in the streets of Gion, Kyoto's old entertainment district. Although touristy, it has an air of tradition. The busiest streets bustle with shops stacked with lacquerware and boxed sweets. But the real journey of discovery begins in its narrow back-lanes. Behind closed doors and shuttered windows of old teahouses, *kaiseki* restaurants and exclusive bars await, signalled by glowing lanterns.

🕊 SEE IT ! *Gion is particularly lovely during cherry-blossom season and at night.*

148

Grand Buddha, Lèshān

IS THAT A BUDDHA?

CHINA // For such a humble man, the Buddha has been reproduced on an epic scale over the centuries. The seated Buddha statue at Lèshān finds him blown up to 40 times normal size, with 7m-long earlobes and 8m-long toes. In fact, this vast representation, created in the 7th century by ascetic monks, is less a statue than a carved mountain. To really grasp the scale of the Grand Buddha, climb the stairway to his right shoulder for a close-up view of one enormous earhole.

🕊 SEE IT ! *Ferries run from the main dock in Lèshān; it's more atmospheric than coming by road. Afternoons are quieter.*

149

Actun Tunichil Muknal

SACRED CAVE

BELIZE // A 45-minute hike through tropical jungle brings you to Actun Tunichil Muknal, the cave of the stone sepulchre. Donning a headlamp, you'll swim across an icy pool guarding the entrance to the Mayan underworld, then you'll walk, climb and crawl past dripping stalactites to the main chamber. Inside lies the calcite-encrusted remains of the maiden for whom the chamber is named. Be reverent. This is one of Belize's – and the Mayas' – most sacred spaces.

🕊 SEE IT ! *The round trip from San Ignaciao (including the jungle drive) takes 10 hours and must be done with a licensed guide.*

150 Haida Gwaii

LOST WORLD OF HAIDA CULTURE

CANADA // To walk among the iconic totem poles of Haida Gwaii staring eerily out to sea is to enter into a lost world. This is Canada as you'll see it nowhere else. It's a place where bears roam and bald eagles soar, where sea lions, whales and orcas frolic offshore and where superb old-growth rainforests feed some of the world's largest spruce and cedars. But the island's real soul lies in the ancient Haida culture itself, which resonates powerfully across this sparsely populated archipelago and particularly in beautiful Gwaii Haanas National Park Reserve, the islands' number-one attraction. Geographically more chummy with Alaska than it is with Vancouver, the best part could be its remoteness, making it a very special place indeed. This is somewhere you'll want to spend several days, which necessitates a decent amount of advance planning.

☞ SEE IT ! *Ferries between Prince Rupert on the mainland and Graham Island take between six and seven hours.*

151 Bairro of Ribeira

A MAGICAL MEDIEVAL WATERFRONT

PORTUGAL // Oh, Porto. So many charms colliding in such a romantic, medieval way. It's difficult to define the mystery behind its Bairro of Ribeira (a Unesco-listed waterfront) and what makes it such a captivating part of Portugal. Perhaps it's the meshing of sensory pleasure that creates a unique atmosphere: the multistoreyed pastel-coloured buildings precariously lining the quay, the accordion-players, the squawking gulls, the traditional Rabelo boats puttering down the River Duoro through the elegant Gustave Eiffel–built bridge, the sizzling aroma of sardines, the cafes, bars and restaurants peeking out from under arches and winding into narrow alleyways. Grab a coffee and a warm *pastel de nata* (egg-tart pastry) and soak it all up. Try sunrise, sunset, noon: in fact, any perspective of the promenade is sure to win your heart.

☞ SEE IT ! *The teleférico from Vila Nova de Gaia offers a fine view. On 23 June, there are festivities and fireworks for Festa de São João.*

151

154

152

Kōya-san

A RELIGIOUS EXPERIENCE

JAPAN // Nestled in Northern Wakayama, Kōya-san is as much about the journey as it is about the destination. The train trip winds through valleys and mountains before the final cable-car leg up to the peaceful setting of thickly forested Kōya-san itself. More than 110 temples make up this monastic complex, the headquarters of the Shingon school of Esoteric Buddhism. Day trips are possible but stay overnight in temple lodging for an insight into the life of a Japanese Buddhist monk.

☛ SEE IT ! *From Osaka's Namba station, take the Nankai Railway to Gokurakubashi then the cable car up the mountain.*

153

Mt Etna

SMOKING SICILY

ITALY // You'd think Catania locals would be always looking nervously over their shoulders at Mt Etna, as the volcano has been destroying settlements on its flanks since Roman times. But they view their smoking overlord as a fact of life, and just get on with it. No visit to Sicily would be complete without a scramble up the summit, where you may be greeted by the full sound and light show, before retreating for a glass of the robust red wine raised on Etna's volcanic soil.

☛ SEE IT ! *All lava-cobbles and Baroque churches, Catania is the gateway to Etna; rent a Vespa and rip up to the mount in style.*

154

Eiger

INFAMOUS ALPINE OGRE

SWITZERLAND // It's not a mountain, it's a monster: Eiger, the Ogre. There are higher peaks, but this 3970m behemoth in the Bernese Oberland is one of the most feared – on account of its North Face. This fearsome flank is steep, exposed and treacherously loose, frequently firing salvos of boulders at anyone on the way up. Since 1935, more than 60 climbers have died on this *mordwand* ('murderous wall'). Better to appreciate it from pretty Grindelwald.

☛ SEE IT ! *Trains run from Grindelwald to Kleine Scheidegg, from where you can join the Jungfrau Railway towards Eiger Glacier.*

155 Walt Disney World

THE WORLD'S HAPPY PLACE

USA // We adore Disney with complete sincerity. It's an utterly immersive fantasy world, planned down to the smallest detail (speakers disguised as rocks, talking trash cans). Ride the Space Mountain coaster, take a spin through Epcot's Spaceship Earth (the giant golf ball), watch the fireworks over Cinderella's Castle, and we dare you not to grin. Just watching other visitors is a delightful experience. The Magic Kingdom is not just about American capitalism, it's about a shared global culture. It's about Pakistani women wearing mouse ears atop their hijabs, about Argentinian teenagers breaking their cool to embrace Donald Duck, about Chinese families picnicking at Tom Sawyer Island. So drop your sophistication, buy yourself a Mickey ice cream, and join them.

☛ SEE IT ! *Orlando, Florida is the gateway to Disney. Just don't visit during American school holidays, when the crowds are even more intense than usual.*

156 Chernobyl

TOUR THE APOCALYPSE

UKRAINE // Conspiracy theorists still go potty for the passage in the Bible that warns about wormwood falling from the skies. When the reactor core went into meltdown in 1986, Chernobyl (wormwood, in Russian) certainly seemed to fit the bill. Thirty years later and the world's worst nuclear accident has become an unlikely tourist attraction, albeit a haunting and very strange one.

Tours offer first-hand views of the apocalypse – whole cities, deserted and overgrown; classrooms with chairs overturned after pupils fled for their lives; a fairground where rides were abandoned in the midst of the catastrophe. It's incredibly eerie, and utterly sobering, but also occasionally beautiful, as wild deer, wolves and elk wander though the now only mildly radioactive wasteland.

Yet you'll have to put aside any ambitions of actually visiting the reactor itself – it is still a radioactive hotspot and no-one is allowed within 200m of the site.

☛ SEE IT ! *Tours (arranged in Kiev) run to Pripyat and Chernobyl inside the exclusion zone; radioactivity is monitored throughout.*

157 Shibuya Crossing

JAPAN // Shibuya Crossing is the Tokyo you've seen in the movies – neon canyons, giant video screens and streets teeming with humanity. It's an electric setting for a spectacle of epic proportions. This is one of the world's busiest pedestrian crossings, where five roads meet and up to 1000 people cross from every direction.

When the man goes green, the scramble begins. But what should resemble a battle-charge of armies from *The Lord Of The Rings* is instead an elegant dance of people dodging their way through the throng. Anywhere else in the world things could get ugly, but such are the good manners of the Japanese that it goes off without a hitch. No sooner has the crossing cleared than all sides are replenished again. And so the shows go on; one you can star in or view from the wings.

☛ SEE IT ! *Go at night, definitely at night, and particularly on Fridays or Saturdays when fleets of fashionable young things crank the whole scene up to 11.*

158 Valle de Viñales

CUBA // Embellished by soaring pine trees and scattered with bulbous limestone cliffs teetering like giant haystacks above placid tobacco plantations, Parque Nacional Viñales is one of Cuba's greatest spectacles. This otherworldly karst landscape was created by the collapse of a vast prehistoric cave system, and the valleys are still wormholed with caverns, offering spectacular caving, rock climbing and trekking.

The juxtaposition of primeval *mogotes* (limestone buttresses) and colonial-era tobacco plantations creates a view found only in Cuba; one best appreciated with a glass of *ron* in one hand and a cigar in the other. Despite drawing day-trippers by the busload, the park's well-protected attractions have somehow managed to escape the frenzied tourist circus of other less well-managed destinations, while the atmosphere around Viñales town is refreshingly hassle-free.

☛ SEE IT ! *Viñales is the portal to the Valle, with abundant* casas particulares *that will take you to the heart of the Cuban way of life.*

159

Schloss Neuschwanstein
Bavaria's fairy-tale made flesh

↓

GERMANY // This confection of turrets was used by Walt Disney as inspiration for his Cinderella castle. Neuschwanstein was the vision of eccentric King Ludwig II, who hired a set designer rather than an architect to help him build it. He lived here for 170 days before dying in 1886. Just 15 of the proposed 200 rooms were finished. These include a show-stopping Singers' Hall, covered in frescoes; a Throne Hall with a 4m-high chandelier; and Ludwig's bedroom, with a bed that took 14 carvers four years to make.

☛ SEE IT ! *The castle can only be visited by guided tour.*

160

Terracotta Warriors
Silent ceramic sentinels

↓

CHINA // Chinese emperor Qin Shi Huang wanted to go out in style, and constructed an army of terracotta warriors to accompany him into the afterlife. Their discovery was accidental; in 1974, peasants drilling a well uncovered a vault filled with 8000 clay soldiers. This is one of China's big hitters, so you may know that no two soldier's faces are alike, or that the first emperor lies buried nearby in an unexcavated tomb, with a scale model of his empire.

☛ SEE IT ! *Buses leave Xī'ān Train Station via Huáqīng Hot Springs and the Tomb of Qin Shi Huang.*

161

Shackleton's Hut

BE A POLAR EXPLORER

ANTARCTICA // The wooden hut erected by Ernest Shackleton in 1908 has been preserved in ice – literally. Hardly a stick of firewood or army ration has been moved in the intervening century; those socks on the line were left by members of the Nimrod team on their way to the South Pole. Shackleton didn't make it to the Pole, but he did leave behind this astonishing time capsule. In fact, a few items have been removed – the missing dining table was almost certainly burned for fuel by a later expedition party. Only in the deep-freeze environment of the Antarctic could such a relic be so perfectly preserved; few places on earth have such a sense of being plucked from history.

🐋 SEE IT ! *Cape Royds is an Antarctic Special Protect Area, so you must join a tour; only eight people are allowed in the hut at one time.*

162 Icehotel

A MAGICAL SUB-ZERO SLEEPOVER

Jukkasjärvi, SWEDEN // There are very few hotels that issue their guests with instructions on how to sleep. But this is what happens at Swedish Lapland's ICEHOTEL, located 200km north of the Arctic Circle. Before you retire to bed, you get a briefing: strip down to just your long johns (sweating is bad); don't use water-based moisturiser (lest it freeze on your face); and don't drink too much in the Ice Bar (you don't want to have to get up in the night to pee). These are the practicalities of spending a night on ice.

Now for the magic. Staying at the ICEHOTEL, which is carved afresh each winter from the frozen Torne River, is a little like stepping into Narnia, *Frozen* and *Sleeping Beauty* combined. Ice beds topped with reindeer skins and expedition-thick sleeping bags will keep you warm despite the -5°C chill; however, the enchantment of laying in a glistening blue-white cocoon, snow-muffled and sparkling all night, may just keep you awake.

🐋 SEE IT ! *Jukkasjärvi is 20km from Kiruna Airport. Transfers from the airport to the ICEHOTEL by husky-sled are available.*

163

Moraine Lake

MORE THAN A 20-DOLLAR VIEW

CANADA // There's a reason this vista in Banff National Park is used to promote Canadian tourism – there's something about the deep-teal depths of Moraine Lake (which has graced the Canadian $20 bill) that knocks your jaw to the floor. Nestled in the Valley of the Ten Peaks, its rugged setting, framed by snow-capped mountains and emerald firs, is magical. Paddle a boat through glacier-fed waters, investigate the great day hikes, or snap some of the best pictures you'll ever take.

🐾 SEE IT ! *Visit in summer, as Moraine Lake Rd and its facilities close October to June. This is grizzly territory, so observe bear safety.*

164

Roman Baths

AWASH WITH BEAUTY

Bath, ENGLAND // It started with King Bladdud and his leprous pigs: when the wallowing porcines were cured here, a healing hot spring was revealed. The Romans arrived in the 1st century AD and called it 'waters of goddess Sulis'; today, the site of their grand temples and baths is called... er, Bath. What the city lacks in imaginative nomenclature it delivers in gorgeousness. The centre is Unesco-listed, and the Baths (now a museum) offers a glimpse into the toga-ed past.

🐾 SEE IT ! *Bath is a 90-minute train ride from London. The Roman Baths open at 9am and the busiest period is from 11am to 3pm.*

Chobe National Park

It's what I didn't see that impressed me the most. I'd long heard about the park's 50,000-strong elephant population, and when boarding the launch for my late afternoon cruise atop the Chobe River I was looking forward to seeing some of the large tuskers face to face. Yet, my initial encounter provided anything but. There were elephants for sure, over a dozen at first count, but I could see next to nothing of them. And that was the best part. Like a choreographed troop of synchronised swimmers, the matriarchal herd was strung out in a perfect line beneath the surface, only their waving trunks emerging from the depths. Several minutes (and many breaths) later, the aquatic marvels reached the far bank and climbed, one by one, onto its grassy fringes. Looking up at the towering terrestrial creatures, I simply couldn't reconcile that they were the same ones who'd just delicately swam beneath me.

Matt Phillips, Destination Editor

165 166 167

Chobe National Park

KINGDOM OF ELEPHANTS

BOTSWANA // At nearly 11,000 sq km, Chobe National Park in northern Botswana is the size of a small country, and there are more elephants here (thousands of them) than anywhere on earth. Then there are the landscapes of Savuti with their lions and leopard-rich rocky outcrops. Or the Linyanti marshes, the best place to see rare African wild dogs. Or the Chobe Riverfront where Africa's megafauna comes to drink. It's one of the continent's great wildlife destinations.

☛ SEE IT ! *Daily flights from Johannesburg make Kasane the ideal base for exploring the park, which has campsites and luxe lodges.*

Inle Lake

BURMA'S LIVING LAKE

MYANMAR (BURMA) // Although the serene Inle Lake is 21km long and 11km wide, it's hard to tell where the water finishes and the land begins. The surface resembles a silver sheet, dotted with stilt-house villages, island Buddhist temples and floating gardens. Traversing this water wonderland by boat is one of Southeast Asia's great pleasures. When you do hit land, you'll encounter white-washed stupas and tribal markets that hop-scotch around the lake on a five-day cycle.

☛ SEE IT ! *The closest town to Inle is Taunggyi, with an airport nearby at Heho; most people stay in pretty Nyaungshwe.*

Mt Kinabalu

MALAYSIA'S MAGNIFICENT MOUNTAIN

MALAYSIA // You probably won't tackle Mt Everest or K2 any time soon. Trekking Kili-manjaro takes a week. But if you want a peak with a perfect ratio of wow factor and feasi-bility, Mt Kinabalu is it. In Malaysian Borneo, Kinabalu rises 4095m above dense tropical lowland. The ascent requires no special equipment and takes two days, including an acclimatisation night at a lodge. The summit push begins pre-dawn, ending in a blue-and-orange sunrise over the Crocker Range.

☛ SEE IT ! *The Kinabalu trailhead is a two-hour bus ride from Kota Kinabalu. Pre-booking your treks is essential.*

168 Phong Nha-Ke Bang National Park

JUNGLES, WAR-RELICS & THE WORLD'S BIGGEST CAVE

VIETNAM // Like Vietnam in general, Phong Nha-Ke Bang National Park has hidden depths – in this particular case, a staggering network of karst caverns, which wormhole beyond the range of human exploration beneath a vast area of pristine primary rainforest. There are hundreds of caves here, including Son Doong, the world's largest: its main chamber is an astonishing 5km long and 200m high.

Even first-time speleologists can stroll through forests of stupa-like stalagmites and petrified waterfalls, or comb the jungles above for tigers, elephants and rare Asian antelopes. The only precondition is that you take a guide – there's too much wartime ordnance lying around to safely wander aimlessly. The park was part of the Ho Chi Minh trail, chosen, no doubt, for its ample number of places to hide.

☞ SEE IT ! *Son Trach village is the main centre, but it's a tiny place; most people arrive on organised trips and stay at lodges and farmstays in the vicinity of the park.*

169 Royal Mile

EDINBURGH'S STORIED SPINE

SCOTLAND // Boasting grand Edinburgh Castle at one end, Scottish Parliament at the other and St Giles Cathedral in the middle, the Royal Mile embodies history like nowhere else in Scotland. It runs up to Castle Rock (the volcanic plug on which the castle sits) like a great, cobblestoned spine, with views stretching across to Arthur's Seat and the Georgian New Town, and down to the Firth of Forth. Its sides are dotted with atmospheric alleyways, or wynds, and beneath its cobbles are catacombs and other remnants of medieval Edinburgh, which you can visit on tours. It's popular with visitors, and throbs with performers, tourists and salesmen hawking shows during Edinburgh's festival seasons. But, thanks to plenty of historic pubs, such attractions as the Camera Obscura and the Scottish Storytelling Centre, shops packed with souvenirs and knitwear, and some fine restaurants, there really is something for everyone on this most iconic of streets.

☞ SEE IT ! *The Royal Mile is in central Edinburgh. There's plenty of accommodation, but it's worth booking ahead, especially around New Year and during festival season (around August).*

171 National Mall

AMERICA'S FRONT YARD

USA // Folks call the National Mall, in Washington DC, 'America's Front Yard', and that's a good analogy. It is indeed a lawn, unfurling two miles of scrubby grass in the heart of the US capital. And it just happens to be dotted with the nation's most iconic monuments and hallowed marble buildings. At the east end, the mighty domed US Capitol rises up. Next come 10 Smithsonian museums that hold everything from the *Star-Spangled Banner* flag to the Apollo Lunar Module. The powerful Vietnam Veterans Memorial and beloved Lincoln Memorial anchor the west end. But it's not only about history. The Mall is also America's great public space, where citizens come to protest their government, celebrate at festivals or go for a run. These miles of green pretty much contain the American experience in one tidy plot.

☞ SEE IT ! *The Smithsonian Metro station is in the Mall's midst. Monuments are open 24 hours, most museums open 10am to 5.30pm. All of them are free.*

170 Cristo Redentor

THE LORD ON HIGH

BRAZIL // Think of all the statues throughout the world – those facing bare walls in museums, or those watching over pigeons in parks. Well, chances are none of them boast a view as sublime as that enjoyed by Rio de Janeiro's Cristo Redentor. Standing atop Corcovado, arms outstretched in peace, this soapstone icon watches out over the Brazilian city's spectacular landscape: a jumble of mountains and beaches, favelas and skyscrapers. It's a view almost as impressive for all the tiny mortals who ride up on the Corcovado rack railway and stand at the statue's holy feet.

Although plans for Cristo Redentor stretched back as far as the 1850s, the statue was only completed in 1931. Since then it has been struck by lightning a few times, visited by Popes, presidents and kings, and mischievously illuminated in the German national colours for the 2014 World Cup – but it still claims its place in the starting line up of Brazilian national treasures.

☞ SEE IT ! *If you plan to take the rack railway up to Cristo Redentor, arrive early or expect long queues – train services are limited.*

172

Prague Castle

LOOK IN ON KING WENCESLAS

CZECH REPUBLIC // Looming over the Vltava's west bank, this crazy collection of spires, towers and palaces dominates the centre of Prague like a set from *Cinderella*. Within its walls lie fascinating historic buildings, museums and galleries holding some of the Czech Republic's great artistic and cultural treasures. Every visitor to the city swings by, but what else would you expect from Prague's answer to the Louvre? Enjoy the treasures rather than seeking peace and quiet.

☞ SEE IT ! *Prague Castle is a steep uphill climb from Charles Bridge; tickets last two days, so don't cram everything into one.*

173

Ghana's Slave Forts

SOBERING SLAVE-TRADE HISTORY

GHANA // On the one hand, these forts are a grim reminder that countless souls arrived here in chains, before being shipped to the New World. On the other, the castles and coastline have an undeniable beauty: hulking whitewashed battlements watch over palm-shaded beaches and colourful fishing boats. Spend time in Elmina and Cape Coast to try to make sense of it all, wandering beneath the ramparts and pondering the fate of those who disappeared over the horizon.

☞ SEE IT ! *Cape Coast and Elmina are the most popular of the 30 or so castles that line the Ghanaian coast.*

174

Brussels' Grand Place

GOTHIC GUILDHALL GRANDEUR

BELGIUM // Europe's full of grand squares – several appear in the Ultimate Travelist – but there's something special about Brussels' World Heritage-Listed Grand Place (Grote Markt). As you stroll through backstreets crammed with seafood restaurants and boutique stores, you might not even realise it's there until you emerge into this awe-inspiring square. Gawp at majestic buildings that huddle side-by-side, reflecting an eclectic mix of architectural styles of opulent guildhalls and neoclassical facades.

☞ SEE IT ! *It's a 20-minute train ride from Brussels airport to the city centre. Brussels is also accessible by Eurostar.*

175

Kinkaku-ji
The golden jewel of Japan

↓

Kyoto, JAPAN //
Kinkaku-ji (the
Golden Pavilion)
is one of the
truly great sights
of Japan. Wrapped
in gold leaf and
shimmering in the
pond below it,
the Zen Buddhist
temple is beautiful,
whether you see
it in autumn to a
backdrop of red
maple leaves, in
winter covered in
snow, or on a shin-
ing summer day.
The temple was
restored in 1955
after a young monk
burned Kinkaku-ji
to the ground five
years earlier. The
tale was immortal-
ised in a novel by
Japanese writer,
Yukio Mishima.

☛ SEE IT !
*Kinkaku-ji is in
northwest Kyoto,
a 30-minute bus
ride from JR Kyoto
station.*

176

Gullfoss
Thunderous falls

↓

ICELAND //
Glorious Gullfoss
is more than a
plummet of water.
It is the symbol of
Icelandic conser-
vation. Yes, this
'Golden Falls' on
the White River,
south-central
Iceland, is one
of Europe's most
powerful cascades.
It also looks damn
pretty, especially
in winter, when
bits are frozen. But
in the early 20th
century, foreign
investors wanted
to buy Gullfoss, to
produce electricity.
Sigríður Tómasdót-
tir, the daughter of
the landowner, was
having none of it,
and fought tireless-
ly to save the falls
from development.

☛ SEE IT ! *Local
tour operators offer
Golden Circle tours
of Gullfoss, Geysir
and Thingvellir
National Park.*

177

Rocky Mountain National Park

GET ROCKY MOUNTAIN HIGHER

USA // Due to its 415 sq miles of mountain terrain, 350-plus miles of hiking trails, horse riding, biking, cross-country skiing and snowshoeing, Rocky Mountain National Park is a national treasure. It is home to some of America's largest mammals, including black bears, mountain lions and moose. Autumn is elk bugling season, when visitors come to see the majestic beasts and hear their mating calls. With 72 peaks above 3500m, you'll get even higher than is the Colorado norm.

🐾 SEE IT ! *Unless you're a serious uphill cyclist you'll need a car to reach the park, which is 78 miles from Denver airport.*

178

Egyptian Museum

EGYPTOLOGY'S TREASURE TROVE

Cairo, EGYPT // Think of it as a hide-and-seek game of world-class artefacts. Brimming with Egyptology's finest discoveries, this museum is a fascinating adventure through time, devoid of touchscreen technology, interactive displays or in-depth explanations. The obvious highlights are Tutankhamun's treasures and Hatshepsut and co in the Royal Mummies Hall, but the real marvels of this old-school maze are the statues, shrines and sphinxes shoved into every dimly lit corner.

🐾 SEE IT ! *The Museum is in downtown Cairo on Midan Tahrir. Sadat Station is the nearest metro station to the entrance.*

179

Gorges du Verdon

EUROPE'S GRAND CANYON

FRANCE // The Gorges du Verdon slice a 25km swathe through Haute-Provence's limestone plateau in the foothills of the Alps. Part of the Parc Naturel Régional du Verdon, the gorges create an incredible habitat for wildlife and a playground for humans. Hike, climb, kayak, raft, cycle, drive, or ride horses through an elemental landscape. The winding roads that cling to the valley sides, looking over perilous drops to the milky Verdon and Jabron Rivers, are not for the faint-hearted.

🐾 SEE IT ! *Jumping-off points are Moustiers Ste-Marie (west) and Castellane (east); canyon floors are accessible by foot, raft or kayak.*

180 Amber Fort

RAJASTHAN IN A FORTRESS

Jaipur, INDIA // A romantic tumble of battlements and bastions on a rocky desert ridge, Amber Fort is Rajasthan summed up in a single building. More palace than castle, this gargantuan fortification was the personal playground of Raja Man Singh, who amassed incredible power and fortune as one of the favoured generals of the Mughal Emperor Akbar. Outside, Amber Fort is fierce and formidable; inside, it's all gorgeous carvings, inlays and perforated marble screens. Although the crowds can sometimes feel like a besieging Mughal army, the fort doesn't look all that different to how it must have looked in Akbar's time, the primary difference being armies of camera-toting tourists in place of, well, armies. None of that matters when you step through the Suraj Pol (Sun Gate) into the lavish courtyards beyond and find yourself in a scene from *Arabian Nights*.

☛ SEE IT ! *The Fort is in Amber, 11km from Jaipur; skip the elephant-ride to the gate; take photos with them in the foreground instead.*

181 Snowdonia

WALES' LEGENDARY MOUNTAINS

WALES // Snowdonia National Park is full of beauty and myth. Snowdon itself is a mountain for anyone – those who don't want to walk can get a train up, while hikers can follow clearly marked tracks or scramble up one of many harder options. But there are several other ranges in this North Wales park, with numerous highlights: craggy Tryfan has invigorating scrambling routes and is topped by rocks called Adam and Eve (jumping between them brings good luck), while Cadair Idris is home to legends of bottomless lakes and giant hounds. Those in search of activities have plenty to get their teeth into, including sandy beaches and an increasing range of adventure sports: Snowdonia is already home to the zip line in Europe, and a cutting-edge inland surfing lagoon that opened in 2015.

☛ SEE IT ! *There are some useful buses – notably the Snowdon Sherpa service linking trailheads – and trains run to Llanberis Junction, but a car is very useful when exploring.*

Volcanoes National Park
Gorillas in the mist

↓

RWANDA // Nothing compares to gazing into the eyes of a gorilla and seeing them look back at you with the same sense of wonder. And there's nowhere better to embrace this experience than in Rwanda's Volcanoes National Park.

The park's stature is impressive, with five steep-sided conical volcanoes, each covered in rainforest, rising out of the East African plains. Their rugged nature becomes apparent as you climb through the thick bush to one of the 10 habituated family groups that live on the Virunga volcanoes' slopes.

☛ SEE IT! *Musanze (Ruhengeri), two hours' drive from Kigali, is the park's gateway.*

183

Xochimilco

VENICE, MEXICAN STYLE

MEXICO // An hour by train to the south of Mexico City, the urban sprawl breaks into a tangle of waterways – the last vestiges of the canals and floating gardens of Tenochtitlán, the Aztec city described as the 'Venice of the New World' by Spanish conquistadors. Colourful canal boats ferry day-trippers along the channels, accompanied by roaming mariachi bands and the bustle of village life. After the hectic buzz of downtown, it's clear why this is Mexico City's favourite escape.

🖝 SEE IT ! *Metro Línea 2 runs to Tasqueña. From here ride the Tren Ligero to Xochimilco and charter a wharfside trajinera for a cruise.*

184

Glen Coe

MONARCH OF THE GLENS

SCOTLAND // Glen Coe may not be cosy or picturesque – just a sullen expanse of rock, heather and thistle; empty and desolate – but this is rugged, spectacular mountain scenery quite unlike anywhere in Western Europe. Snow-dusted Munros rise sheer along the valley, bearing down fearsomely on hikers who trudge along the boggy, barren floor. Don't leave without hearing stories of massacres past – when Highland clans fought to the death in this godforsaken spot.

🖝 SEE IT ! *Some of the best views of Glen Coe are from atop Buachaille Etive Mor – reached by a challenging ascent.*

185

Mont Blanc

DANCING WITH LA DAME BLANCHE

FRANCE // From Nid D'Aigle trailhead, you can hike endless switchbacks to Refuge de Tête Rousse, survive crossing 'Death Gully' and climb to Refuge du Goûter. Using crampons and an ice axe, the next vertical kilometre is a marathon, but finally you'll reach the the summit ridge, where the mountain drops to France on your left and Italy on your right. The 4810m peak is in sight, it's -15°C, your head and stomach are spinning. And you wouldn't want to be anywhere else on the planet.

🖝 SEE IT ! *Chamonix is the gateway to the Mont Blanc massif. Engage a professional mountain guide.*

186

Karnak

A SACRED SITE ON STEROIDS

EGYPT // Karnak, near Luxor, was once known as Ipet-Sut – 'The Most Esteemed of Places'; quite a claim in a country that boasts Abu Simbel and the Pyramids of Giza. To ancient Egyptians, it was the earthly home of the god Amun, an enormous religious complex with 25 chapels, abundant obelisks and an avenue of sphinxes once 3km long. Everything – particularly the 134 papyrus-shaped columns in the hypostyle hall – is gigantic. Architecture on steroids, it still wows after 3500 years.

☞ SEE IT ! *Karnak is open 6.30am-5.30pm in winter, 6am-6pm in summer; a Sound and Light Show runs many times every evening.*

187

Gardens by the Bay

THE BOTANIC GARDEN OF THE FUTURE

SINGAPORE // This 101-hectare fantasyland of space-age bio-domes and whimsical sculptures is simply unmissable. Singapore's show-stopping green space has a Flower Dome replicating the dry Mediterranean climate, and a Cloud Forest with a waterfall, but it's hard to trump the huge vertical gardens known as Supertrees, six of which are joined by a skyway with knockout city views. These vegetated pillars twinkle nightly during the Garden Rhapsody light-and-sound show.

☞ SEE IT ! *Located behind Marina Bay Sands (Bayfront MRT/metro station), the outdoor gardens are free to visit.*

188

iSimangaliso Wetland Park

AFRICA'S WATERLOGGED WONDERLAND

SOUTH AFRICA // The name iSimangaliso means 'miracle' – apt for this spectacular wetland reserve, stretching for 220km from the Mozambique border to the southern end of Lake St Lucia. As well as amazing wildlife, it's pretty magical for human beings, with stunning ocean beaches pulling in seasonal crowds for scuba diving, deep-sea fishing, and kayaking, river-boating and horseback trips into the interior. Where else can you find whales *and* rhinos in one national park?

☞ SEE IT ! *The town of St Lucia is the nominal entrance, but there are lodges and camping sites scattered through the reserve.*

191

189

York Minster

FAIRY TALE OF OLD YORK

ENGLAND // The walls of York circle a beautiful city steeped in stories, and this mighty medieval minster (Northern Europe's largest) is the place to start exploring. Begin with the new subterranean experience in the Undercroft, leading you through 2000 years of local history from the remains of Roman barracks to the foundations of the Norman building you're standing in. Emerge to pass through the Orb, a display of stunning stained glass, and finish by climbing the cathedral's central tower for views across Yorkshire.

☛ SEE IT ! *Admission tickets last a year, so you can enjoy multiple revisits.*

190

Van Gogh Museum

TRACE THE TORTURED ARTIST'S LIFE

NETHERLANDS // He epitomised the artist's struggle through poverty and obscurity – only selling one painting in his lifetime – but Vincent van Gogh was the greatest 19th-century Dutch painter. Housing the world's largest collection of his works, the Van Gogh Museum in Amsterdam shows masterpieces from early works in the Netherlands to his final years in France. Trace the artist's life from floor to floor as you marvel over vivid yellows and deep purples and blues in such paintings as *Sunflowers* and *The Potato Eaters*.

☛ SEE IT ! *Queues can be long so book tickets online to get fast-track entry.*

191

Sigiriya Rock

SRI LANKA'S ROCK STAR

SRI LANKA // Rising from plains, the iconic outcrop of Sigiriya is perhaps Sri Lanka's most dramatic sight. Near-vertical walls soar to a flat summit containing the ruins of an ancient civilisation, with carvings and frescoes as well as spellbinding vistas across forests. Sigiriya (lion rock) is named after the huge lion paws that mark the site of the old palace gateway. The surrounding landscape – lily-pad-covered moats, water gardens and quiet shrines – only adds to Sigiriya's appeal.

☛ SEE IT ! *Sigiriya is east of Inamaluwa, between Dambulla and Habarana. Buses run to the gardens; it's 1200 steps to the top.*

192

Meenakshi Amman Temple
Meet 10,000 gods

↓

Madurai, INDIA //
The home of the triple-breasted goddess Meenakshi is considered to be the crowning glory of South Indian architecture, as vital to the aesthetic heritage of this region as the Taj Mahal is to North India. The 12 *gopurams* (temple towers) are encrusted with gods, goddesses and demons. Peer closely and you'll find most of the heroes and villains of Hinduism rendered in Technicolour. This is a living place of worship, with mingling priests and throngs of pilgrims.

☛ SEE IT ! *The temple sits in the heart of Madurai. Dress modestly: no shorts or bare shoulders please.*

193

Tbilisi Old Town

THE HEART OF EURASIA

GEORGIA // A tangle of winding lanes, wooden houses, leafy squares and handsome churches overlooked by the 4th-century Nariqala Fortress, Tbilisi's Old Town is a charming corner of the Caucasus. Virtually untouched for a century, its delightful art nouveau–style houses lean at such angles it's a wonder they still stand. Indeed, due to a lack of support for their preservation, many won't be for long. Grab a steaming cheese bread from one of the busy cafes and soak up the scene while you can.

☞ SEE IT ! *Witnessing an Eastern Orthodox service at one the Old Town's many churches is a truly humbling experience.*

194

Changdeokgung Palace

SEOUL'S MOST REGAL RESIDENCE

SOUTH KOREA // Principles of feng-shui dictate the architecture at this Joseon palace, adopted as the seat of the Korean royal family after the Japanese destroyed the original in the 1590s. Framed by a mountain and a stream, it is a gateway to a 14th-century world of refinement, exemplified by the Biwon (Hidden Garden), where the royals came to write poems inspired by their surroundings. It's amazing something so fragile survives amid Seoul's urban sprawl.

☞ SEE IT ! *You can reach the palace by subway; ride Line 3 to Anguk station and leave via Exit 3.*

195

Korea's DMZ

THE MOST DANGEROUS PLACE ON EARTH?

NORTH KOREA/SOUTH KOREA // To set foot in totalitarian North Korea without going there, visit Korea's DMZ (Demilitarized Zone). This heavily guarded, landmine-lined 240km-long buffer cuts through the country. Join a tour from Seoul to the Joint Security Area for a surreal experience. Blue office buildings straddle the ceasefire line, guarded by South Korean soldiers. Inside the building you cross into North Korea's territory, where intimidating soldiers peer through the glass at you.

☞ SEE IT ! *Recommended tour operators are Panmunjom Travel Center and USO (United Services Organizations).*

196

Bodhnath Stupa

WHERE LIFE IN KATHMANDU REVOLVES

NEPAL // Prior to the earthquake that hit Nepal in 2015, life in Kathmandu revolved around Bodhnath. For thousands, each day started and ended with a ritual circumnavigation of Nepal's largest Buddhist stupa. Though the stupa was damaged, not destroyed, this act of devotion has been interrupted. But there's hope that joining this human tide, and spinning a prayer wheel while gazing on Bodhnath's golden Buddha-eyed tower, will once again be an electrifying experience.

☛ SEE IT ! *Bodhnath is 7km from central Kathmandu, and ringed by guesthouses.*

197

Rynek Główny

TRUMPETER OF KRAKOW

Krakow, POLAND // Nearly 800 years old, the Rynek Główny is paved with cobblestones and circled by original buildings, with the old marketplace at its heart. Lined with shops and cafes, the plaza is abuzz. A window opens in the tower of the Mariacka Basilica, and a trumpeter plays a mournful melody. Below, the crowds stop to listen. Suddenly, the song is cut short, mid-note, as if the trumpeter were shot by a Mongol invader, a re-enactment of a legend that's also 800 years old.

☛ SEE IT ! *Though stunning all year, Rynek Główny sure is cold from December to March.*

198

Mògāo Caves

RUGGED ROMANCE ON THE SILK ROAD

CHINA // For all its romance, the Silk Road was dangerous for travellers – all the more reason to drop in at Mògāo Caves to pray for safe passage. This warren of 492 caverns and chambers was hollowed out in the 4th century and later abandoned... until 20th-century explorers discovered one of the world's greatest repositories of Buddhist art. The mesmerising murals and tower-block-sized Buddha statue tell of a people creating their own beauty in the desolate Gobi Desert.

☛ SEE IT ! *Reach the caves by bus or long, hot desert bike ride. Entry is via tour only.*

199

Wat Phou

LAO'S ANSWER TO ANGKOR

LAOS // The People's Democratic Republic of Lao is better known for laid-back escapes than ancient ruins, but at Wat Phou you get both. This complex of Khmer-era temples is hidden in the pristine jungles of southern Laos, on the banks of the Mekong River. The tumbledown pavilions, graceful Buddhist and Hindu carvings, and tall trees shading the site give Wat Phou a mystical ambience. It's still a place of worship today, a calm version of the end-of-the-river temple in *Apocalypse Now*.

☛ SEE IT ! *Pakse, the provincial capital of Champasak, is the closest town; rent a motorbike or take the boat to get here.*

196

200—
299

200 Island of Gorée

SENEGAL // An eerie calm shrouds Gorée. Bougainvillea-flushed lanes and bright colonial buildings fill the sand-swept, car-less island. But the stillness is meditative, as its structures bore witness to the slave trade. The House of Slaves is the era's chilling memorial; the Door of No Return opens to the sea. Debate exists about how many victims passed through, but no-one disputes the stark reminder it evokes.

☞ SEE IT ! *Gorée Island is 3.5km off the coast from Dakar. Ferries depart every one to two hours for the 20-minute journey.*

201 Mont St-Michel

FRANCE // Mont St-Michel only really merits this list in low season when calm envelops Normandy's abbey-island. *Sans* crowds, it's possible, at low tide, to stroll barefoot across the bay. Centuries of history seep through your soles as you trace the path of ancient pilgrims who crossed the sands to reach the turrets. It's almost a disappointment to reach its church-spire summit – it's more romantic from afar.

☞ SEE IT ! *Pontorson, the nearest town, is 9km south and you'll need wheels to get there. Bring some cider and a picnic.*

202

202 Blue Mountains National Park

HAZY AUSSIE MOUNTAINS

AUSTRALIA // To call the Blue Mountains our third favourite national park in Australia, after Kakadu and Cradle Mountain-Lake St Clair, isn't to damn with faint praise. The bar is set high. The park earns its place not only through its natural beauty but also its proximity to Australia's most populous city, Sydney. This is prime weekending territory when you need to swap the sand and surf for a leg-stretching hike among the eucalyptus trees that give the park its name through the fine mist of oil they exude.

The park itself sits on a sandstone plateau around 1100m high that is riven with forested gorges. Walks here often involve steep descents and ascents, but while your legs pay the price, your senses are rewarded with the scents (lemon myrtle, eucalyptus) and sounds (cockatoos and kookaburras) of the Australian bush. Many of the key sights, such as the Three Sisters rock formation, are close to the towns of Katoomba and Leura but the crowds dissipate the further you go from the car parks. Hikes for every fitness level are mapped; stop at Katoomba's visitor centre.

☛ SEE IT ! *The Blue Mountain's hub of Katoomba is around a 90-minute drive from Sydney. Avoid the heat and fire risk of summer.*

203

Mozambique Island

VIBRANT GHOST TOWN

MOZAMBIQUE // Tiny in size, powerful in presence, this historical island – the capital of Portuguese East Africa for centuries – has charmed all who've stepped ashore since Vasco da Gama landed here in 1498. The European powers and Arab traders may have gone, but relics of the past loom large, such as the 16th-century Fort of São Sebastião. A fishing community now calls the island home, its colourful nets dry on beautiful beaches that welcome barefoot explorers.

☛ SEE IT ! *Nampula, about 180km from the island, is the closest international airport.*

204

Erg Chebbi Dunes

THE SAHARA'S STUNNING CREST

MOROCCO // The wild red-gold sands that have piled up at Erg Chebbi are menacing enough to be deemed – even by sand-savvy Moroccans – a punishment sent by God. Winds have whipped the dunes here up into a swathe of 150m-high peaks. These waves of sand roll for 50km along the Morocco–Algeria frontier in a *Star Wars*-esque landscape justifiably touted as the quintessential Sahara experience.

☛ SEE IT ! *Merzouga is the main dune gateway. Visit outside of July and August, when the sands get unbearably hot.*

Erg Chebbi Dunes

The shifting sands of the Sahara sweet-talked my inner Lawrence of Arabia for years before I finally reached Erg Chebbi at the end of a hot and dusty road to Merzouga, a frontier village close to where Morocco ends and Algeria begins. From a loo with a view I got my first glimpse of the dunes through a hole in a wall – empty, vast and undulating orange ripples. The end of the world? It was a bizarre, spine-tingling introduction but just a prelude to the exquisite sensation of stepping into the void as that tantalising whisper of Arabian adventure was swallowed whole by the vacuum of nothingness. The desert silence was deafening. As our camel-led caravanserai arrived at a candlelit Bedouin camp for songs, dinner and jasmine tea, the sound of silence crescendoed into a howling wind I'll never forget, making sleep impossible and sending my imagination running riot under the darkening sky, away with the whipping grains of sand.

Lorna Parkes, Destination Editor

204

205 Historic Centre of San Gimignano

ITALY'S FIRST SKYSCRAPERS

ITALY // One-upmanship is a core part of the human psyche. Some people like to get one up on the neighbours with a bigger car; in San Gimignano, it's all about towers. Over centuries of internecine squabbling, rival clans built ever taller towers in a bid to be king of the *castello*, leaving a garden of looming towers looking out over this wheat-field-coloured Tuscan town and the rolling farmland.

Here are towers to climb, churches full of frescoes, gorgeous cobbled squares, ancient city walls and pavement *trattorie* serving the delicious local vino. It's about as Italian as you could possibly imagine,

and best appreciated in the languorous days of early summer, when the surrounding landscape is at its most quintessentially Tuscan.

As with everywhere in Tuscany, San Gimignano is unimaginably beautiful and unimaginably crowded with day-trippers; stay over to catch it in the early morning or late light of evening, when the streets are at their most magical.

☛ SEE IT ! *Staying over is the best way to experience San Gimignano, but you can day-trip from Siena; buses run via Poggibonsi.*

207

206

Vasamuseet

SWEDEN // When the mighty Swedish warship *Vasa* sank in Stockholm harbour, just 1300m into her maiden voyage in 1628, it was an embarrassment. When she was salvaged and restored, she became a source of national pride and a symbol of the Swedish Empire at its pinnacle. Now on display in full regalia, *Vasa* is glorious. You'll gawk at her size and lavish ornamentation, and also learn about the sinking and salvage, and the efforts to preserve this piece of Swedish history.

☛ SEE IT ! *Vasamuseet is on the island of Djurgården in Stockholm. From June to August, arrive early to avoid summer crowds.*

207

Portmeirion

WALES // If you've ever seen 1960s TV series *The Prisoner*, you might find yourself looking out for giant bouncing balls as you explore Portmeirion, where the cult show was filmed. Its colourful Italianate buildings were created by Welsh architect Sir Clough Williams-Ellis, who believed that beauty is a necessity. This was also once home to the Portmeirion pottery factory, producer of florid tableware. It's all rather captivating and slightly odd – it could only be in Britain.

☛ SEE IT ! *Portmeirion is two miles east of Porthmadog; public transport isn't great, so if you don't fancy the walk, catch a taxi.*

208

Times Square

New York, USA // There are two types of people: those who love Times Square, and those who just haven't learned to love it yet. The intersection of Broadway and Seventh Avenue is crammed with more iconic New York moments than a Woody Allen movie. You've already seen it a thousand times, so set aside your inhibitions and step through the silver screen. Whether it's the real New York, or real in any sense, will cease to matter in a blur of neon billboards and yellow cabs.

☛ SEE IT ! *Alight at the busy Times Square–42nd Street subway station, where numerous subway converge.*

209 Bacuit Archipelago

PICK A PARADISE ISLAND...

PHILIPPINES // With 7107 islands to choose from, the challenge in the Philippines has always been which island to pick for that perfect mix of sand, palms and coral. We'll make it easy for you – from the laid-back dive resort of El Nido, you can roam around a karst limestone wonderland of jungle-capped islets in a perfect turquoise bay. The Bacuit Archipelago has hidden beaches, secret caverns, lost lagoons, archaeological sites and spectacular dive sites. You can swim with whale sharks, manta rays and dugongs, along with other denizens of the deep, in one of the last truly relaxing tropical island destinations.

The main form of transport around the archipelago is the outrigger canoe, and it's a wonderfully atmospheric way to travel, but you can also get around by rented kayak or by using your own mask, snorkel and fins. Take an island-hopping cruise or charter a boat to drop you on an uninhabited island and go Robinson Crusoe; either way, you'll reconnect with what travel in Southeast Asia was meant to be about.

☛ SEE IT ! *El Nido is the doorstep to the Bacuit Archipelago; it's pretty paradisical in its own right, and served by flights from Manila.*

210

Robben Island

WALK IN MANDELA'S FOOTSTEPS

SOUTH AFRICA // A prison might seem an unlikely tourist sight, but Robben Island is synonymous with the struggle against apartheid thanks to Nelson Mandela, who was held here for 18 years, writing and hiding the memoirs later published in *Long Walk to Freedom*. Tours of the former gaol are led by other ex-prisoners, adding a personal aspect to proceedings. Visiting is a challenging but uplifting experience; a tour of the human spirit as much as some faded old buildings.

☞ SEE IT ! *Tours of Robben Island last four hours, and ferries depart daily from beside the clocktower at Cape Town Waterfront.*

211

Borgarfjörður Eystri & Seyðisfjörður

FJORDTASTIC!

ICELAND // Fjord-lovers, prepare to worship this pocket of east Iceland. Surrounded by mountains and waterfalls and nestled at the bottom of a steep valley, stunning Seyðisfjörður rewards all those who make the (sometimes challenging) trip into her secluded haven. Kayakers, mountain-bikers and hikers are in paradise here, hikers even more so at nearby Borgarfjörður Eystri, with its spectacular routes untouched by the masses, and its sustainable-tourism focus.

☞ SEE IT ! *A car ferry from Denmark sails into Seyðisfjörður via the 17km-long fjord. Borgarfjörður is a two-hour drive north.*

212

Sossusvlei

MOUNTAINS OF SCULPTURED SAND

NAMIBIA // The Namib Desert is the world's oldest, and the mammoth dunes at Sossusvlei in Namib-Naukluft National Park are stunning. Rising up to 380m above the parched pans and sculpted by the wind, the parabolic dunes are adorned with what seem like razor-sharp crests. At sunrise and sunset, the play of light is mesmerising, as orange hues are juxtaposed against black shadows. There's no better place to watch the show than from a seat in the sand atop a dune.

☞ SEE IT ! *Sossusvlei is a scenic 365km-drive from Windhoek. You must sleep in the park for sunrise/sunset access.*

213

Wieliczka
Salt Mine

VAULT OF SALT

POLAND // Deep underground in this unusual museum, all of the artistic, architectural and even spiritual treasures are fashioned from salt. Wieliczka operated as a salt mine for more than 700 years. Reaching depths of 327m, the mine has 287km of tunnels. It now includes a mining museum, sculptures and a vast chapel hung with chandeliers (all made from salt). There's an underground lake and a subterranotherapy spa too: the mine's microclimate supposedly has health benefits.

☛ SEE IT ! *Wieliczka is 14km from Krakow. Whatever the weather outside, it's chilly when you're 135m underground.*

214

Parque Nacional
Nahuel Huapi

PRETTY ALPINE CROWD-PLEASER

ARGENTINA // The siren call of Nahuel Huapi resounds from the tops of its snow-dusted mountains down to the depths of its huge glacial lake and the many hiking trails in-between. Who's surprised that it's one of Argentina's most visited national parks? Sitting pretty at its heart, Bariloche is a thriving alpine resort town in a gorgeous setting. Both winter wonderland and summer playground, the skiing, rafting, fishing, cycling, climbing and ambling on offer will have you hooked.

☛ SEE IT ! *Bariloche is in Argentina's Lake District, a short hop southwest from Buenos Aires by plane or a very long ride by bus.*

215

Jellyfish
Lake

MARINE MIRACLE

PALAU // The 21-million softly pulsating landlocked jellyfish of Micronesia's Palau, trapped in a saltwater lake for many thousands of years, are an outright miracle of evolution. Don't worry – they won't sting, although they could well make your hair stand on end. Boat into their uninhabited rock isle, hike the jungle, don your snorkel and dip into the warm waters to make like a sea cucumber and float with these marine marvels until you start to wrinkle.

☛ SEE IT ! *Palau's Rock Islands are 7500km southwest of Hawaii. It's popular; get there early for one-on-one time with the jellies.*

216

Vigelandsparken

SCULPTURE IN THE BUFF

Oslo, NORWAY // Norwegian sculptor Gustav Vigeland was an artist of raw talent, and this park bearing his name is the manifestation of his naked ambition. Vigelandsparken is filled with statues engaged in all manner of human activity, from conversing and caressing to wrestling and waxing philosophical. All share one common trait – nudity. Most photographed of the sky-clad figures are the angry baby and a surreal god-like figure who seems to be hurling children from all limbs. On a raised stairway stands the most famous of the sculptures, *Monolith*, a 14m-tall carved column consisting of 121 people connected in a writhing, orgiastic pose. Some see it as a representation of man's eternal struggle. Others see a huge wang. Visit and decide for yourself.

☛ SEE IT ! *The park is a short walk from Majorstuen metro station, and bus 20 and tram 12 both pass the entrance. Admission is free.*

217

216

217

Summer Palace

IMPERIAL CHINA'S SUMMER RETREAT

CHINA // Běijīng's splendid Summer Palace was a refreshing breeze for emperors and court-holders who would decamp here every year to shake off the old Imperial City's stifling summers. The palace – which has a huge lake and hilltop views – feels like a pastoral escape into the landscapes of traditional Chinese painting. Once you've hit up the Forbidden City and Great Wall, this is your next mandatory stop in Běijīng. Trashed twice by foreign soldiers and repaired under Communist rule, it's an OTT mix of temples, gardens, pavilions, bridges and gate towers built by 100,000 workers for 18th-century Emperor Qianlong, who clearly didn't like doing things by halves. Come summer, locals flock here to indulge in strolling and lake boating followed by much beer quaffing and *shāokǎo* (barbecue).

☛ SEE IT ! *The Palace fringes the Hǎidiàn and Wǔdàokǒu districts. In summer, visit the beer garden near the Wǔdàokǒu subway stop.*

219

218

Old Québec City

THE NEW WORLD'S ELDERLY EXCEPTION

CANADA // 'Old' in North America is relative. So Québec City's historic heart is all the more special. The city, founded in 1608, is the only one on the continent to have preserved its old defensive walls, gates and bastions. Inside these ramparts is a twisty, tumbledown, cobbled cluster of 17th- and 18th-century streets and houses more suited to France. Sitting at a pavement cafe with a vin rouge and plate of poutine (chips, cheese and gravy) is the best way to take it in.

🕿 SEE IT ! *Walking tours, with maps, instructions and background info, can be downloaded from www.quebecregion.com.*

219

Canterbury Cathedral

CHURCH OF ENGLAND'S HISTORIC HOME

ENGLAND // Already the country's pre-eminent place of worship, when Canterbury's then- archbishop, Thomas Becket, was murdered in 1170 by four knights seeking favour with King Henry II, the cathedral became a place of pilgrimage, famed throughout Christendom. Today's pilgrims won't be disappointed. The seat of the Church of England is fittingly grand, from its Gothic Southwest Porch to the strikingly modern altar marking the spot where Becket was slain.

🕿 SEE IT ! *It's £10.50 to enter the Cathedral, unless you're attending a service. Regular guided tours run Monday to Saturday.*

220

Carthage

AFRICA'S ANCIENT PUNIC CAPITAL

TUNISIA // The remnants of this grand Punic city lie scattered across a quiet seaside suburb northeast of Tunis. Wander through the excavated residential quarter of Byrsa to capture a glimpse of what life was like in this capital, then head up to Byrsa Hill past the forum built by the Romans after Carthage's defeat in the Third Punic War. Once an ancient superpower that grew fat from its trading prowess, Carthage's scant remains are a glimpse of how empires can crumble.

🕿 SEE IT ! *Carthage can be reached using the TGM train network that connects Tunis Marine Station with Hannibal-Carthage.*

DEM DEUTSCHEN VOLKE

221

221 Reichstag

TEUTONIC SHAPESHIFTER

GERMANY // You can see right across Berlin from the glass dome atop the Reichstag building, but beneath your feet is a bricks-and-mortar metaphor for the bumpy journey the German nation has experienced since its birth in 1871. This neo-baroque pile began sprouting on the banks of the Spree in 1884. The power-laden words *'Dem Deutschen Volke'* (To the German People) were etched into the frieze above the main façade in 1916, to the chagrin of Wilhelm II, and when the kaiser abdicated after WWI, Philipp Scheidemann proclaimed a republic from a balcony of the building. Unloved by the Nazis, it was battered

during the Battle of Berlin in 1945. (Graffiti left by Soviet soldiers – such as 'Hitler kaputt' – can still be seen.) Caught in the crosshairs of the Cold War, the Reichstag was on the seam of East and West Berlin, and in 1961 was closed by the erection of the Berlin Wall. When the wall fell, the building was redesigned by Norman Foster, and now you can watch the *Bundestag* (German government) at work.

☛ SEE IT ! *Admission to the roof terrace and dome is free, but you must register in advance: www.bundestag.de*

222 Virupaksha Temple

ANCIENT SACRED SKYSCRAPER

INDIA // Not so very long ago, Hampi's Virupaksha Temple and be-witching ancient city ruins represented the sacred beating heart of an inhabited village, Hampi Bazaar. For better or worse, the Indian government served the locals with an eviction order and now you'll just find (relative) peace and quiet among the Dravidian skyscrapers – it can be an unreal place to linger, amid a landscape marbled with giant boulders. Constant worship ensures Virupaksha, Hampi's only working temple, is still the life and soul of the party. Its intricately carved main *gopuram* (gateway tower), which is almost 50m high,

is a superb example of the temple architecture that is so typical of southern India. Completed in 1442, these days it bows slightly under the weight of time and usage, but the thin veneer of grime only adds to its persona as a granddaddy of the Dravidian empire in the capital of the last great Hindu Kingdom of Vijayanagar. All who enter here are certain to be spellbound.

☛ SEE IT ! *Bangalore and Goa are international airports; rail links to nearby Hospet abound. Stay in Virupapur Gaddi, across the river.*

223

223

Malecón

CUBA // Havana's most soulful and quintessentially Cuban thoroughfare, the 8km-long seafront esplanade has been a meeting place for lovers, philosophers, minstrels and fishermen since it was laid out in the early 20th century. The Malecón is where the whole city comes to meet, greet, date and debate on the salt-sprayed promenade sandwiched between the seawall and the wave-dodging vintage Buicks and Chevrolets cruising the road on the other side.

☛ SEE IT ! *Find a seaside perch at sunset, when the weak yellow light from Vedado filters on to the buildings of Centro Habana.*

224

Brú na Bóinne

IRELAND // When it comes to significant mounds of rock, England's Stonehenge (p78) has the historical fame but Ireland's Brú na Bóinne, in County Meath has the clout of a thousand extra years. It's an extraordinary sight: a vast Neolithic necropolis of squat rotund tombs set in emerald plains. These mystical beauties were the largest structures in Ireland until the construction of Anglo-Norman castles 4000 years later – a mind-boggling achievement of prehistoric humankind.

☛ SEE IT ! *Buses go via Drogheda from Dublin. Visits are by tour only: just 750 tickets are sold on the day, so arrive early.*

225

Museo del Prado

SPAIN // The Museo del Prado, in a stately 18th-century palace, is a window to the historical vagaries of the Spanish soul: imperious in the royal paintings of Velázquez while darkly tumultuous in Goya's *Las Pinturas Negras*. The collection of Spanish masters, from El Greco to Francisco de Zurbarán, would rank the Prado among Europe's elite galleries. But its European portfolio – from Rembrandt to Rubens, Brueghel to Bosch – reads like a roll call of stellar masterpieces.

☛ SEE IT ! *Madrid is well-connected by air. The Prado can be reached on foot from most hotels. Book tickets online to avoid queues.*

226

Lago de Atitlán

THE HEART OF THE GUATEMALAN HIGHLANDS

GUATEMALA // Surrounded by volcanoes, its shoreline dotted with Mayan villages, this vast lake serves as an irresistible invitation to kick back and soak up the serenity. With plenty of Spanish schools, bars and good accommodation, San Pedro La Laguna is a popular town in which to bed down. Hike the San Pedro volcano, kayak between villages or relax and enjoy the beautiful views with a freshly brewed espresso – it's one of Guatemala's premier coffee regions, after all.

☛ SEE IT ! *The gateway town of Panajachel is 2½ hours from Antigua by shuttle bus.*

227

Gunung Leuser National Park

ORANG-UTAN FANTASY JUNGLE

INDONESIA // It's a sad fact that Gunung Leuser's primeval forests are one of the few places on earth where it's still possible to spy wild orang-utans. If our wonderful auburn-locked cousins don't do it for you, tigers, rhinoceros and elephants make up the rest of the big four found here. It's one of the world's most important conservation areas and it receives barely a trickle of visitors. If you want to re-enact *The Jungle Book*, then swing by here.

☛ SEE IT ! *The nearest base is tiny Ketambe; Medan in Aceh is the gateway town.*

228

Alcatraz

LEGENDARY GANGSTER PRISON

San Francisco, USA //Alcatraz: the name alone has given innocents the guilty cold sweats. 'The Rock' was a one-time Civil War jail, A-list gangster penitentiary (Al Capone did a spell here) and contested territory between Native Americans and the FBI, not to mention a Clint Eastwood film set. Its run as escape-proof fortress extraordinaire ended in 1963 when it was abandoned to the birds. No wonder that first step you take off the ferry seems to cue ominous music...

☛ SEE IT ! *Buy tickets weeks ahead. Avoid crowds by booking the day's first or last boat.*

227

229

Piazza del Campo

Medieval stage for a wild race

↓

Siena, ITALY // A bird's-eye view makes Siena's *Campo* look like a massive crater squished into this cute terracotta-tiled Tuscan town. The sloping piazza, hemmed in by tall buildings and a medieval palace, has been Siena's centre since the 12th century. Students and tourists picnic on its pie-piece paving – until it's time for the Palio, a spectacle dating from the Middle Ages, involving pageants and a horse race that lasts barely one exhilarating minute, but never fails to make spectators' hair stand on end.

☛ SEE IT ! *Siena is 3.5 hours from Rome by bus. The Palio is in July and August.*

230

Postojna Cave & Predjama Castle

CAVE-&-CASTLE COMBO

SLOVENIA // Postojna has an enviable swag bag of tourist traps. First there's brooding Predjama Castle, wedged into the gaping mouth of a cavern halfway up a 123m-high cliff, looking unconquerable. Drawbridge? Tick. Dank dungeon? Tick. Ancient treasure haul? Tick. Less than 10km down the road, the awesome karst cave of Postojna swallows crowds in a series of caverns, halls and passages some 20km long and two million years old. Together, they're fantastically popular.

👉 SEE IT ! *Postojna is an hour by bus from Ljubljana. In July, the castle hosts the Erasmus medieval games tournament.*

231

Rila Monastery

HEAVENLY HIGHLAND HAVEN

BULGARIA // The Unesco-listed Rila Monastery is a sacred, sylvan symbol of Bulgarian identity. Emerging from the Rila Mountains like a divine vision, its comely cloisters were a stronghold of Bulgarian culture during Ottoman rule. If the mountain views, fresco-plastered interiors and 220-year-old Rila Cross – a wooden masterpiece of carved biblical scenes so tiny they cost the artist his sight – don't leave you breathless, a hike up to the tomb of St Ivan, its founder, certainly will.

👉 SEE IT ! *Rila is an easy day-trip from Sofia (public transport options abound), or stay overnight in a spartan monk's cell.*

232

Bund

HISTORIC CITY PROMENADE

CHINA // The grand sweep of the riverside Bund is symbolic of colonial Shànghǎi and is the city's standout landmark. The Bund was the city's Wall St, a place where fortunes were won and lost. Originally a towpath for dragging barges of rice, it's been the first port of call for visitors since passengers began disembarking here more than a century ago. Today, it's the boutiques, bars and restaurants, and the hypnotising views of Pǔdōng (new Shànghǎi) that pull crowds.

👉 SEE IT ! *The Bund Sightseeing Tunnel runs under the Huángpǔ River, connecting the Bund to Pǔdōng. Best strategy? Stroll.*

233 Rijksmuseum

NETHERLANDS' TREASURE CHEST

Amsterdam, NETHERLANDS // One of the world's premier art troves, the Rijksmuseum stuffs masterpieces galore into its 1.5km of galleries. The crowds huddle around Rembrandt's humongous *Night Watch* and Vermeer's *Kitchen Maid*, and who can blame them? The former is a Golden Age icon, the latter so dreamy it continues to pique Hollywood's interest centuries later. But step into the 100 or so rooms beyond, and the most eye-popping treasures await: antique ship models, savage-looking swords, crystal goblets and magic lanterns from the 17th century, when the Dutch sailed the world and brought

back riches. Other galleries display Delftware, the delicate blue-and-white pottery from the era, and Golden Age dollhouses with such exquisite furnishings they cost more than a full-scale house. You could spend days gaping at the beautiful and curious collections tucked into the nooks and crannies. Browse deep enough and you'll even stumble upon works by Van Gogh and the 20th-century CoBrA artists.

👈 SEE IT ! *The Rijksmuseum is in the Old South area, easy to reach via tram. Queues can be long; buying tickets online saves time.*

234

Pont du Gard

PASTORAL ROMAN ENGINEERING MARVEL

FRANCE // Those Romans knew a thing or two about grandiose engineering. Take Pont du Gard, southern France's three-tiered aqueduct, which was once part of a 50km-long system of channels. It's a gasp-inducing beast that's 275m long (you can walk atop its tiers) and graced with 35 arches towering almost twice as high as its cousin in Segovia, Spain. Straddling two bushy banks with sandy river beaches to swim off and a walking trail nearby, it's a popular place to gawp and play.

☞ SEE IT ! *The bridge, stunningly floodlit early evening, is an easy trip from Avignon.*

235

Real Alcázar

ANDALUSIAN ARCHITECTURAL PERFECTION

Seville, SPAIN //Built over centuries of Islamic and Christian rule, the architecture of Seville's Alcázar is close to perfection. See the Mudéjar plasterwork and the *artesonado* (ceiling of interlaced beams with decorative insertions) in the Sala de Justicia; the refined sensibilities of the Palacio de Don Pedro; or the elegance of the archways, decorated ceilings, vivid tilework and elaborate wood carvings that adorn this tapestry of interlocking palaces, patios and oasis-like gardens.

☞ SEE IT ! *It's two hours from Madrid by train. Avoid midsummer's high temperatures.*

236

Singapore Zoo

WHERE WILD THINGS ROAM

SINGAPORE // Due to an 'open enclosure concept' offering animals humanely spacious habitats (in a city not known for spacious humanly habitats), Singapore Zoo might win your respect. Eleven climate zones, from Arctic tundra to Australian outback, allow animals a natural setting. From aardvarks to zebras, they seem less stressed than most Singaporeans. Visit after dark, when the zoo becomes a night safari, offering the chance to get up close to its nocturnal residents.

☞ SEE IT ! *Ang Mo Kio is the nearest metro; after the Night Safari you'll need to taxi it.*

234

237

Wadi Rum

JORDAN'S MAJESTIC DESERT-SCAPE

JORDAN // TE Lawrence called this expanse of desert 'vast, echoing and godlike', and the wild, raw beauty of this landscape continues to enthral. Wadi Rum seems to have fallen straight off a painter's canvas: its craggy rock outcrops rim a plateau of sand tinted in a spectrum of pinks, oranges and yellows. After sunset, when the shadows of the giant rock formations have withered into blackness, sleeping under the star-strewn sky amid the silent desert sands is awe-inspiring.

🐫 SEE IT ! *Buses run from Aqaba (one hour) and Petra (two hours) to the Visitors' Centre where tours are booked on arrival.*

238

Luxor Temple

ABODE OF ANCIENT GODS

EGYPT // The giant columns raised by New Kingdom pharaohs Amenhotep III and Ramses II preside over the Nile, at the heart of modern Luxor. Enclosing the sacred sanctuary of the god Amun, this stone monument of reliefs, statues, obelisks and shrines reveals the power and wealth of the Pharaonic era. Come late afternoon to wander through the vast chambers and courts as the stones take on a shimmering glow, and again after dark when the columns are illuminated.

🐫 SEE IT ! *Luxor airport has flights from Cairo as well as some European destinations. Trains connect Luxor with Cairo and Aswan.*

Natural History Museum

Fossils, skeletons, not my thing, I thought. And was I wrong. My love for this museum is distinctly seasonal; I first fell under its spell during London's Christmas festivities, stunned by a late-afternoon sunset illuminating the terracotta beauty of the building, bathing the nearby skaters on the ice rink in a glittery, golden glow. I went snap-happy trying to capture the magic of the moment. I took even more photos when I entered the Hintze Hall, awed by the dramatic combination of the grand architecture with the gigantic Diplodocus dinosaur as centrepiece. In summer, it's a different kind of unbridled joy for me – that of the English countryside – when the Wildlife Garden and Sensational Butterflies take up residence. This museum doesn't just impress with its preservation of the past, the simple act of an owl butterfly landing on your nose as honey bees buzz by can also charm you in the present.

Karyn Noble, senior editor

239

Natural History Museum

WONDROUS EXHIBITS & ARCHITECTURE

ENGLAND // Eighty million specimens, billions of years – London's Natural History Museum manages to squeeze eons into its formidable space. Here you can learn about dinosaur bones and butterflies, blue whales and human babies, volcanoes and the big bang. This den of knowledge, treasures and research is housed in a majestic building, opened to the public in 1881. It's a glorious German Romanesque edifice, adorned with zoological gargoyles and reliefs.

☛ SEE IT ! *The museum is five minutes' walk from South Kensington Tube. Admission to the main collection is free.*

240

Old Delhi

CHAOTIC JUMBLE OF LIFE

INDIA // The motorcycle chaos, the barrage of noise, the searing aromas and the in-your-face colours: Old Delhi is quite an assault on the senses. Sprawling around the Red Fort, this medieval-era neighbourhood is a tangled web of narrow lanes and clusters of temples anchored by action-packed bazaars, all seeped in Hindu, Sikh and Islamic history, yet brushed over with modern Delhi life. It will certainly make your head whirl but, boy, is it memorable.

☛ SEE IT ! *The best vantage point is the minaret of Jama Masjid – Delhi's largest mosque, which provides a calm respite.*

241

Cinque Terre

CLIFFSIDE VILLAGES STEEPED IN HISTORY

ITALY // If you ever tire of life, decamp immediately to Cinque Terre. You might be hightailing it there with all the other world-weary, but these five crazily con-structed medieval fishing villages, set amid dramatic coastal scenery, still ought to bolster jaded spirits. Sinuous cliffside paths wind past castles, churches and clinging gardens, while a 19th-century rail line ferries tourists village to village. Cars? No thanks: they were banned more than a decade ago.

☛ SEE IT ! *Trains trundle through to the Italian Riviera's Cinque Terre from Genoa daily; in summer, go by boat.*

The 9th-century temples of Borobudur with the volcano Gunung Merapi in the background.

242

Borobudur

BUDDHA'S MEGA MONUMENT

INDONESIA // If you've seen any travel images of Indonesia you probably already know what Borobudur looks like. Along with Angkor Wat in Cambodia and Bagan in Myanmar, Java's colossal Buddhist temple complex makes the rest of Southeast Asia's spectacular sites seem almost incidental. The monument's tiered quadrant of bell-like structures has survived Gunung Merapi's eruptions, terrorist bombs and the 2006 earthquake to remain as enigmatic and as beautiful as it must have been 1200 years ago. Nearly 1500 narrative relief panels on the terraces illustrate Buddhist teachings and tales, while 432 Buddha images sit contemplatively in chambers on the terraces. Locals call the site's surrounding countryside the garden of Java, so supremely beautiful is the landscape of green rice fields and traditional rice-growing *kampung*, all overlooked by soaring volcanic peaks. It can easily hold you entranced for a day or two.

☞ SEE IT ! *The gateway town of Yogyakarta is a 1¼ hour bus ride. Borobudur is Indonesia's most popular attraction; the site is quietest and most photogenic between sunrise and 6am. There's a hill 100m south of the temple, from where you can study the monument in peace.*

243

Bosque Nuboso Monteverde

CLOUD CUCKOO LAND

COSTA RICA // The first of a pair of Costa Rican parks in our list, Monteverde's name alone – 'Green Mountain' cloud forest – evokes a magical place, where life is abundant but concealed. It's a land where trees are draped in epiphytes, so it's impossible to distinguish between forest floor and canopy; where the undergrowth is seemingly impenetrable but punctuated by orchids and bromeliads; and where the silence is amplified by the dripping from the canopy, then shattered by the clang of the three-wattled bellbird. Monteverde sits atop the Continental Divide, acting as a watershed and providing a habitat for hundreds of species. Swirling with mist and pulsing with life, it has a sensual, unique aura.

☛ SEE IT ! *The main entrance is 6km south of Santa Elena. It rains least (but still a lot) from December to April.*

244

Parque Nacional Manuel Antonio

PERFECTLY FORMED PARK

COSTA RICA // The country's tiniest national park is only 20 sq km, but it is 20 sq km of pure bliss. Well-marked trails wind through the rainforest where birds squawk and monkeys scamper. The trails emerge on to dreamy palm-fringed beaches, yielding glorious views across the turquoise sea. Brown boobies and brown pelicans nest on the rocky islets off the shore. The embodiment of a tropical paradise, Manuel Antonio is no secret, and you're likely to find yourself sharing this idyllic spot with 600 of your closest friends. But despite the park's small size, it's possible to find solitude, as long as you're willing to wander a little bit farther. And for that, it's all the more rewarding.

☛ SEE IT ! *The park is 7km from Quepos, with the smaller village of Manuel Antonio at the edge. February to April is the dry season.*

243

247

245

Milan's Duomo

MILAN'S CREATIVITY & AMBITION

ITALY // Any building that took nearly 600 years to complete has to be pretty special. Milan's extravagant Duomo lives up to expectations. A vision in pink Candoglia marble, this multispired Gothic cathedral is at the centre of this one-time imperial Roman capital and expresses the love of beauty and power that still drives the city today. Commissioned in 1387, it has 135 spires and 3200 statues, and a vast interior punctuated by massive stained-glass windows. Underground, you'll see the remains of saintly Carlo Borromeo in the crypt, and ancient ruins in the Battistero di San Giovanni. Up top, the spiky roof terraces offer stunning views. Squint, and on a clear day you can see the Alps.

☞ SEE IT ! *Milan's spiderweb of streets fan out from the Duomo. To the north, Brera's old buildings and cobbled streets deserve exploring.*

246

Burj Khalifa

POTENT SYMBOL OF POWER

DUBAI // From the world's highest observation deck, slicing through the slipstream of the sky's superhighways, the dizzying view from the Burj Khalifa tower is testament to Dubai's ambitious nature. At 828m high, this giant pointy engineering masterpiece is shockingly high; the world's tallest building (for now). Clad in 28,000 glass panels that reflect Dubai's sapphire skies, it holds several world records. Hell, it's seven times the height of Big Ben. A rocketing ascent to the outdoor viewing point on the 148th floor (555m) is a must, but there's also a restaurant-bar on the 122nd if you want to savour the experience of looming over Dubai's great phalanx of futuristic skyscrapers.

☞ SEE IT ! *Timed tickets for a VIP package at the highest of two observation decks are available online up to 30 days in advance.*

247

Djenné Mosque

FAIRY-TALE MUD MOSQUE

MALI // Djenné's incomparable Grande Mosquée – the world's largest mud-built structure – rises from the banks of the Bani River like an apparition from a child's imagination. It's the highpoint of Sahel-style mud-brick architecture, and a symbol of a time when Mali was one of Africa's great trading and cultural crossroads. Faithful to the original 13th-century design, the mosque is a forest of turrets, towers and wooden struts. These struts support the planks and ladders used during the rainy-season repairs to the mud-render when, overseen by specialist masons, up to 4000 locals voluntarily assist. And every Monday, Djenné throngs once again with people who come to market.

☞ SEE IT ! *Buses run from Bamako but it may be quicker to go via Mopti. Most transport is on market day. Monitor the security situation.*

248 Naoshima

ART ISLAND ESCAPE

JAPAN // The tiny tranquil island of Naoshima lies in Japan's Inland Sea, far from Tokyo's deafening pachinko parlours and blaring department store songs. This once sleepy fishing community is home to an impressive contemporary art collection scattered around the island. Works by Claude Monet, Yukinori Yanagi, James Turrell, Tadao Ando, Yves Klein, Andy Warhol and Hiroshi Sugimoto pop up in hotels and galleries, or surprise you outdoors as you work your way around the white sandy beach and wooded hills. Perched at the end of a pier jutting into the Inland Sea is Yayoi Kusama's impressive yellow pumpkin sculpture – the symbol for Naoshima itself.

☛ SEE IT ! *The main port for Naoshima is Miyanoura – ferries travel here from the port close to Uno station (on the JR Uno line). Visit for the day or stay overnight in the boutique Bennesse House or opt for a Mongolian yurt near the beach.*

249 Tajik National Park

ROOF OF THE WORLD

TAJIKSTAN // This sparsely populated wilderness of 2.5 million hectares encompasses the Pamirs, a jagged Central Asian landscape of alpine deserts, deep lakes and glacial valleys that make up the world's third highest mountain ecosystem. The epic tectonic forces that pushed up these hulking massifs, along with the world's other highest ranges – the Himalaya and Karakorum – radiate from right here, at a point called the 'Pamir Knot'.

Awe-inspiring geography aside, Tajik National Park is a tranquil land, where Siberian ibex and yaks graze, snow leopards roam and Pamiris villages lie deep within dramatic rocky valleys. Those who venture here bed down in homestays or yurts (most of the tourist accommodation is located in the villages of Badakhshan, Khorog and Murgab). The area's local nickname is Bam-i-Dunya (the Roof of the World) and, with a plateau above 3000m, Tajik National Park will quite literally take your breath away.

☛ SEE IT ! *To visit the Pamirs in eastern Tajikistan you need a permit. Transport is scarce; a trip here requires planning.*

251 Bwindi Impenetrable National Park

APE ATTRACTION

UGANDA // Home to almost half of the world's surviving mountain gorillas, the World Heritage-listed Bwindi Impenetrable National Park is one of East Africa's most famous and significant national parks. Arrayed across 331 sq km of steep mountain rainforest, this stunning realm provides refuge for an estimated 360 gorillas. The Impenetrable Forest, as it's known, is one of the continent's most ancient habitats, having thrived through the last Ice Age (12,000 to 18,000 years ago) when many of Africa's other forests disappeared. In conjunction with the altitude span (1160m to 2607m), this antiquity has produced an incredible diversity of flora and fauna, even by normal rainforest standards. And we do mean rainforest; up to 2.5m of rain falls every year. Add in some 120 mammal species and more than 360 bird species and the result is a near-perfect blend of beauty and biodiversity.

☛ SEE IT ! *Getting here is best done through a safari operator. Reserve permits in advance. Avoid March to May and September to November.*

250 Silfra

TAKE THE PLUNGE WHERE CONTINENTS DIVIDE

ICELAND // Everything about this adventure just sounds wrong. On a day when the air temperature is barely above freezing, you're about to plunge into water that's even colder, in order to swim through a crack between shifting continents. This could only be Iceland. Silfra is a fissure between the North American and Eurasian tectonic plates, which are drifting apart at a rate of 2cm each year. And it's filled with glacial run-off that has been filtered though underground lava for decades and, consequently, is the very crystal-clearest blue – the visibility is about 100m.

Despite the cold, it's difficult to resist the chance to dive or snorkel between continents, finning through a sub-aqua world where towers of rock soar and crumble, and colours ebb from turquoise to sapphire to inky indigo. A dry suit that covers everything except your face will keep you warm(ish); the knowledge that you're bobbing between worlds will give you chills.

☛ SEE IT ! *Silfra is in Thingvellir National Park, about one hour's drive east of Reykjavík. The water temperature is 2°C-4°C year round.*

251

252

250

252

La Citadelle la Ferrière

DESERTED HILLTOP FORTRESS

HAITI // This battleship-like *citadelle* doesn't enjoy the stardom it deserves. Epic in concept and execution and hidden from the world's gaze, it holds its own against the best historical sites the Americas can offer but, as this is Haiti, it's mercifully underexplored. Built to mark the country's independence and the world's first black republic almost 200 years ago, it sits atop a mountain crag, bedecked with 160 cannons and shielding a Versailles-like ruined palace at its base.

☛ SEE IT ! *The citadelle is an hour from Haiti's northern city of Cap-Haïtien.*

253

Gallipoli Cemeteries

MOVING MEMORIALS OF WAR

TURKEY // The Gallipoli Peninsula is a place of remembrance for the WWI battles that took place on its rugged shores. The nine-month campaign resulted in half a million casualties, and the cemeteries scattered across the pine-clad countryside are a stark reminder of the sacrifice and heroism of the soldiers who fought on both sides. This is an important pilgrimage site for Turks and foreigners, and the thousands of graves are more poignant for their serene surroundings.

☛ SEE IT ! *When visiting the battlefields and cemeteries most visitors base themselves in either Eceabat or Çanakkale.*

254

Davit Gareja

MONASTERY AT THE EDGE OF THE EARTH

GEORGIA // Destroyed by the Mongols in 1265, revived in the 1300s, sacked by Timur, then devastated in 1615 when Shah Abbas' soldiers killed 6000 monks, Davit Gareja (set in a semi-desert landscape) must be the world's most resilient monastery. Of its 15 cave complexes, Lavra is the only one still inhabited. On the hill above, Udabno's colourful frescoes (which suffered further when used as target practice by the Soviets) are somehow still a stunning sight to behold.

🕭 SEE IT ! *Davit Gareja is an easy day trip from Tbilisi. Allow three hours to explore Lavra and Udabno; bring your own food.*

255

Rhodes Old Town

ECLECTIC FORTIFIED PORT

GREECE // Bygone eras and fallen empires lurk in every corner of Rhodes Old Town, permeating the classical, medieval, Byz-antine and Ottoman architecture of this ramparted port. Its cobbled streets are evocative, as black-clad octogenarians loom from doorways, and the scent of leather competes with bougainvillea. Half the fun is getting lost: start at the pedestrian moat walk and plunge in, punctuating navigational head-scratching with shops and restaurants.

🕭 SEE IT ! *Rhodes is in the Dodecanese islands. The New Town, to the north, has smart shops, bars, bistros and the best beach.*

256

Church of the Holy Sepulchre

HOLY HEAVYWEIGHT

ISRAEL // Venerated as the site of Jesus of Nazareth's crucifixion as well as his tomb, Jerusalem's Church of the Holy Sepulchre is one of the holiest places in the world for Christians. This is a location that has been a focal point for pilgrims from around the world for centuries, and custodianship has been a source of debate for even longer. It is a special place, even in a city that's full of them, attracting the crowds and the intensity to match.

🕭 SEE IT ! *The church is in the Christian Quarter of Old Jerusalem. Dress modestly and bring small denomination notes as alms.*

257

257 Registan

EXQUISITE SILK ROAD PLAZA

UZBEKISTAN // Even in Islam's competitive repertoire of important-looking mosques and glittering *madrassas* (Islamic schools), Samarkand's Registan plaza stands out. It's an ensemble of majestic, tilting *madrassas* and mosques – a near overload of majolica, azure mosaics and vast, well-proportioned spaces – that make up the most awesome sight in Central Asia. These beleaguered treasures have been battered by time and earthquakes, but their incredible craftsmanship and restoration under Soviet rule have kept them standing. Lovers of symmetry will be bowled over by the exquisite edifices flanking three

sides of the plaza, which in medieval times would have been wall-to-wall bazaar. Ulugbek Medressa, on the west, is the original madrassa, finished in 1420. Opposite is Sher Dor (Lion) Medressa, finished in 1636 and decorated with roaring felines. In-between is the Tilla-Kari (Gold-Covered) Medressa, completed in 1660 with a mosque decorated with gold, to symbolise Samarkand's wealth at the time it was built.

☞ SEE IT ! *Samarkand city was a key post on the Silk Road. Visit the galleries of Tilla-Kari and Ulugbek Medressa, depicting old Samarkand.*

258 Itsukushima-Jinja gate

JAPAN // On the sacred island of Miyajima floats a stilted shrine. Standing out in the bay shielding the shrine is this towering vermilion *torii* (shrine gate), which rises 16m and glows orange at night like a lighthouse signalling to seafarers. At high tide, the *torii* appears to float on water, attracting camera-wielding crowds. At low tide the shrine and *torii* wallow less romantically in mud, but it's possible to walk right up to the gigantic structure.

Standing there, it is easy to imagine what it was like for the commoners who at one time were not allowed to set foot on Miyajima and had to approach by boat through the *torii*'s wide embrace. It is well worth staying on the island overnight in order to avoid the crowds and to see the shrine and the gate beautifully illuminated at sunset and after dark.

☛ SEE IT ! *Miyajima island is an easy day trip from Hiroshima by train then ferry, or a direct high-speed ferry that takes 30 minutes.*

259 Lincoln Memorial

Washington, DC, USA // There's something extraordinary about climbing the steps of the Doric-columned temple to Abraham Lincoln, staring into his dignified eyes, and reading about the 'new birth of freedom' in the Gettysburg Address chiselled beside him. Then feel the sweep of history as you stand where Martin Luther King Jr gave his 'I Have a Dream' speech (there's a marker 18 stairs from the top), and take in the famous view. The memorial to the 16th president remains wildly popular, with six million people every year coming to gaze at the man. Lincoln's face and hands are particularly realistic, since they are based on castings done a few years before he died. At dawn, nowhere is as serene and as lovely, which is why the Lincoln Memorial is a favourite place for marriage proposals.

☛ SEE IT ! *The memorial is at the National Mall's west end, closest to the Foggy Bottom-GWU Metro station. It's open 24/7.*

260

260 Chateau de Chenonceau

FRANCE // The turrets... the supremely graceful river-spanning archways... the exquisite formal gardens... *sacré bleu*! To say this place is grand would be an understatement. The castle of Chenonceau is one of the most elegant and unusual in all of the Loire Valley in central France. It dates back to the 16th century, and many a wild party has been thrown here by a succession of tenants from the French court, including Catherine de Médicis.

You can't help but be swept up in the magical architecture and the glorious surroundings. The *pièce de résistance* at the chateau's heart is its 60m-long window-lined Grande Gallerie spanning the Cher River. During WWII, the Cher marked the boundary between free and occupied France; local legend has it that the gallery was used as an escape route for many refugees fleeing Nazi occupation.

☞ SEE IT ! *From Chenonceaux, the town just outside the chateau grounds, frequent trains run to Tours, taking 25 minutes.*

261 South Luangwa National Park

ZAMBIA // This country flies under the radar when it comes to name recognition – how else to explain why South Luangwa National Park is not celebrated as one of Africa's premier safari parks? In actual fact, for scenery, variety of animals, accessibility and selection of accommodation, South Luangwa is the best park in Zambia and one of the most majestic in Africa. Among the varied terrain of dense woodland, oxbow pools and open grassy plains lurk beasts of all shapes and sizes, from massive elephants to an abundance of lions.

Part of the park's appeal also lies in its walking safaris – taking place from June to September – that heighten the senses and quicken the pulse. But South Luangwa National Park's greatest attraction has to be its simple call of the wild, for here is an untamed landscape that can be explored without crowds, and where you can get up closer and more personal with all manner of megafauna than just about anywhere else on the entire planet.

☞ SEE IT ! *Safari operators minimise travel hassle. Rains can disrupt visits from December to April. Lusaka is the international gateway.*

262

262 Valle de la Luna

PARCHED DESERT LUNARSCAPE

CHILE // Welcome to the driest place on earth. From atop a giant sand dune in Atacama Desert's otherworldly Valley of the Moon, you'll begin to get a strong inkling of what that really means. To say it's a parched and barren land would be an understatement that hardly does justice to its baking sand valleys and dusty rock formations. It's an area that struggles to record even 1mm rainfall a year; some corners have never seen a drop.

Coincide your visit with sunset and witness the distant ring of volcanoes, rippling Cordillera de la Sal and surreal lunar landscapes of the valley suddenly become suffused with intense purples, pinks and golds. The desert village of San Pedro de Atacama is where you'll find tourist accommodation and be able to arrange tours.

🐾 SEE IT ! *The nearest overland transport hub to Valle de la Luna in northern Chile is Calama, or hop on a flight from Santiago.*

263 National September 11 Museum & Memorial

POIGNANT GROUND ZERO TRIBUTE

New York, USA // Glued to television sets watching the World Trade Center's twin towers crash down, millions were aware that the world had changed forever that fateful day in 2001. Once the wreckage was cleared, it was also obvious that a memorial honouring the victims was the only appropriate structure to fill the gaping, silent void. This museum and memorial finally rose from the ashes exactly 10 years after 9/11, and also remembers victims of the 1993 World Trade Center bombing.

Titled 'Reflecting Absence', the Memorial's two massive reflecting pools are as much a symbol of hope and renewal as they are a tribute to the thousands who lost their lives to terrorism. Beside them, the state-of-the-art Memorial Museum is a striking, solemn space, documenting the tragic events and consequences of that day.

🐾 SEE IT ! *The museum and memorial are in Lower Manhattan. Download a 9/11 Memorial Guide mobile app before arrival.*

266

264

Glaciar Perito Moreno

ARGENTINA // As glaciers go, Perito Moreno, 80km west of El Calafate in Patagonia's Parque Nacional Los Glaciares, is one of the most dynamic and accessible on the planet. This creaking blue-tinged behemoth is 30km long, 5km wide and 60m high, but what makes it exceptional is its constant advance – up to 2m per day. Its slow but constant motion creates incredible suspense as building-sized icebergs calve from the face and spectacularly crash into Lago Argentino.

☛ SEE IT ! *You can get close to the action via an extended network of steel catwalks and platforms, or approach by boat.*

265

Ningaloo Marine Park

THE LIFE AQUATIC

AUSTRALIA // The Great Barrier Reef gets all the attention, but discerning Australian aquanauts head west – just like the mighty migratory whale sharks that visit the waters of Ningaloo every year (March–July). It's possible to explore Ningaloo Reef straight from idyllic beaches in Cape Range National Park, and all you need is a snorkel and mask. Share the water with an astonishing ensemble of aquatic animals, from giant turtles, immense manta rays, dugongs and dolphins, right down to exquisitely coloured nudibranchs.

☛ SEE IT ! *The town of Exmouth is the gateway to Ningaloo.*

266

Lóngjǐ Rice Terraces

SPECTACULAR DRAGON'S BACKBONE

CHINA // For hundreds of years, these 1000m-high terraced paddy fields remained unknown to travellers, then everything changed in the 1990s when a photographer named Li Yashi moved here. His amazing images put mesmerising Lóngjǐ (literally 'Dragon's Back') firmly on the tourist trail. The fields cascade in swirls down hills dotted with minority villages that can be hiked between, or there's a cable-car connecting the principal viewing points.

☛ SEE IT ! *Guìlín is the gateway city. Píng'ān, Dàzhài and Tiántóuzhài villages offer the most spectacular views.*

267

267 268 269

Mt McKinley (Denali)

ALASKA'S TAKE ON EVEREST

USA // Fact: although Mt Everest is the world's highest mountain, Alaska's Mt McKinley (20,237ft) actually soars 6000ft higher because it starts from a much lower base. The sheer independent rise of its bulk will have you transfixed by more than 18,000ft of ascending rock, ice and snow. In Denali National Park, it is one of the world's great scenic mountains, perfectly framed by the odd moose – if you're lucky. If you're not so lucky, it could just be clouds you see.

☛ SEE IT ! *Denali National Park is two hours south of Fairbank. The most enjoyable approach is aboard the Alaska Railroad.*

Athabasca Glacier

ICY ADVENTURES

CANADA // Foaming waterfalls, aquamarine lakes and hulking mountains flash by on the Icefields Parkway in the Canadian Rockies of Alberta. But glaciers are the road's star sight, and none is more accessible than Athabasca. The frosty toe of ancient ice drops down near the parkway where you can gawp from afar, or board a jumbo-wheeled 'Snocoach' that crunches on to its craggy surface. The bold don crampons and walk the ice-carved landscape with a guide.

☛ SEE IT ! *Athabasca Glacier is 105km south of Jasper. The closet airport is in Edmonton, 450km east.*

Timgad ruins

SYMBOL OF ROME IN AFRICA

ALGERIA // A Roman military colony extraordinaire, the ruined city of Timgad is difficult to gain a perspective of, such is its sprawl of barracks and bathhouses, chapels and colonnades. Conceived as a perfect square, it lurched into new territory during its 2nd- and 3rd-century heyday. The city is an expression of Roman power in Africa, though it also housed a Byzantine fort. The most impressive surviving structure is Trajan's Arch, a chariot gateway soaring from the rubble.

☛ SEE IT ! *Timgad is in Algeria's Aurès Mountains; Batna is the jumping-off point, 40km away. Don't miss Timgad's museum.*

270

Selous Game Reserve

WILD HEART OF AFRICA

TANZANIA // Vast Selous, with its tropical climate, profuse greenery and huge Rufiji River, is one of Africa's largest yet most underrated wildlife reserves. Take a boat safari and, as you glide past borassus palms, hippos and elephants, you'll only skim the surface of a wilderness that covers some 5 percent of Tanzania. Other Selous trademarks include rich birdlife, river dolphins and close to 20 percent of all Africa's lions. The size and remoteness of Selous only add to its appeal.

☛ SEE IT ! *Fly or drive from Dar es Salaam or drive from Morogoro and avoid the March to May wet season when many camps close.*

271

Volcán Arenal

VOLCANO VIEWS

COSTA RICA // Imposing Volcán Arenal looms over this region. No matter what you're doing – exploring lava trails, windsurfing on Lake Arenal or biking remote roads – the volcano is your backdrop. Gone are the days of nightly firework displays, when molten lava spewed from the volcano's mouth and down its slopes: Arenal has been dormant since 2010. What's left is a picture-perfect peak, docile but still steaming, surrounded by animal-rich forests, waterfalls and hot springs.

☛ SEE IT ! *The main gateway to Volcan Arenal is La Fortuna, Costa Rica. Dry season is from February to April.*

272

Asa Wright Nature Centre

CARIBBEAN BIRD SANCTUARY

TRINIDAD & TOBAGO // Even if you can't tell a parrot from a parakeet, the diversity of our feathered friends at this 80-hectare reserve will blow your mind. Cocoa and coffee used to thrive at this one-time plantation, but now birds – such as blue-crowned motmots, chestnut woodpeckers and channel-billed toucans – flit along lush hiking trails. Add in a natural swimming pool and rum-punch-touting lodge, and Asa Wright presents eco-living at its best, Caribbean style.

☛ SEE IT ! *The Centre is about a 90-minute drive from Port of Spain. Tour companies can ferry you here by day, but why not stay?*

273

Parque Nacional de los Picos de Europa

HEAVEN FOR HIKERS

SPAIN // Venture inland from the Atlantic north coast of Spain and the roads swiftly gain altitude and become claustrophobically narrow. Etched into the side of limestone mountains, they skirt precipices as they wind upwards towards pretty mountain villages. These are the Picos, an especially jagged mountain range spanning southeast Asturias, southwest Cantabria and northern Castilla y León.

The Picos confound Spanish stereotypes: cider is the local tipple not sangria, and cows amble the village streets not sightseers. The pace of life may be slow here but the range, and the national park within, is fast gaining fans. The reason is that some of the finest walking in the country can be enjoyed on the 647-sq-km Parque Nacional de los Picos de Europa's trails, including one of the most of the popular paths in Spain, the Ruta del Cares. This 11km trail cuts through the Garganta del Cares, a limestone gorge that splits the Picos.

You won't be limited to hiking here either: rivers can be run on rafts and kayaks and the off-road tracks are popular with mountain bikers.

☛ SEE IT ! *Fly into Bilbao and drive about 3hr west. Shoulder seasons, with fewer visitors and more accommodation, are May to June and September to October.*

274

Angel Falls
Inaccessible waterfall wonder

↓

VENEZUELA // Back off Iguazú and Victoria: it's Angel Falls that wins the title of world's highest waterfall. At 979m-high, it's about 16 times loftier than Niagara (p110). Unlike its brash brothers, you'll find no road access here and no looming hotels. Set in a *Lost World*-style wilderness, most visitors who approach by boat stay overnight in hammocks at camps near the base of the falls. The canoe trip up-river and the camp experience are nearly as memorable as the waterfall itself, which spills into Devil's Canyon.

🕿 SEE IT ! *Parque Nacional Canaima is a plane hop from Ciudad Bolívar (a nine-hour bus ride from Caracas).*

277

275

Yakushima

CEDAR-CARPETED HIKERS' PARADISE

JAPAN // If ever there were a real-life equivalent of *Lord of the Rings'* Fangorn Forest, Yakushima's primeval mossy woods is it. The craggy mountains of the island's interior are home to the famous *yakusugi* (ancient cedar trees), which embrace explorers with eerie twisted limbs. It's a wet, rugged land beloved by hiking folk but also sea turtles, who come here to lay their eggs. Seaside *onsen* (hot springs) and sandy beaches make the trip all the more worthwhile.

☞ SEE IT ! *Kagoshima is a hub of ferries and flights to Yakushima, off southwest Japan. Avoid local holidays, when trails are busy.*

276

Whakarewarewa

STEAMED-UP SPECTACLES

Rotorua, NEW ZEALAND // This place offers an eye-popping combo of authentic Maori culture and geothermal wonders that bubble from beneath the central North Island's crust. Whakarewarewa is a living Maori village, where *tangata whenua* (people of the land) have resided for centuries, while Mother Nature throws a tantrum of steaming vents, boiling mud pools and fickle geysers. Visitors feel the heat on walkways, guided by villagers who tell tales of old and demonstrate traditional Maori arts.

☞ SEE IT ! *Rotorua is three hours from Auckland on the Thermal Explorer Hwy, a road trip of North Island highlights.*

277

Memento Park

CEMETERY OF SOCIALISM

HUNGARY // Memento Park in Budapest can only be described as a well-manicured trash heap of history, or perhaps a socialist Disneyland. It's home to about four dozen statues, busts and plaques of notable Communists, including Lenin and Marx, that have been collected from around the city. Here you'll even find the replicated remains of Stalin's boots – all that was left after a crowd pulled the enormous statue down from its plinth during the 1956 uprising.

☞ SEE IT ! *The park is in southern Buda; there's a dedicated bus (admission included) that runs year-round from central Budapest.*

278

Death Valley National Park

LAND OF EXTREMES

USA // Who can resist the challenge of visiting somewhere with such a foreboding name? There's something invigorating and even life affirming about being out of your element and in an environment so punishing that even the rocks try to escape.

Straddling California and Nevada, Death Valley National Park is a land of extremes. It claims the USA's hottest temperature (134°F/57°C), its lowest point (Badwater, 282ft/86m below sea level), and is the largest national park outside of Alaska (more than 5000 sq miles/13,000 sq km). The valley itself isn't actually a valley but a graben – an elongated slice of the earth's crust wedged between two faults and pushed down by tectonic forces. The misnomers don't stop there either, for despite its chilling name, Death Valley is also home to plenty of endemic wildlife, and even spectacular spring wildflower blooms when conditions are right.

Other natural spectacles here include eerie canyons, sand dunes that sing and the afore-mentioned 'sailing rocks' that mysteriously slide across the surface of Racetrack Playa. It's a crazy place to visit, but perhaps not to live – as attested by the relics left by pioneering miners who eventually gave up the ghost.

☛ SEE IT ! *Peak seasons are winter and spring. If you visit in summer, spend the hottest part of the day by the pool or head for the hills where it's cooler.*

279

280

279
Ko Phi-Phi

THE PEARLS OF THE ANDAMAN

THAILAND // Thrust to the top of every backpacker's bucket list when *The Beach* hit cinemas in 2000, the azure waters of Ko Phi-Phi Leh's Maya Bay, encircled by a crown of jungle-covered limestone cliffs, is one of Thailand's most beautiful – if crowded – pilgrimage sites. By sundown, day-trippers (you can't stay overnight on Leh) flock back to the hedonistic HQ of neighbouring Phi-Phi Don, where long, lazy days on powder-white beaches ooze into sweaty nights sipping cocktails to bone-rattling beats in heaving bars. Climb to the 300m Phi-Phi Viewpoint to admire the butterfly-shaped island's lush brilliance, or take a long-tail boat tour on the cerulean sea. Having suffered minimal reef damage in the 2004 tsunami, Phi-Phi still boasts great diving.

🦶 SEE IT ! *Phi-Phi is hot, crowded, but most beautiful from November to April. The rains and ocean swells pick up from May to October.*

280
Waitomo Caves

A GALAXY OF GLOWWORMS

NEW ZEALAND // Proving you don't have to rocket into space to discover alien landscapes, Waitomo Caves are all the more surprising for their location under workaday New Zealand farmland. There are various portals into this underworld. At Ruakuri Cave, a futuristic stairway corkscrews down into labyrinthine passageways and huge caverns. Nearby is Glowworm Cave, with its acoustically sweet chamber and underground boat ride beneath a 'sky' twinkling with a galaxy of glowworms. The most geologically striking cave is Aranui, with its array of limestone formations and thousands of 'straw' stalactites resembling dragon's teeth. For the ultimate deep-space exploration, embark on a Black Water Rafting trip where you don a wet suit and inner-tube to clamber through cavities and float through subterranean waterways.

🦶 SEE IT ! *Waitomo is less than three hours' drive south of Auckland, within close reach of Rotorua, Taupo and Tongariro National Park.*

282

Kizhi Pogost

RUSSIA // Groaning under the weight of historic buildings, Russia can induce fatigue in even the most ardent architecture aficionados. But Kizhi Pogost, built in the 18th and 19th centuries, is one complex worth riding a river (and braving poisonous snakes) for. Sitting pretty on a small island on Lake Onega, Kizhi's collection of log buildings is crowned by the Transfiguration Church, bubbling with 22 domes and – at 37m high – said to be one of the tallest wooden structures in the world; apparently the unknown builder threw away his axe after completing it, rightly assuming its glory could never be matched. Getting the logs to Kizhi by boat was a remarkable feat; even more astonishing is that not a single nail was used in the buildings' construction.

☞ SEE IT ! *Kizhi is a daytrip from Petrozavodsk, 425km north of St Petersburg. Hydrofoils visit the island daily from May to September.*

281

Eden Project

Cornwall, ENGLAND // What do you do with an enormous clay pit when it has run out of clay? Why, ship in some banana palms and build a really big bubble, of course. The Eden Project is a garden on an immense scale. Where others have greenhouses, Eden has biomes, huge clear-plastic domes – like gigantic space beetles – that can nurture whole continents of plants. Whatever the Cornish weather, the Rainforest Biome keeps the leafy, lush life inside, from coffee bushes to kapoks, at the perfect temperature; the Mediterranean Biome is a profusion of cacti, citrus and olive trees. But there's more to Eden than domes. It's a charity, and a centre for conservation and research; it hosts music, storytellers, exhibitions and ice skating; it's colourful, innovative and flamboyant, always nurturing something new.

☞ SEE IT ! *Eden is three miles from St Austell train station; bus 101 runs from St Austell. Arrive by public transport for discounted entry.*

283 Mt Kailash

THE WORLD'S MOST SACRED MOUNTAIN

TIBET // Dominating the mythology of a billion people just as it dominates the landscape of western Tibet with its sheer four-sided black-rock summit, Mt Kailash (6638m) is one special peak. In Tibetan, its name is Kang Rinpoche, or 'Precious Jewel of Snow'. Shrouded in the myths of ancient Asia, Mt Kailash could be the world's most venerated holy place. Hindus believe it's the home of Lord Shiva (legend has it he practises yoga here), and myths that predate Hinduism and Buddhism speak of it as the birthplace of the whole world. For such a holy heavyweight it draws relatively few

pilgrims because of its inaccessibility, although improving tourist infrastructure, road conditions, and an airport just a few hours away could change that. Once you've marvelled at its awesome aura, make like a pilgrim and complete a *kora* (circumambulation) around the mountain's base – a journey across a stark, cold landscape that takes three days but will be emblazoned in your memory forever.

☛ SEE IT ! *Mt Kailash is accessed via the small town of Darchen, the starting point of the kora and a lonely 1200km from Lhasa.*

284

Rainbow Reef
Psychedelic coral forests

↓

FIJI // Divers are spoilt for choice in Fiji's archipelago, but the Rainbow Reef has achieved Shangri-La status above all others. Strong tidal currents push the deep water back and forth through the Somosomo Strait, providing such rich nutrients for the soft corals and sea fans that they form psychedelic underwater forests. Drift dives are the way to travel here. Highlights include the luminescent Great White Wall, and Annie's Brommies – an outcrop teeming with fish.

SEE IT ! *Flights service Taveuni, from where the reef is easily accessed. Avoid January and February.*

285

Te Papa Tongarewa

NEW ZEALAND // Like a good schoolteacher, New Zealand's national museum makes learning so much fun you'll forget you're getting an education. Translating as 'container of treasures', Te Papa Tongarewa is the colourful architectural centrepiece of the capital Wellington's waterfront. Its four floors of exhibits are hands-on, with plenty of digital bits and buttons to push, plus good old-fashioned interactions. Children of all ages love it. At its heart are New Zealand's stories – from dinosaurs and volcanoes to a carved Maori meeting house and an impressive collection of Number 8 wire. The national art collection is a fitting finale to a visual feast that includes such freakishness as a blue-whale heart that the kids can clamber through, and a colossal squid preserved in formaldehyde. Fun, friendly and multicultural, Te Papa is how New Zealanders like to see themselves.

☛ SEE IT ! *The museum is within walking distance of the capital's other major attractions, including the City Gallery, Cuba Street, the Cable Car and Botanic Gardens.*

286

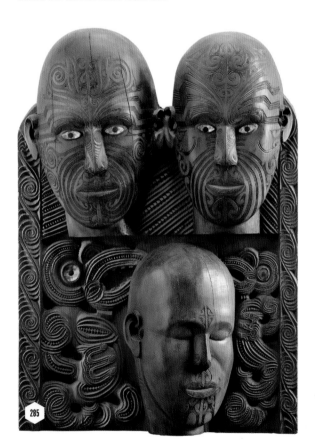

285

286

Ross Ice Shelf

ANTARCTICA // Could this be the end of the world? It sure looks like it. Covering some 520,000 sq km, an area that is approximately the size of France, the Ross Ice Shelf stretches as far as the eye can see. When Captain James Clark Ross discovered it in 1841, he called it the Victoria Barrier (in honour of Queen Victoria). And 'barrier' is an appropriate description for this gigantic shelf because up close it resembles a natural fortress that practically screams 'get back!'; in places, it's up to 1000m thick.

For such a gigantic lump, it's surprisingly nimble and moves as fast as 1100m per year. It actually *floats*, and calves about 150 cu kilometres of icebergs annually. If this was *Game of Thrones*, we'd be asking what's on the other side...

☛ SEE IT ! *Most visitors reach Antarctica via group tours on a ship, many of which board in Ushuaia at the southern tip of Argentina.*

289

287

Ras al-Jinz

IMPORTANT TURTLE-NESTING SITE

OMAN // Rugged Ras al-Jinz beach is renowned for one thing: turtle nesting. At the easternmost point of the Arabian Peninsula, it's an important site for 20,000 endangered green turtles who return in droves each year to lay their eggs. Oman takes its conservation responsibilities seriously, and it's a magical thing to watch these gentle domed giants slog their way up the broad beach in the thick of night, although at times the viewing can almost seem too intrusive.

☞ SEE IT ! *The only way to visit Ras al-Jinz is on an evening or dawn trip from nearby Sur. July is the best viewing month.*

288

Anse Vata

FANTASY CITY BEACH

NEW CALEDONIA // Not many capitals can boast a beach as sublime as Anse Vata. Residents of Noumea have a lot to be thankful for in this seemingly never-ending arc of sand. On breezy days, kite- and windsurfers skim up and down the bay. On calm days you'll find children building sandcastles. At all times you'll see locals and tourists alike hanging out with toes dipped in the perfect white sand, splashing in the turquoise sea and lolling in its restaurants and bars.

☞ SEE IT ! *New Caledonia is a French overseas territory in the Pacific. Flights land at Tontouta, 45km northwest of Noumea.*

289

Kilwa Kisiwani

SWAHILI PORT RUINS

TANZANIA // In its 13th-century heyday Kilwa Kisiwani was the seat of sultans and the centre of an extensive trading network linking the old Shona kingdoms and the gold fields of Zimbabwe with Persia, India and China. For a settlement of such historical riches and glory, it's a little bit incongruous that these days it's a quiet fishing village baking in the sun. Still, gold dust lingers on the crumbling Swahili palaces and mosques that whisper of a bygone era.

☞ SEE IT ! *Kilwa Kisiwani is a short sailing dhow trip from Kilwa Masoko on Tanzania's east coast; guides are compulsory.*

290

Socotra Island

GALAPAGOS WITHOUT THE CROWDS

YEMEN // The Middle East's most otherworldly landscape? Take a bow Socotra Island, where fuzzy dome-topped dragon's blood trees rise out of the boulder-strewn landscape, creating a sci-fi worthy scene. One of the world's most biodiverse spots, Socotra should be as famous as the Galapagos Islands (p39), with some 700 unique species of flora and fauna. But regional instability keeps tourists away. For the intrepid, this wacky eco-wonderland is waiting to be explored.

☞ SEE IT ! *Yemenia Airways flies here from Dubai and Sana'a. Eco-tourism-focused operators on the island can arrange tours.*

291

Old Dhaka

BANGLADESH'S THROBBING HEART

BANGLADESH // No matter where in the world you've rocked up from, Old Dhaka will sideswipe you with its overwhelming intensity and leave impressions that will never fade. It's a maze of photogenic incense-clouded bazaars and incredibly crowded alleyways, packed with dilapidated historic sights. Running through its centre is Buriganga River – Dhaka's lifeblood and a fascinating vantage place from which to grab a tour and observe Bangladesh at its most raw and gritty.

☞ SEE IT ! *Hotels are poor in Old Dhaka and many cheap lodgings won't accept foreign tourists. Central Dhaka is a better base.*

292

Underwater Sculpture Park

EERIE ARTIFICIAL REEF ART

GRENADA // Think art galleries are all the same? Wrong. Grenada's flourishing Underwater Sculpture Park is 2m beneath the surface of the sea, for starters. The idea was to create an artificial reef to help regenerate an area of storm damage. Works include a circle of women clasping hands, a man at a desk, and a sole mountain-biker, all slowly becoming encrusted with coral growth. It's a spooky sight to see the lifelike statues, fixed to the ocean floor, consumed by the sea.

☞ SEE IT ! *Just north of Grenada's capital St George's, in Molinière Bay, the park is situated in clear, shallow water.*

293

Pulau Sipadan

BORNEO'S DIVING PARADISE

MALAYSIA // Located 36km off Sabah's southeast coast, Sipadan is the shining star in the Semporna Archipelago's constellation of islands. The elliptical islet sits atop an extinct volcanic cone surrounded by near- vertical walls. Blanketed in Technicolor corals, they form a veritable way-station for all types of sea life, from barracuda to bumphead parrotfish and, from around March to May, whale sharks. Sea turtles and reef sharks are a given during any dive, and divers might spot mantas, eagle rays, octopus and scalloped hammerheads. At the time of press, night diving was off the cards until further notice, but if you aren't blown away by the daytime diving, we'll eat our snorkels. Just remember to book ahead – only 120 Sipadan passes (required for both divers and snorkellers) are issued each day.

☛ SEE IT ! *Nearby Mabul island, which offers terrific macro-diving, is the region's accommodation centre; you can't sleepover on Sipadan.*

294

St Davids Cathedral

MEDIEVAL MIRACLE

WALES // Purple is a peculiar colour for a cathedral, but that's the hue of the dusky Welsh sandstone that you'll see at St Davids. The next thing that strikes you – besides the cathedral's stunning location on the bucolic banks of the River Alun, on the wild Pembrokeshire coast where Wales looks across the Celtic Sea to Ireland – is its epic scale, way out of proportion to the tiny Pembrokeshire town of the same name (the UK's smallest city). Thanks to the miraculous performances of the local man who became St David – and whose bones are behind the High Altar – this became one of Europe's most important Christian sites in the 12th century, when the cathedral was built where David's 6th-century monastery once stood. Tourists have always outnumbered residents, ever since Pope Calixtus II decreed that two pilgrimages to St Davids were the equivalent of one to Rome, and three were worth one to Jerusalem.

☛ SEE IT ! *St Davids is a two-hour drive northwest from Cardiff.*

295
Dead Sea

JORDAN/ISRAEL/PALESTINE // Part of the Great Rift Valley's vast geological slash, the Dead Sea marks the lowest point on the earth's surface at 412m below sea level. Its exceptional salinity is what allows a surreal floatation ability. Once you enter the water you'll notice the difference. The sea's salt content is more than 20 percent and the water feels more like wading into syrup. Kick your legs off the bottom and the magic begins. Without any effort you're naturally buoyant and able to sit, roll over, and lift arms and legs in the air while staying afloat. And the visceral landscape – all glittering blue water and blinding-white salt deposits rimmed by swooping craggy mountains – is one of the world's most dramatic settings in which to take a dip.

☞ SEE IT ! *You can access the Dead Sea at beaches on the Jordanian side and from both the Israeli and Palestinian West Bank shores.*

296
Kilimanjaro

TANZANIA // Stumbling across a permanent glacier when you're three degrees south of the equator is surprising, but climbing Kilimanjaro is all-round astonishing, and full of contrasts. Take the surge of euphoria you feel beholding the glowing plains of Tanzania at sunrise on summit day, followed by an urge to be sick. Depending on which of the six trails you take, it's possible to ascend from park gate to Uhuru Peak in fewer than four days, climbing through five ecological zones from African savannah into an alpine region where temperatures can drop to -25°C. At 5895m, Kili is the planet's tallest free-standing mountain, and the quick elevation gain scuppers many attempts. Often it's the fittest who fail. Listen to the repeated words of your guides – 'pole, pole' (slowly, slowly) – and you might reach the roof of Africa.

☞ SEE IT ! *Moshi and Arusha are Kilimanjaro's gateway towns. Choose your guide and route carefully.*

297

297

Cologne Cathedral

GOTHIC KING DOM

GERMANY // As world-class landmarks go, the spectacular spires shooting from the roof of Cologne's dramatic *Dom* are right up there – which is apparently why Allied aircraft left them standing, as a navigational aid during aerial bombardments. Or perhaps they couldn't bear to destroy one of the planet's finest Gothic creations – a cathedral partially built in 1248 but left unfinished for the entirety of the Middle Ages, and only completed 60 years before WWII erupted.

🖝 SEE IT ! *Climb the 509-step spiral staircase to the cathedral viewing platform to admire incredible views over Rhineland.*

298

Drakensberg Amphitheatre

LAND OF CLIFFS & CANYONS

SOUTH AFRICA // There's a bit of poetic licence in the name: Drakensberg's prized Amphitheatre is no Roman structure, but a natural rock arena where the Tugela Falls drop 850m in five stages (in winter, the top one can freeze over). It's a sublime 8km wall of cliff and canyon that's spectacular from below and even more so from up on high. It's the crowning glory of the 8000-hectare Royal Natal National Park, where rustic camps, great hiking and horse trails abound.

🖝 SEE IT ! *The park abuts the northern border of Lesotho, about three hours' drive from Durban in the Drakensberg Range.*

299

Parque Nacional Cotopaxi

VERTIGINOUS VOLCANIC VISTAS

ECUADOR // Get ready to enter a world of fire and ice. The world's highest active volcano is the crown jewel of Ecuador's most popular national park: a snowcapped summit that nevertheless has belched out over 50 eruptions since the mid-19th century. The lower slopes boast pre-Columbian ruins, glacier fields and a still, lonely lake that reflects in breathtaking symmetry the 5897m-high peak above: the pièce de résistance, and an arduous-but-magnificent six-hour climb.

🖝 SEE IT ! *Thursday through Sunday, you can take the train from Quito to the park entrance. Keep an eye on weather conditions.*

300–
399

300

Chatuchak Weekend Market

THAI TEMPLE TO CONSUMERISM

THAILAND // Bangkok's biggest marketplace gets off on bartering and Thai baht, uniting everything that is buyable. Fluffy puppies and fighting cocks may line one market lane, while vintage shoes or hill-tribe crafts could proliferate another. Thousands of shoppers flock here each weekend and, deep in the bowels of the market, it can seem like there is no order and no escape. The experience could be utterly fatigue-inducing if it wasn't for Thailand's famous street-food and drink.

🐟 SEE IT ! *Chatuchak is in Bangkok's northern suburbs and accessible by metro. Come early to beat the crowds and the heat.*

Chatuchak Weekend Market

It's easy to spot someone who has been to Bangkok's fabulous and frenetic Chatuchak Weekend Market. The mottled palm wood chopsticks should be the first pointer – they'll most likely be propped up on elegant chopstick stands, beside silk napkins, poised beside delicately carved wooden bowls of soy sauce or *nam phrik* (fish sauce with chilli). When I returned home after my first trip to Chatuchak, my flat was transformed into a Royal Thai restaurant overnight. It took two or three more trips to Chatuchak to get over the initial 'oh-my-god-everything-is-amazing' vibe and become a more discerning weekend market shopper. These days, I'll head straight for the antique section in the heart of the market, to stock up on lacquerware tiffin pots and opium weights to add to my growing collection of latter-day Chinoiserie. Every trip, I'll make time for a bowl of fiery *tom yang* soup, a bottle of freshly squeezed Thai orange juice from Uncle Add, and a potently-mixed cocktail at Viva 8.

Joe Bindloss, Destination Editor

301

Parque Nacional Tortuguero

TURTLE ISLANDS

COSTA RICA // This is where the coastal rainforest feels like the Amazonian jungle: humid, clamorous and teeming with life. Lazy lagoons host crocodiles on logs, sloths in trees, otters, vocal howler monkeys and hundreds of birds. Watch a sea turtle haul herself on to a beach, laboriously dig out her nest and drop in dozens of eggs. Then, catch a glimpse of the hatchlings scurrying to the sea. In Tortuguero, you'll witness the cycle of life, playing out on a dark stretch of beach.

🐟 SEE IT ! *Tortuguero is the best base for exploring the park. The turtle-nesting season is from March to October.*

303

Capri

WHERE THE GLAMOROUS GO TO PLAY

ITALY // This 3km-by-6km rugged rock, off southern Italy's Sorrentine Peninsula, has long been the playground of the beautiful people: Emperor Augustus made it his private retreat in the 1st century BC; in the 1950s and '60s, Taylor, Garbo and Gable jet-setted here. These days, Capri is a little overrun with tourists – but who can blame us for seeking a touch of *dolce vita*? Even with the crowds, the island's pretty piazzas, chichi cafes, sandy coves, vertiginous lookouts and famed Blue Grotto offer a tiny taste of how the fabulous other half live.

🐾 SEE IT ! *Ferries run all year from Naples and Sorrento; plus other crossings in summer.*

302

Parc National d'Andringitra

UNSPOILT SECLUSION

MADAGASCAR // This park's greatest feature? There's hardly anyone here! Andringitra encompasses a majestic central mountain range with two valleys on either side nibbled by natural pools, inhabited by lemurs, dotted with villages and graced by three extraordinary peaks. The two-day Imarivolanitra Trail stretches from one side of the park to the other via the summit of Pic Boby. Its natural wonder and unspoilt seclusion makes Andringitra a world-class destination.

🐾 SEE IT ! *Both park entrances are a three-hour drive from the town of Ambalavao. The park is closed from January to March.*

304 305 306

Bamburgh Castle

CAMELOT BY THE SEA

ENGLAND // Mighty Bamburgh Castle stands sentinel over one of England's finest stretches of sand, dominating the Northumbrian coastal landscape for miles. Generations of Brits come every summer to brave North Sea breezes, use the castle as inspiration for sand imitations, and scoff crab sandwiches. One of the best views of the castle is from the sea itself. Alternatively, stand on the ramparts to appreciate the outstanding vista of Farne Islands and the Cheviot Hills.

☛ SEE IT ! *The National Cycle Way's Coast and Castles route is one way to see the coast, or take a bus from Berwick-Upon-Tweed.*

Lake Geneva

WINE-INFUSED LAKESIDE LIFE

SWITZERLAND // Western Europe's biggest lake stretches like a liquid mirror along the French–Swiss border, but the Swiss side tugs most at the heartstrings. Lined by the elegant student city of Lausanne and pretty smaller enclaves, it presents the spectacle of terraced Lavaux vineyards where wines can be quaffed, and vines walked among. The lakeside is graced with fairy-tale chateaux, luxurious manor houses and modest beaches framed by a classic mountain backdrop.

☛ SEE IT ! *Lake Geneva is in Switzerland's southeast. A Regional Pass will get you free and discounted travel on buses and trains.*

Cu Chi Tunnels

THE WARRENS OF WAR

VIETNAM // This network of three-storey-deep hand-dug passages, stretching from Ho Chi Minh City to Cambodia, was used to facilitate Viet Cong control of the area, and attacks on American forces: thousands of Vietnamese lived, died, wed and gave birth here in cramped conditions underground. Portions of the tunnels are open today; crawling through subterranean passages is not for the claustrophobic, but this is an astonishing testament to Vietnamese tenacity.

☛ SEE IT ! *Regular tours run from HCMC to tunnels at Ben Dinh and Ben Duoc: the latter, slightly farther afield, is less crowded.*

307 Art Institute of Chicago

USA // Chicago's art museum has the kind of celebrity-heavy collection that draws gasps from patrons. Wander the endless marble corridors and Grant Wood's *American Gothic* appears (his sister and dentist were the models, FYI). Around the corner hangs Edward Hopper's lonely *Nighthawks*. Further on, Georges Seurat's big, dotted *Sunday Afternoon on La Grand Jatte* tricks your eyes. Then come Monet's *Stacks of Wheat*, Van Gogh's *The Bedroom*, Picasso's *The Old Guitarist* – the big-name roster goes on. The collection of Impressionist and post-Impressionist paintings is second only to those in France, and the number of surrealist works blows the mind. But wait, we haven't even gotten to the odd bits and bobs, such as the galleries stuffed with Japanese prints, Grecian urns and suits of armour. The basement holds rooms of miniatures – haven't you always wanted to see a tiny French boudoir circa 1740? – and 800 bejewelled glass paperweights. Sculptures and architectural relics stud the outdoor gardens.

☛ SEE IT ! *The Art Institute sits in downtown Chicago. Public transport trains stop a block away. Queues are rarely an issue.*

308

Gros Piton
Iconic Caribbean climb

↓

ST LUCIA // The sky-scraping twin towers of rock known as the Pitons are St Lucia's tourism poster pin-ups. Jutting from the sea like shark's teeth, the views from the summits are just as bewitching as the experience of first clapping eyes on them. Though Gros Piton (797m) is taller than Petit Piton (749m), it's easier to climb – but not for the faint-hearted: the trek involves switchbacks and steps carved from volcanic stone. The reward is a panorama of southern St Lucia and a cold Piton beer after the descent.

🕿 SEE IT !
December to April is the best time to climb. Pick up mandatory guides in Soufrière.

309

309

Louisiana Museum of Modern Art

DENMARK // It's not only what's inside this long, low, white building – itself a masterpiece of modernist Danish design from the 1950s – that guarantees its place in the Ultimate Travelist. It's what is outside.

Louisiana sits right on the shore of the Øresund coast in a small town north of Copenhagen, with views towards lots of slow-turning wind turbines. When you've meandered through its long glass corridors and rooms containing work by Pablo Picasso, Yves Klein and David Hockney – one of Scandinavia's most important collections of modern art (post-1945) – head outdoors to explore a sculpture park packed with hidden corners and work from the likes of Henry Moore, or simply to dangle your toes in the sea. Like the Museum of Old and New Art (p40) in Tasmania, though without its edginess, Louisiana's location makes it unmissable.

☛ SEE IT ! *From Copenhagen, take a 35-minute train ride to Humlebæk. The museum is a short walk from the station.*

310

Lower Zambezi National Park

SAFARIS SHAKEN & STIRRED

ZAMBIA // Most things are a lot more fun when water is involved, and safaris are no exception. And water is what makes the Lower Zambezi so very special. Here, guests are not limited to traditional wildlife drives – they can instead climb into a canoe and paddle silently down the mighty Zambezi River, past bathing elephants, bobbing hippos and Nile crocodiles. Without the disturbing drum of a 4WD – and benefiting from being at eye level with animals on the bank – the experience is intimate. And because most lodges sit right on the riverbank, you can plug into this marvellous safari scene easily. For those with energy to burn, it's also possible to join expert guides for walking safaris in the park or for hikes up the steep Zambezi escarpment, which offers views over the river valley and Zimbabwe.

☛ SEE IT ! *Zambia's Proflight airline services all the park's airstrips from Lusaka. Best times to visit are from late May to early October.*

311

Temppeliaukio Kirkko

MODERN PIECE OF HEAVEN

FINLAND // Do my eyes deceive me? Nope. From the air, Helsinki's futuristic Rock Church looks like a sunken spaceship that has collided with earth at great force, slap bang in the middle of a classic Finnish square. That there is enough creativity in the world to build such an inspired piece of architecture should give solace to even the glummest soul, it's that unique and uplifting. Designed by Timo and Tuomo Suomalainen in 1969, it is one of Helsinki's foremost attractions. Hewn into solid stone, its interior feels closer to a Finnish ideal of spirituality in nature than a spaceship – you could be in a rocky glade were it not for the stunning 24m-diameter roof covered in 22km of copper stripping, soaring overhead like a window into heaven.

☛ SEE IT ! *Excellent acoustics make this a popular concert venue; opening times depend on events. Midweek is a better time to visit.*

312

Petronas Towers

WORLD'S TALLEST TWINS

MALAYSIA // Kuala Lumpur's identical 88-storey cloud-tickling towers are unignorable, drawing incoming visitors to their leggy embrace as soon as they appear on the hazy horizon. Don't fight it. Go climb them. But go early – as humidity rises, the view evaporates beneath KL's pea-*laksa* smog. Walk through the air on the double-decker Sky Bridge on levels 41 and 42, or shoot to the 360m-high Observation Deck on level 86 for a gander over the Golden Triangle. But KL's best vista is one featuring the towers. Select an elevated vantage point, such as the open-air Sky Bar and pool in Trader's Hotel, and drink in a view of the twins from there.

☛ SEE IT ! *Observation-deck tickets, on sale from 7am, go quickly – buy them in advance. Visit KL around Malaysia's independence day (16 September) to see the Towers lit up like rockets about to launch.*

313

313

Calakmul

MEXICO // Lesser known but more grandiose than the ancient Mayan cities of Tulum or Chichén Itzá, Calakmul is deep in the jungles of Campeche near the base of the Yucatán Peninsula. Known as the Snake Kingdom for the proliferation of Kaan (snake-head) glyphs among the exquisite limestone stelae, Calakmul was rivalled only by Guatemala's Tikal for dominance during the Classic era. Rising through the jungle canopy, the huge Estructura II is the tallest known Mayan pyramid.

☞ SEE IT ! *Calakmul is about 100km from Xpujil, where day trips can be booked. Keep watch for toucans, monkeys and jaguars.*

314

Murchison Falls

UGANDA // Uganda's largest national park, Murchison Falls offers some of the country's best wildlife viewing on safari drives or boat cruises down the mighty Nile. Spot hippos' bulbous eyes bobbing from the water's surface while a herd of elephants amble on the riverbank behind, as you cruise toward the raging falls. The river squeezes itself through a 7m-wide (23ft) rock chasm to crash down 43m (141ft) with an intense force.

☞ SEE IT ! *If you're not on a tour, your best bet is to hire a vehicle from Kampala or the town of Masindi, on the park's outskirts.*

Murchison Falls

I first visited Murchison Falls National Park as a wide-eyed teenager, when the sight of its cartoonish animals – officious baboons with red bottoms; fat, hulking hippos; great crocs, lying low in the water like logs – was like finding proof of an outlandish urban myth. We approached the park's eponymous waterfall by boat from below, before scrambling up the steep riverbank – not a handrail to be seen, even at the top, where it seemed that one misstep on the slippery rocks could see you tumbling into the furious waters of the Nile. From above, the thundering cascade was so close I could feel the spray, and the white water's glare in the equatorial sun was hypnotic, like a campfire's flame and crackle. In many return trips since, that sense of exhilaration has never diminished. With Murchison Falls, Nature beckons us, cracks open the door, and gives us a sneak preview of the big show.

Jessica Cole, Commissioning Editor

315

Caernarfon Castle

WALES // When majestic Caernarfon Castle was erected between 1283 and 1330, its design and scale were quite unlike those of any other royal stronghold of its time. In fact, they were quite extraordinary. Inspired by the dream of Macsen Wledig recounted in the *Mabinogion* (a literary work of medieval Celtic mythology), Caernarfon echoes the 5th-century walls of Constantinople, with colour-banded masonry and polygonal towers, instead of the traditional round towers and turrets. Despite its fairy-tale aspect, this military stronghold, seat of government and royal palace of Edward I is thoroughly fortified; it resisted three sieges during the English Civil War before surrender to Cromwell's army in 1646. These days, it's still relatively intact and you can walk on and through the interconnected walls and towers, imagining the bloody battles that once took place here.

☛ SEE IT ! *Caernarfon is a 20-minute drive from Bangor in North Wales. The castle grounds include exhibitions and a military museum.*

316

Ben Nevis

SCOTLAND // Like a repentant rabble-rouser on the morning after Hogmanay, Scotland set about positively revolutionising its reputation a few years ago, and has morphed from a place famed for golf, whisky and deep-fried monstrosities to one of Europe's outdoor capitals (in-the-know adventure types have been quietly enjoying the country's alfresco pursuits for decades). At the epicentre of this action-packed eruption is Britain's tallest peak, 1344m-high Ben Nevis, which towers over the Highland town of Fort William. Nevis and Aonach Mòr have long attracted mountain-sports fans to the world-class hill walking, skiing and mountain biking. Nevis genuinely has something for everyone – from an easy walking path to the sensational summit (potentially lethal in bad conditions) right through to technical ice climbing.

☛ SEE IT ! *Fort William is the best place to make your base camp – then go forth and explore.*

317

Chitwan National Park

NEPAL // Chitwan National Park may have lost its 'royal' moniker since the abolition of the Nepali monarchy, but this is still the top spot in the Himalayan foothills to spot a one-horned Indian rhinoceros or a royal Bengal tiger. Generations of trekkers have finished a trip to the highest peaks on earth with a recuperative safari through the elephant grasses that lines the Rapti river. This swishing sea of green hides Nepal's largest population of rhinos – 503 at the latest count – plus herds of deer and other critters that serve as a movable feast for Chitwan's tigers. Seeking these creatures from the back of one of the park's working elephants or, even better, on foot led by a local guide, is everything a safari should be: thrilling and full of anticipation. Every rustle could be something as mundane as a jungle fowl or as electrifying as a royal Bengal tiger.

☛ SEE IT ! *Chitwan's front door to the world is the village of Sauraha, with dozens of rustic jungle resorts along the Rapti River.*

318

Museo Guggenheim
Breathtaking temple of modern art

↓

SPAIN // One of the most eye-catching architectural creations on the planet, Bilbao's Museo Guggenheim almost single-handedly lifted the Basque city out of its post-industrial depression and into the 21st century. Canadian architect Frank Gehry drew on Bilbao's historical industries of shipbuilding and fishing for design inspiration. Gehry's use of flowing canopies, cliffs, promontories, towers and fins is simply irresistible. With so much to admire about the structure, it can seem almost incidental that 'El Goog' is also a world-class gallery.

☛ SEE IT ! *Buses, planes and trains link Bilbao to the rest of Europe.*

320

319

Pulpit Rock

FINEST VIEW ON EARTH

NORWAY // Perched atop sheer cliffs, 604m above one of Norway's most beautiful fjords, Preikestolen, or Pulpit Rock, is arguably the world's most spectacular lookout. Reached by a two-hour, 3.8km hike, it's a place where you'll barely be able to look, as travellers dangle more than seems advisable over the precipice, even as you find yourself drawn to the edge. The view is remarkable: the granite rock lining the 42km-long Lysefjord (Light Fjord) glows with an ethereal, ambient light.

☛ SEE IT ! *Stavanger, with domestic and global flights, is the gateway town. Trips to Pulpit Rock are possible via public transport.*

320

Bay of Fundy

DRAMATIC TIDAL SHAPE-SHIFTER

CANADA // Two sites in one, this inlet between New Brunswick and Nova Scotia is swept by the world's greatest tides, giving it a schizophrenic personality. Twice a day, 160 billion tonnes of seawater flows in and out of the 270km-long bay, varying the water level between high and low tide by up to 15m. To grasp this extreme oceanography, kayak the coast. You'll find rock arches you rowed under on the way out marooned on the return, and cliffs that were submerged now aren't.

☛ SEE IT ! *Check online for tide times. Fundy's whale-watching season is from June to October; numbers peak in August.*

321

Reed islands

FLOATING ISLANDS

PERU // Meeting the Uros people on the reed islands of Lake Titicaca is a ground-moving encounter – partly because the floating islands they live on do actually bob a bit, but mostly because theirs is an existence that's absolutely unique. The islands are made from dried totora reeds, which the Uros also use to construct their boats and houses. As the reeds at the bottom rot, new ones are added on top. The islands feature a reed watchtower and, traditionally, if a threat was spotted, the islands could be moved. Today, about 300 families live on them.

☛ SEE IT ! *The gateway town is Puno.*

323

322

Sheikh Zayed Grand Mosque

HOUSE OF THE HOLY

ABU DHABI // Covering an area equivalent to 17 football pitches, and with a capacity of 40,000, Abu Dhabi's Grand Mosque is only number eight in the world's biggest mosque chart (Saudi Arabia's Al-Masjid al-Nabawī accommodates 900,000), but it does boast the planet's largest handmade carpet (weighing 35 tonnes). The vast marble mosaic courtyard, complete with floral motif, is also unrivalled. Arab, Persian, Mughal and Moorish influences are all evident in the mosque's architecture.

☛ SEE IT ! *The Grand Mosque is between three main bridges connecting Abu Dhabi City to the mainland. Arrive by cab or bus.*

323

Cape Cod National Seashore

DUNES, WHALES & OYSTERS

Massachusetts, USA // Thank JFK for this unspoilt goodness, where salt marshes and shifting dunes step the landscape and humpback whales spout offshore. He preserved some 40 miles of his home-state coastline, so it remains a vista of sand and sky. Beachcombers wade among sandbars, surfers ride the waves and hikers hop on trails edged by saltspray roses and scrub pine. Characterful towns, such as gallery-laden Provincetown and oyster-rich Wellfleet, enhance it all.

☛ SEE IT ! *The shore is a 3½-hour drive from Boston. Fast ferries make the trip from the city to Provincetown in 90 minutes.*

324

Isla de Ometepe

LAKE NICARAGUA'S VOLCANO-CAPPED JEWEL

NICARAGUA // The two obvious reasons to visit Ometepe, the largest island in Central America's biggest lake, are volcanoes Maderas and Concepción. Challenging hikes lead past howler monkeys and through cloud forests to the exposed summits. Ometepe also offers rock carvings, beaches and blissed-out accommodation. It has a history of pirates and conquistadors, and a reputation as a holy place. With a massive canal project set to transform Lake Nicaragua, get here quick.

☛ SEE IT ! *Ferries run from San Carlos, Granada and San Jorge. The volcanoes represent a serious climb/hike: hire a guide.*

325 Wat Pho

BUDDHIST TEMPLE NIRVANA

Bangkok, THAILAND // If the ginormous Reclining Buddha at gorgeous Wat Pho isn't enough to make you come over all Zen, how about an on-site massage? In addition to being the country's biggest temple, Wat Pho is also the national headquarters for the teaching and preservation of traditional Thai medicine, which includes Thai massage. Pavilions housed within the temple complex, located in Bangkok's Ratanakosin district, facilitate that elusive yet wonderful convergence of sightseeing and relaxation (thank you Thailand, you're the best). The Reclining Buddha's pretty special, as well. Almost too

big for its shelter, the genuinely impressive statue, which stretches out 46m long and 15m high, illustrates the passing of the Buddha into nirvana. It positively glows with gold leaf, while mother-of-pearl inlay ornaments the massive feet. From the outside, Wat Pho is equally as fanciful, displaying an array of beautiful *chedis* (stupas) and several more Buddhas to ogle.

🕮 SEE IT ! *Get up early and take the Chao Phraya Express Boat to Tha Tien to reach Wat Pho. Directly opposite is the Grand Palace.*

326 Golden Temple

PUNJAB'S SPIRITUAL HOME

INDIA // Amritsar's Golden Temple is a defining image of India: a vision of golden perfection rising from a shimmering pool the waters of which are believed by Sikhs to be the nectar of immortality. And yet the Golden Temple is only one part of a greater *gurdwara* (religious complex) that includes mighty minarets, monumental arches, museums and even noisy dining rooms. Built in the 16th century under the guidance of the fifth of Sikhism's 11 gurus, the Harmandir Sahib (or Temple of God, as it is formally known) is laid out on the principles of equality and a casteless society – as symbolised by the gates that open on to the temple from every direction. In practice, it means the Golden Temple is arguably more welcoming than any major place of worship in the world. Everyone, regardless of faith, is invited to a simple meal in the *langar* (dining room), and Sikh pilgrims are especially keen to discuss their religion with visitors – conversations best enjoyed among shady colonnades, while chants echo gently along the marble surfaces.

☛ SEE IT ! *Amritsar's airport has connections to other Indian cities and regional airports. There are also train and bus services.*

329

327
Central Kalahari Game Reserve

SOULFUL KALAHARI HEARTLAND

BOTSWANA // The dry heart of the dry south of a dry continent, the Central Kalahari Game Reserve is epic in scale. Covering 52,000 sq km, this is a vast world of shimmering salt pans and ancient river valleys bathed in desert sands. The Kalahari is the largest expanse of sand on the planet, but the surprising abundance of greenery shelters black-maned lions, secretive leopards and some true desert specialists that include the gemsbok and the bat-eared fox.

☛ SEE IT ! *Gaborone or Maun are the main international gateways, but from either you'll need your own wheels or a safari operator.*

328
Beit She'an

SNAPSHOT OF PROVINCIAL ROME

ISRAEL // In Israel, provincial Roman life after Jesus was a time of grandeur, self-confidence and decadence, and nowhere shows this more clearly than Beit She'an's extraordinary ruins. Colonnaded streets, a 7000-seat theatre that looks much as it did 1800 years ago (the original public bathrooms are nearby) and two bathhouses can be found here, along with huge stone columns that lie right where they toppled during the AD 749 earthquake that levelled the city.

☛ SEE IT ! *Buses from Jerusalem take two hours. Don't miss the after-dark multimedia spectacular that brings the ruins alive.*

329
Majorelle Garden

RAINBOW-HUED BOTANICAL GARDEN

Marrakesh, MOROCCO // This haven of tall palms and bamboo groves is a psychedelic desert mirage accented by candy-coloured trails and lashings of cobalt blue. Created by artist Jacques Majorelle and later owned by Yves Saint Laurent, the botanical refuge oozes style cred. More than 300 plant species are grown here, while the dazzling blue art-studio where Majorelle worked is home to the Berber Museum. This tranquil spot is a heavenly break from Marrakesh's hubbub.

☛ SEE IT ! *Majorelle Garden is in the Guéliz district in Ville Nouvelle. It's a 20-minute walk (or short cab ride) from Djemaa el-Fna.*

330

Bioluminescent Bays

LUMINOUS MARINE PHENOMENON

PUERTO RICO // Who knew micro-organisms could be this beautiful? They're phosphorescent dinoflagellates, to be exact, and if you've seen that famous swim in the film *The Beach*, you'll know what we're talking about. A trip among these tiny stars is nothing short of psychedelic, with hundreds of fish, small sharks and rays whipping up bright-green sparkles below the surface as your kayak or boat glides through the inky night water – like a reflection of the Milky Way.

SEE IT ! Of three bioluminescent bays in Puerto Rico, the one at Mosquito Bay on Vieques (fly from San Juan) is most lauded.

331

Tian Tan Buddha

HILLTOP BRONZE GIANT

Hong Kong, CHINA // When flying into Hong Kong, take a peek out of the window and you may spot this giant Buddha perched atop Lantau island. There are larger Buddha statues elsewhere in the world, but none that are seated, outdoors or made of bronze like this one, weighing 202 tonnes and towering over 23m high. Slog your way heavenwards up 268 steps to his bird's-eye throne and you will appreciate Lantau as Buddha sees it: gloriously green and pretty.

SEE IT ! Reach Lantau by bus, metro or ferry from Hong Kong Island. Approach the plateau via the scenic bayside cable car.

332

Makhtesh Ramon

ISRAEL'S GRAND CANYON

ISRAEL // To simply say that Makhtesh Ramon is a crater makes this nature reserve sound far duller than it really is. Featuring multicoloured sandstone, volcanic rock and fossils, this geological phenomenon is 300m deep, 8km wide and 40km long: you'll feel like an extra in a sci-fi movie exploring it. The landscape resembles a *Star Wars* desert planet and the wide-open spaces, far from city lights, are equal fantasy fodder for solitude- and adrenaline-seekers.

SEE IT ! Mitzpe Ramon, on Makhtesh's northern edge, is 136km north of Eilat and the best base for hikes, drives or rides.

334

333

Grotte De Lascaux

VAST PREHISTORIC GALLERY

FRANCE // Less a cave and more a gallery, Grotte de Lascaux is a network of chambers adorned with the most complex prehistoric paintings ever found, and has been referred to as the prehistoric Sistine Chapel. The 600-strong menagerie of technicolour animal figures are renowned for their artistry. Discovered in the 1940s, the original cave has been closed since the 1960s to protect it; what you'll see is a centimetre-by-centimetre replica of the most famous sections.

☛ SEE IT ! *Lascaux is hidden in wooded hills outside the town of Montignac in France's Dordogne region.*

334

Jokhang Temple

ATMOSPHERIC SPIRITUAL HEART

TIBET // The atmosphere of hushed awe hits you first as you inch through the dark medieval passageways of the 1300-year-old Jokhang. The central golden Buddha here is the most revered in all Tibet. Queues of wide-eyed pilgrims shuffle up and down the stairways, past medieval doorways and millennium-old murals, pausing briefly to top up the hundreds of butter lamps that flicker in the gloom. It's the beating spiritual heart of Tibet. Welcome to the 14th century.

☛ SEE IT ! *Jokhang Temple is in Lhasa, the capital of Tibet. Visit in the morning to be swept along with the crowds of pilgrims.*

335

Kigali Memorial Centre

REMEMBERING RWANDA'S DARKEST HOUR

RWANDA // The lush, rolling green hills, clean streets and smiling faces of Rwanda belie the horror that occurred here just two decades ago, when some one million Tutsis and moderate Hutus were systematically butchered by the Interahamwe and army. This memorial honours the estimated 250,000 people buried here in mass graves and tries to explain how the genocide unfolded. The powerful exhibits serve as a sobering reminder of an atrocity that should never be forgotten.

☛ SEE IT ! *Located in the northern Kisozi district of the capital, just a short moto ride from the centre, the memorial is free to visit.*

336

Lisbon's Alfama
Heart of a city

↓

PORTUGAL // Whether you ride the canary-yellow tram 28 up its winding streets, almost touching the front doors of houses that you pass, or wander its maze of twists and turns, the Alfama will enchant. This is Lisbon's heart and soul. By day you're negotiating flapping laundry outside locals' windows, fighting the throngs gathering at *miradouros* (viewpoints) to admire the Tejo river below. By night, when the sounds of fado penetrate the bars, a deeper significance sets in; day or night, the Alfama merits several visits.

🕿 SEE IT ! *You'll get lost in the Alfama; it's all part of the fun. But take care at night and stick with others.*

337

Museo del Oro

COLOMBIA // Bogotá's Gold Museum will floor you with a sensation of Indiana Jones proportions. It was here in Colombia that conquistadors first heard a whisper of 'El Dorado', the legendary lost city of gold that inspired centuries of explorers and treasure hunters. It's no surprise then that the country's capital is one of the few places in the world where you can get a sense of what finding a long-lost buried treasure might be like. Although the lost city was never found, plenty of other loot was, and Museo del Oro contains more than 55,000 glittering pieces of gold and other materials from pre-Hispanic cultures. If anything is going to make you want to hack off into the jungle in search of fame and fortune, this museum is it.

☛ SEE IT ! *Museo del Oro is in the city centre. Although descriptions are in Spanish and English, it's worth taking a guided tour.*

338

MuseumsQuartier

AUSTRIA // If only every major European city could neatly package its best museums in one purpose-built district, tourism would be so much easier. Vienna's MuseumsQuartier is a grand affair indeed, boasting airy creative spaces, a remarkable ensemble of museums, and a sprinkling of cafes, restaurants and bars that serve as a breeding ground for the city's cultural life. With more than 60,000 sq metres of exhibition space, a top-notch kids' museum and Vienna's first dance institution, it's one of the world's most ambitious arts spaces. Highlights include the world's largest collection of Egon Schiele paintings in the striking, light-filled Leopold Museum, and MUMOK, an establishment at the vanguard of modern art that has a collection as serious as its brooding dark-basalt and sharp-cornered facade.

☛ SEE IT ! *The MuseumsQuartier is best tackled by purchasing a combined ticket that includes entry to every museum.*

337

338

340

339

798 Art District

CHINA // Red Maoist slogans and statues of lantern-jawed workers show Běijīng's premier art district is proud of its proletarian environs. Set inside the cavernous buildings of an old electronics factory, the workshop setting is the perfect canvas for ambitious projects requiring lots of space, and the area is a landmark for China's leading artists. Cafes dot the streets, providing relief between gallery hopping. Prepare to be alternately bemused and captivated.

☛ SEE IT ! *Located in the Cháoyáng district, exploring 798 is easy. There are signboards with English-language maps to guide you.*

340

D-Day Beaches

FRANCE // Wandering the windswept expanse of Normandy's Omaha Beach at dawn, as the English Channel strokes French sand, all seems serene. This is in contrast to 6 June 1944, when Operation Neptune sent a wave of 150,000 Allied soldiers crashing into this coast, as the largest seaborne invasion in history began. D-Day helped change the course of WWII – an exploration of the bunkers, and a sombre stroll through cemeteries dedicated to the fallen, begins to bring home the horrific magnitude of the sacrifice.

☛ SEE IT ! *The D-Day beaches are 24km from Bayeux, 90-minutes from Le Havre.*

341

Białowieża Forest

POLAND // Green and Middle-earth-like, Poland's oldest national park owes its existence to royalty, as it was a private hunting ground for kings and tsars. The hunting must have been good: Białowieża is the original home of the European bison, the continent's largest land mammal. Though the bison died out in 1919, it's been successfully reintroduced here, and the chance of spotting one is reason to visit. Another is the walking and biking trails that burrow into the zingy foliage.

☛ SEE IT ! *Białowieża straddles the Belarusian border in eastern Poland, 230km from Warsaw.*

342

N Seoul Tower

BELOVED LANDMARK TOWER

SOUTH KOREA // As iconic as *kimchi*, the spindle of N Seoul Tower teeters over Seoul, offering panoramic but hazy views of the immense metropolis. It's the star attraction of Namsan mountain, beloved by locals as a place for exercise, peaceful contemplation and hanging out with loved ones; thousands of padlocks festooned around the tower's railings are inscribed with lovers' names. Several restaurants are housed within the spire and there's a popular cable car.

☛ SEE IT ! *Namsan is the most central of Seoul's mountains. Visit at sunset and watch the city morph into a galaxy of lights.*

343

Lake Manasarovar

HOLIEST OF HOLY LAKES

TIBET // It is said that some of Mahatma Gandhi's ashes were sprinkled into Lake Manasarovar, the most venerated of Tibet's many lakes and one of its most beautiful. It's a sacred place for Indian pilgrims and Tibetans, extolled in literature and writ large in Buddhist legend. A walk along its banks, dotted with Buddhist shrines, cave retreats and the fantastical Chiu Monastery would be appealing anywhere, but in this snow-capped mountain terrain it is simply special.

☛ SEE IT ! *Manasarovar is in Western Tibet. The best base is picturesque Chiu village on the northwestern shore of the lake.*

344

Grossglockner Road

ULTIMATE ROAD TRIP

AUSTRIA // Like the Matterhorn (p103) and Mont Blanc (p118), Grossglockner is a European peak that mountaineers love to conquer. But what makes this snow-dusted hulk more fun is the road that twists and turns beneath it. A stupendous feat of 1930s' engineering, the 48km Grossglockner Road swings around 36 switchbacks, passing jewel-coloured lakes, forested slopes and glaciers from Bruck in Salzburgerland to Heiligenblut in Carinthia. Buckle up for one of the great Alpine drives.

☛ SEE IT ! *The road can be bumper-to-bumper, particularly in July and August, so set off early and always check the weather.*

345

345

Pelourinho

HISTORIC NEXUS WITH RHYTHM

BRAZIL // Salvador's pulsating heart, Pelourinho is the historic core of Brazil's first capital, the New World's first slave market and a melting pot for European, African and Amerindian cultures. A slick restoration added a glossy sheen but Pelourinho still grooves. Stucco-fronted Renaissance architecture provides a backdrop for wild festivals, buzzing pavement bars and capoeira dancers glimpsed inside studios crammed into the pastel-hued colonial buildings.

☞ SEE IT ! *Salvador, in Bahia, northeastern Brazil, has an international airport connecting to Europe and the US.*

346

Glacier Skywalk

FLOATING IN THE ROCKIES

CANADA // Jasper's Glacier Skywalk requires a leap of faith. The arcing glass walkway melts into the valley beneath your feet to give you the impression of being suspended in thin air. It's a multimillion-dollar engineering feat of glass, steel and wood that floats above the Sunwapta Valley. Thrust 30m from the cliffside, it's a sublime way to experience the panoramic vista of snowcapped mountains and glacier-carved valleys that will make you feel very, very small.

☞ SEE IT ! *Jasper National Park, the largest in the Canadian Rockies, is in Alberta province, eight hours inland from Vancouver.*

347

Casino de Monte Carlo

GLITZY, GLAM HEDONISM

MONACO // In the cashed-up principality of Monaco, attitude is everything. Nowhere is this more apparent than at the legendary marble-and-gold Casino de Monte Carlo. This is not just any casino: the 1910 building and atmosphere are an attraction in their own right. Gambling here – or just watching the poker-faced gamble – is part of the Monaco experience, and living out your James Bond fantasies doesn't get any better than in these monumental, richly decorated rooms.

☞ SEE IT ! *Monaco is in the south of France. To enter the casino, you must be at least 18; a jacket-and-tie dress code kicks in after 8pm.*

350

348 349 350

Lahore Fort

ATMOSPHERIC MUGHAL COMPLEX

PAKISTAN // There's an appealing sense of abandon about gritty Lahore Fort when there are few visitors. The star attraction of the Old City, it's believed the site conceals some of its most ancient remains. Its current form dates to the 16th century and partial restoration means an atmospheric grimi- ness pervades. Although not as elaborate as the great Mughal forts at Delhi and Agra in India, a comparable succession of graceful palaces, finely decorated halls and tranquil gardens give sightseers plenty to explore.

☛ SEE IT ! *Lahore Fort is in the historic centre of Lahore, capital of Punjab Province.*

İshak Paşa Palace

STORYBOOK TURKISH PALACE

TURKEY // As if lifted from a page of *One Thousand and One Nights*, İshak Paşa Palace is a romantic vision of honey-toned stone perched on a tiny plateau, backed by soaring cliffs. Once home to Kurdish chieftains, the vast courtyards and ornate salons are a blend of Seljuk, Ottoman, Persian, Georgian and Armenian architecture that fizz with exuberant decoration. The views – facing the rugged contours of Mount Ararat across the Anatolian plains – are worth the visit alone.

☛ SEE IT ! *İshak Paşa Palace is 6km from the city of Doğubayazıt in eastern Turkey. Catch a minibus or taxi from the centre.*

Mo'orea

POSTCARD-PERFECT TROPICAL ISLE

FRENCH POLYNESIA // Mo'orea is so beau- tiful you'll be rubbing your eyes at your first glimpse of it from Tahiti. That turquoise la- goon that you were sure was Photoshopped in the brochure? It's better in real life. Bora Bora might be better known, but glimpsing the near-vertical emerald cliffs, brilliant sun- sets and underwater playground of sloping reefs at Mo'orea will still make you feel as if you're the luckiest person in the world.

☛ SEE IT ! *Less than 20km of Pacific from Tahiti, Mo'orea can be reached by air or boat. May to October is driest; whale- watching season runs July to October.*

351

Snæfellsnes
Eerie volcanic majesty

↓

ICELAND // A windswept promontory inhabited principally by rain-soaked sheep, the Snaefellsnes Peninsula casts a spell on all who visit. Jules Verne set his novel *Journey to the Centre of the Earth* here; presiding over the whole peninsula is the white mass of Snaefellsjokull, a glacier-topped active volcano that featured in Verne's book. Take a snowmobile ride to its tip for Iceland's most epic views: long beaches stretching into oblivion, glaciers gathering on the eastern horizon and the surging Atlantic tides on three sides – all with barely a soul around.

🖝 *SEE IT ! A good base is the harbour town of Stykkishólmur.*

354

352

Himeji Castle

SAMURAI STRONGHOLD

JAPAN // The graceful contours and lustrous white facade make multi-tiered Himeji-jō look more like a wedding cake than a military stronghold for samurai and shoguns. Japan's most magnificent castle is gleaming after a lengthy restoration. It's the best example of what are only a handful of original castles left in Japan and, with its pretty five-storey main-keep surrounded by moats and defensive walls, it looks good enough to eat.

☛ SEE IT ! *Himeji-jō towers over the city of Himeji, an hour from Kyoto by train. Come in cherry blossom season (early April) and see the castle adorned with flowers.*

353

Sedlec Ossuary

MONASTIC GOTHIC HORROR

CZECH REPUBLIC // The macabre 'bone church' of Sedlec Ossuary would stretch the imagination of the most accomplished horror novelist. Garlands of skulls hang from the monastery's vaulted ceiling, bones adorn the altar and pyramids of skeletons squat in each of the corner chapels. Who would have thought it was all the work of a local woodcarver, let loose on Sedlec in 1870 with the remains of 40,000 people found in the crypt? Creepy, yes – but utterly captivating.

☛ SEE IT ! *Sedlec is in the medieval city of Kutná Hora, an hour east of Prague by train; an easy day trip from the capital.*

354

Aït Benhaddou

MOROCCAN MUD FORTRESS

MOROCCO // Art imitates life at Aït Benhaddou, rising from the southern foothills of the Atlas Mountains like a fortress from *Arabian Nights*. Myriad films (from *Lawrence of Arabia* to *Gladiator*) have used Aït Benhaddou as a canvas, so perfectly does this red mudbrick kasbah conjure the exotic. Born in the 11th century as an Almoravid caravanserai, its tangle of medieval lanes climbs to a summit from where a panorama of mountains, palm groves and desert stretches out into eternity.

☛ SEE IT ! *Aït Benhaddou is a short hop from Ouarzazate, which has excellent transport links to the rest of the country.*

355

355 Fatehpur Sikri

HEAVENLY SAINT'S CITY

INDIA // Passing through one of Fatehpur Sikri's soaring castle-keep gates is a grand affair in itself, but what lies beyond is an Indo-Islamic masterpiece. This fortified ancient city was the short-lived capital of the Mughal empire in the 16th century, during the reign of Emperor Akbar. According to Muslim history, Akbar built the magnificent city as a tribute to local Sufi saint Shaikh Salim Chishti, who accurately predicted the birth of an heir to the Mughal throne.

An ethereal gleaming white tomb honouring the saint languishes within the walls of the immense Jama Masjid mosque, a highlight of the city and the only part that's still in use today. Enter via the expansive flight of stone steps and towering 54m-high Buland Dar-waza (Victory Gate) and it is clear you're following in the footsteps of emperors and saints. The rest of the city is now a ghost town, albeit a very beautiful one indeed.

☛ SEE IT ! *Lying 40km west of Agra, Fatehpur Sikri is easy to visit as a day trip. The red-sandstone palace walls are at their most atmospheric and photogenic at sunset.*

356

356

Blyde River Canyon

WATER-SOAKED GIANT GORGE

SOUTH AFRICA // Moulded by river water, carved by whirlpools and lashed by water-falls, Blyde River Canyon in Mpumalanga is an awesome sight. As the third largest canyon in the world and one of South Africa's most outstanding natural sights, its reputation is growing. Driving around the canyon's rim is a memorable experience; jumping out to explore the surrounding nature reserve's hulking great rock formations and swimming spots on foot is even better.

☛ SEE IT ! *The canyon is a two-hour drive from Kruger National Park (p130). Access it from nearby towns or stay in the reserve.*

357

Ancient Persepolis

PERSIA'S FINEST MOMENT

IRAN // Few ancient ruined cities beguile like Persepolis. This World Heritage–listed site was the epicentre of the great Persian empires, and the monumental staircases and gateways underline how grand these empires were, just as the broken columns attest that their end, at the hands of Alexander the Great, was emphatic and merciless. The exquisite bas-reliefs of the Apadana Staircase and the remains of the Palace of 100 Columns come close to perfection wrought in stone.

☛ SEE IT ! *Shiraz is a convenient base for Persepolis – rent a taxi or book a tour for the day. Arrive early to beat crowds and heat.*

358

Ao Phang-Nga

A VIEW TO KILL

THAILAND // With turquoise bays peppered with limestone rock towers, brilliant-white beaches and tumbledown fishing villages, Phang-Nga Bay is perhaps Thailand's most exquisite landscape. It was here, among the towering cliffs and swifts' nests, that James Bond's nemesis, Scaramanga (*The Man with the Golden Gun*), chose to build his lair. Come to kayak, climb, dangle off the back of a yacht or live out your own island fantasy in a hammock on Ko Yao Noi or Ko Yao Yai.

☛ SEE IT ! *November to February has good weather but gets busy. March to September is warmer, wetter, cheaper and quieter.*

359

Geysir

THE GREAT GEYSER

ICELAND // Geysir is part of Iceland's 'Golden Circle' of natural wonders. Gullfoss (p150) commands all the waterfall glory, naturally. This one is a highlight for the explosion-lovers. That's right. If you want to see boiling hot water suddenly erupt from the ground, spurting as high as 70m into the air, this is the place for you. There's no danger, it's been happening for quite some time now, around 10,000 years in fact. It's still hugely impressive, all the same.

☛ SEE IT ! *In summer there are regular buses from Reykjavik for day-trippers.*

360

Lake Malawi

AFRICAN QUEEN

TANZANIA // Kayaking to a desert island on a lake in the middle of Africa – not a bad way to spend an afternoon. A drowned section of the Rift Valley, Lake Malawi (or Nyasa as the locals had called it for centuries) was 'discovered' by Livingstone, so thank the good doctor as you lie on a freshwater beach, munching fresh banana bread in Africa's friendliest country. Rich in fish life and as clear as gin, the lake offers fantastic snorkelling and even diving opportunities.

☛ SEE IT ! *There are many lodges, resorts and campsites along the 480km lake front.*

361

Teatre-Museu Dalí

WONDERFUL WORLD OF DALÍ

Figueres, SPAIN //No-one but Salvador Dalí could have conceived of this confection, a red castle-like building topped with giant eggs and Oscar-like statues, its entrance guarded by medieval suits of armour balancing baguettes on their heads. It's an apt resting place for the master of surrealism, and 'theatre-museum' is a fitting label for this trip through his fertile imagination. It's full of surprises and illusions, and contains a substantial portion of Dalí's life's work.

☛ SEE IT ! *Visit on a day trip from Girona or Cadaqués as there's little else in Figueres.*

360

362

Karlštejn Castle

CZECH REPUBLIC // Clip-clopping in a horse's cart through Karlštejn's hilly streets to its model-like castle might feel like a throw-back to Disney World at times, but it's no surprise that this is Prague's most popular day trip. The fairy-tale medieval fort started life in 1348 as a hideaway for the crown jewels and treasury of the Holy Roman Emperor, Charles IV. Although it fell into disrepair over the centuries, it was returned to its former glory in the 19th century, and these days it's justifiably swoon-inducing for hordes of weekending visitors from the capital – particularly from the upper levels of its crowning Great Tower, where visitors can drink in stunning views of the castle's enveloping forested fringe.

☛ SEE IT ! *Karlštejn lies 30km southwest of the capital and is reachable by train. Try to visit midweek to escape the crowds, and avoid queues by buying tickets in advance online.*

363

362

363

Danube Delta

ROMANIA // The Danube appears to be a quiet, relaxing sort of place, but looks can be deceiving: this 4187 sq km wetland of marshes, floating reed islets and sandbars is a constantly evolving network of channels and a busy ecosystem. It's a haven for wildlife lovers, birdwatchers and fishers who come to submerge themselves in this sanctuary for 160 species of fish and 300 species of bird, including Europe's largest white pelican and Dalmatian pelican colonies. Spotting the impressive roll-call of protected species and migrating populations that flock here is only part of the allure. Beautiful, secluded beaches, swathes of marshland and tranquil lakes beg to be explored before you chow down on the best seafood in Romania.

☛ SEE IT ! *The delta is in far eastern Romania, abutting the Black Sea. There is no rail service and few paved roads, meaning ferry is the primary mode of transport.*

364

364 **Blue Ridge Parkway**

PARKWAY TO HEAVEN

USA // Snaking for 469 glorious miles through the undulating peaks of the Appalachian Mountains, the Blue Ridge Parkway is the scenic drive to end all scenic drives. Begun in the 1930s as a Depression-era jobs-creation project, the Parkway took more than 50 years to complete. Today it attracts more than 15 million visitors a year, from families in minivans to Harley-straddling bikers. The Parkway is jaw-dropping all year round: in fall, the landscape flames with gold and scarlet foliage; in winter, the peaks wear a sugary dusting of snow; in spring, the mountainside blooms with trillium, hawthorn and Indian paint-brush; and in summer the trees grow so lush they form shaded canopies. Along the way are hiking trails, historic homesteads, pick-your-own orchards, craft centres, swimming holes and campsites. To make things even sweeter, the Parkway is capped at both ends by two of America's loveliest national parks – Virginia's Shenandoah to the north, and North Carolina's Great Smoky Mountains to the south.

☛ SEE IT ! *The Parkway's northernmost access is near Waynesboro, Virginia. Its southernmost access is near Cherokee, North Carolina.*

367

365

Brecon Beacons

MOUNTAINS, MARKET TOWNS & MONUMENTS

WALES // Brecon Beacons National Park won't win any awards for altitude, but you don't need dizzying mountains when you host a Unesco World Heritage site (the iron-works town, Blaenavon) and thousands of listed buildings. Shaped by 8000 years of human settlement, Roman burial chambers and medieval castles are found here along with waterfalls, caves and forests. In its towns, events like the Hay Festival of Literature and Arts continue the Beacons' cultural legacy.

☞ SEE IT ! *Trains run to Abergavenny, Brecon or Merthyr Tydfil. When there, buy an Explore Wales Pass for transport deals.*

366

Kalemegdan

BELGRADE'S BLOODY BASTION

SERBIA // Looming over Belgrade, Kalemegdan Fortress is a glorious and gory time machine. Positioned above the confluence of the Sava and Danube Rivers, the 1500-year-old citadel has been fought over by the Celts, Romans, Huns, Slavs, Byzantines, Hungarians, Ottomans, Serbs, Austro-Hungarians and Germans. The juxtaposition between still-standing prison gates, torture towers and a military museum, and new funfairs, zoos and bars, makes this a spellbinding site.

☞ SEE IT ! *Ask local tourism officers about seeing what lies beneath; a cryptic maze of tunnels, chambers and dungeons.*

367

Punakha Dzong

DING DONG, WHAT A DZONG!

BHUTAN // It's hard to pin down what makes Punakha Dzong inspire such feelings of inner peace and harmony. Perhaps it's the gently swishing waters of the Pho Chhu (Father) and Mo Chhu (Mother) rivers, which meet beneath the monastery walls. Perhaps it's the timeless jacaranda trees, which paint the riverbank a vivid mauve as they burst into blossom every spring. Whatever it is, the memory of a visit is worth every penny of the steep tourist fee required to visit Bhutan.

☞ SEE IT ! *You need to be on an organised trip to visit Punakha, three hours by road from the capital Thimphu.*

368

Glover's Reef

GILLIGAN'S ARCHIPELAGO

BELIZE // From the sky, the partially submerged atoll (which forms the easternmost part of Belize's protected barrier reef) resembles a string of green-flecked white pearls floating in the endless blue of the Caribbean. In a nation priding itself on an abundance of paradise, Glover's Reef is a cut above. Spend your days swimming, snorkelling, scuba diving, then feasting on seafood and drinking tropical drinks. Naturally, the reef is a perfect spot for that most hallowed of Belizean sports, the zero-yard hammock dash. This enchanted atoll lies further offshore than Belize's other cays and islands, thus offering visitors who make the 35-mile trip from the mainland a chance to live out their personal *Cast Away* fantasies.

☛ SEE IT ! *Glover's Reef is accessible by boat from Dangriga, Hopkins and Sitter River; transport is usually arranged by the resorts, ranging from campsites at Glovers Atoll to eco-friendly Off-the-Wall.*

369

Meeting of the Waters

COLOURFUL CONFLUENCE

BRAZIL // The *Encontro das Águas* (Meeting of the Waters) is a natural phenomenon that occurs throughout the Amazon, but nowhere as dramatically as near Manaus in northern Brazil. Here, the warm, dark Rio Negro pours into the cool creamy Rio Solimões, but because of differences in temperature, speed and especially density (the Solimões carries eight times more sediment than the Negro) their waters don't mix, instead flowing side by side for several kilometres. The result? It's really quite trippy and makes for an absorbing natural oddity that has to be seen to be believed. The colour contrast is so stark that the waters of the Amazon look like two worlds colliding for as far as the eye can see.

☛ SEE IT ! *The Meeting of the Waters occurs just beyond Manaus, an incongruous pocket of urbanity in the middle of the Brazilian jungle and the largest city in the Amazon, accessible by plane, boat and bus.*

370 Baalbek

CITY OF THE SUN

LEBANON // The ruins of one of the Roman Empire's most audacious building projects lies not in Rome but on the high plateau of the Bekaa Valley. This incredible collection of colossal temples, which became the Holy City of the Sun, eclipse, in sheer size, any other construction work the Roman Empire attempted. Climb the staircase to the Temple of Jupiter and be reduced to an ant amid the towering granite columns. Stand under the high entrance portal of the Temple of Bacchus to marvel at the dizzyingly rich carvings and then sit on one of the oversized limestone slabs in the peristyle outside to take

in the scope and vision of this monument made for giants. Why the Romans decided to build their most ambitious temples in a backwater of their empire remains a mystery. But the well-preserved remnants – which have survived earthquakes, pillage and war down through the centuries – are today one of the Middle East's most spellbinding sights and an awesome feat of ancient engineering and architecture.

☞ SEE IT ! *Baalbek is a two-hour drive from Beirut. The security situation in the Valley changes quickly. Seek advice before visiting.*

371

372

373

Museu Picasso

PICASSO IN BARCELONA

SPAIN // Pablo Picasso spent his formative years in Barcelona, and this 3500-strong collection of paintings is a fitting tribute to the master. Spread across five contiguous medieval stone mansions, Museu Picasso's pretty courtyards, galleries and staircases are almost as delightful as the collection inside. The exhibition focuses on the artist's early years but there is enough material from subsequent periods to truly portray the man's versatility and genius.

☞ SEE IT ! *Visit over two days to soak it up, arriving early to beat the crowds. It's easily reached on foot from anywhere in town.*

Mosteiro dos Jerónimos

ORGANIC ARCHITECTURAL FANTASY

PORTUGAL // Wrought for the glory of God, Jerónimos was once populated by monks and is the stuff of pure fantasy, commissioned by the spice and pepper dosh of King Manuel I to trumpet Vasco da Gama's discovery of a sea route to India in 1498. Cloisters drip with organic detail, and gargoyles and fantastical beasties hang from the upper balustrade. It's one of Lisbon's undisputed heart-stealers and it's just... wow.

☞ SEE IT ! *Mosteiro dos Jerónimos is in the Belém district of Lisbon, 6km west of the centre, where it is best reached on one of the zippy trams.*

Tintern Abbey

ARTISTIC INSPIRATION ON THE WYE

WALES // Cloaked in romance, this Cistercian monastery, resplendent next to the River Wye, was founded in 1131, but entered the public imagination in the 18th century, via the paintings of Turner and poetry of Wordsworth, both of whom were inspired by its fairy-tale air. Nibbled by lichen and ruined to just the right degree, the great church, with its arches and ornamental tracery, stands tall against green hills and fields. It's enough to make anyone pen a verse or two.

☞ SEE IT ! *Tintern is just off the A466, 4 miles north of Chepstow, south Wales. The abbey is open year round.*

375

374

Tōshō-gū Shrine

JAPAN // Protected by Deva kings, prowled by mythical beasts and aglow with gold leaf, Tōshō-gū is a brilliantly decorative shrine in a beautiful natural setting. Among its notable features is the 'Sunset Gate', Yōmei-mon, which has intricate carvings and colourful depictions of flowers, dancers, fantastical animals and Chinese sages. Beyond a succession of gateways, inner courtyards unfold to reveal ancient halls of worship where 100 painted dragons crawl across the ceilings.

🔊 SEE IT ! *Tōshō-gū lies above the town of Nikkō, north of Tokyo and accessible from the capital by train in a couple of hours.*

375

Pamukkale

COTTON CASTLE MOUNTAIN

TURKEY // The calcium terraces of Pamukkale ('cotton castle') are a natural wonder, a powder- white mountain sitting incongruously amid pastoral green plains. Stroll across the weird calcite surface and wade through its saucer-shaped travertines of turquoise blue water to reach the summit ruins of the ancient spa-town of Hierapolis. Here, do as the Romans did and dip in the mineral-rich waters, decorated by half-sunk marble columns in the baths of the Antique Pool.

🔊 SEE IT ! *Buses run to Pamukkale village from Denizli (40 minutes), which has bus services from Antalya, Bodrum and Fethiye.*

376

Diocletian's Palace

LIVING HISTORY ON THE ADRIATIC

CROATIA // Many cities have Roman ruins, but they form the very fabric of modern Split. The palace at the heart of this lively Dalmatian port was built by the emperor Diocletian, who imported marble from Italy and Greece, and columns and sphinxes from Egypt for his grand retirement home. It's a fine place to wander. Some of the passageways are deserted and others buzz with bars and cafes, while locals hang their washing, and kids play football within the ancient walls.

🔊 SEE IT ! *It's free to enter the palace. Split is served by flights from many European destinations, and ferries along the coast.*

379

377

Ruta de las Flores

AN ACHINGLY SCENIC HIGHLAND DRIVE

EL SALVADOR // This 36km-long winding route through a handful of colourful colonial *pueblos* is famed for lazy weekends of gastronomy and gallery-hopping, as well as such adventurous pursuits as mountain biking and hiking to waterfalls scattered throughout the glorious Cordillera Apaneca. So-called for the blooms that blanket the hills from October to February, the 'Flower Route' is home to coffee plantations, local artisans and a weekly food festival in the village of Juayúa.

☛ SEE IT ! *The drive can be done in one long day or two, but it's worth scheduling a few days to soak up the vibe.*

378

Cliffs of Moher

OLD WORLD'S END

IRELAND // Europe ends abruptly in Ireland's west, where County Clare plunges off 214m-high cliffs into the Atlantic. With 2000 miles of ocean between here and Newfoundland, the swell is immense and the offshore break Aill Na Searrach draws big-wave surfers. Gaze across Galway Bay and the Aran Islands from O'Brien's Tower, and observe the sea stack An Branán Mór, home to guillemots and razorbills, and Goat Island's puffin colony. The walking trails are stunning; dawdle into Doolin for a black pint.

☛ SEE IT ! *The cliffs are an hour's drive from Limerick and 90 minutes from Galway.*

379

Isla del Sol

CRADLE OF THE SUN

Lake Titicaca, BOLIVIA // Birthplace of the Sun God. No address will ever top that, especially if you're Incan, which is why Isla del Sol boasts more than 180 pre-Columbian ruins, including Chicana, Kasa Pata and Pilco Kaima. Titicaca is an inland sea, the biggest lake in South America and the world's highest navigable stretch of water. One of its largest islands, del Sol offers fine treks across terraced hillsides containing the remains of a culture that once dominated this region.

☛ SEE IT ! *Boats regularly travel to Isla del Sol from the Bolivian town of Copacabana. Accommodation is available on the island.*

381

380

Jesuit missions of Trinidad and Jesus

PARAGUAY // Testimony to the Christianisation of South America during the 17th and 18th centuries, the mission ruins of La Santísima Trinidad de Paraná Jesús de Tavarangue stand out of the farmland of southern Paraguay in red-brown complexes of baroque and Romanesque architecture. These mini-cities comprising churches, houses, schools and workshops must have seemed surreal to the native populations, amid a then-wilderness containing little besides mud huts.

🐾 SEE IT ! *Trinidad's ruins have the easiest access, with buses from Encarnación. For the Jesus ruins, you may need a tour/taxi.*

381

Parque Nacional dos Lençóis Maranhenses

BRAZIL // Surely this can't be planet earth? The Lençóis Maranhenses is like something from another world. Of all Brazil's spectacles, this 70km-long, 25km-wide expanse of dunes resembling *lençóis* (bed sheets) spread across the landscape is the most unexpected. From March to September the dunes are pockmarked by thousands of clear blue lagoons made by rainwater filling the hollows. The result is a unique terrain that can be visited by 4WD, boat or on foot.

🐾 SEE IT ! *Lençóis Maranhenses is in Brazil's northeastern state of Maranhão. The lagoons are at their best in July and August.*

382

Polonnaruwa

SRI LANKA // The garden-city of Polonnaruwa had its heyday in the late 12th century under King Parakramabah, after the plundering of Sri Lanka's first capital, Anuradhapura (which can still be visited). It's the sense of the ancient everyday that makes this ruined city irresistible: its complex irrigation systems and sublime architecture, from giant stupas and carved Buddhas to lotus ponds and libraries. Explore by bicycle; the crumbling grandeur of this medieval metropolis is captivating.

🐾 SEE IT ! *Polo is four hours from Kandy by bus or six hours from Colombo by train. Set off early to avoid crowds and the heat.*

384 Komodo National Park

WHERE DRAGONS STILL ROAM

384

INDONESIA // From the rugged natural beauty of its volcanic islands to its magnificent coral reefs teeming with marine life, Komodo National Park is one of Indonesia's most dramatic landscapes. But this faraway place, nestled between Sumbawa and Flores in the centre of the Indonesian archipelago, is most commonly known for being the home of the world's most formidable lizard. Known locally as *ora*, Komodo dragons can reach over 3m in length and weigh more than 100kg. Although capable of taking down a deer (and yes, a person too) with their dagger-sharp teeth and claws (not to mention toxic venom) these majestic monitors – about 5000 of which are scattered between Rinca, Komodo and several surrounding islands – can be safely observed from a distance. Throw in some seriously world-class diving, and this exotic park is a traveller's wildest dream.

☛ SEE IT ! *Diving and dragon-spotting day trips, usually to Rinca, can be booked from Flores, but stay on Komodo for at least one night.*

383

Cathedral, Santiago de Compostela

THE FLAMBOYANT CLIMAX TO THE CAMINO

SPAIN // They say the journey is more important than the destination, but – wow – what a destination. The Cathedral of Santiago de Compostela is the end-point of the Camino, the fabled pilgrim trail across northern Spain. Many a *peregrino* will have walked from the French Pyrenees for a month or more, fuelled by the local almond cake, to reach the gates of Galicia's triumphal church. They're confronted with dominating Praza do Obradoiro, the cathedral's main 18th-century facade, a baroque flourish adorned with statues of St James, carrying his signature staff and scallop shell. The flamboyant outer conceals the medieval building: first, the masterfully carved Pórtico da Gloria, then the main nave, where a gilded High Altar bears a statue of the saint – the devout queue to kiss this effigy, while his actual remains rest (allegedly) in the crypt below.

☛ SEE IT ! *A pilgrim mass is held at midday. In Holy Years (when St James's Day, 25 July, falls on a Sunday) the incense burner is swung.*

383

385

Kelvingrove Art Gallery & Museum

CATHEDRAL OF SCOTTISH CULTURE

SCOTLAND // Scotland's biggest city, Glasgow, might lack Edinburgh's classical beauty, but it more than makes up for it with its cultural big-guns, and leading the way is Kelvingrove. Housed in a magnificent stone building, this grand Victorian cathedral of culture is a fascinating and unusual museum, containing a bewildering variety of exhibits. You'll find fine art alongside stuffed animals, and Micronesian shark-tooth swords alongside a Spitfire plane, but it's not mix'n'match: rooms are carefully and thoughtfully themed, and the collection is a manageable size. There's an excellent room of Scottish art, a room of fine French Impressionist works, and quality Renaissance paintings from Italy and Flanders. Even Salvador Dalí has a spot here, with his superb Christ of St John of the Cross.

☞ SEE IT ! *Kelvingrove is in Glasgow's West End area. Free hour-long guided tours run twice daily. Glasgow is just over an hour from Edinburgh by train.*

385

386

386

Copán

HONDURAS' MAYAN GEM

HONDURAS // It may have only one major Mayan ruin, but Honduras is home to an absolute beauty. Known for its remarkable stone sculptures, especially the enormous and intricately carved stelae depicting former leaders, Copán contains the remains of 3450 (and counting) structures in a 27 sq km radius, most of them within about half a kilometre of the *Grupo Principal* (Principal Group). The final phase of construction, dating from AD 650 to 820, is what we see today. But buried underneath the visible ruins are other ruins, which archaeologists are still exploring by means of underground tunnels. This is how they found the Templo Rosalila, below it the Margarita, and below that, Hunal, which contains the tomb of the founder of the dynasty, Yax K'uk' Mo' (Great Sun Lord Quetzal Macaw). It's housed in a lush jungle setting – look out for the macaws that hang out in the trees by the entrance.

☞ SEE IT ! *Get to the site, just a short walk from the lovely village of Copán Ruinas, early to avoid the heat and the crowds.*

388
Wolf's Lair

POLAND // From June 1941 – the beginning of Operation Bar-barossa, Germany's attempted invasion of the Soviet Union – to November 1944, Adolf Hitler was frequently hunkered down in *Wolfsschanze*, the Wolf's Lair, in what is now northeastern Poland. These days, the site comprises an eerie 18 hectares of overgrown forest, peppered with massive concrete bunkers, most of which were at least partially destroyed by the retreating Nazis. The site has not been maintained particularly well, and there is very little in the way of explanatory or educational materials, which can leave you feeling lost – emotionally, if not physically. It makes for a strange and sobering pilgrimage site. (It's not clear: are you supposed to smile when posing for a photo atop Hermann Göring's bunker?)

🐾 SEE IT ! *The Wolf's Lair is 8km east of Kętrzyn in Masuria, Poland. There is a bus service, but it's easier to rent a vehicle or take a tour.*

387
Hill of Crosses

LITHUANIA // On this legendary hillock, broad thickets of crosses sprout from the ground to give the impression of a graveyard forest. Some of the crosses are devotional, others are memorials (many for people deported to Siberia by the Soviets) and some are finely carved folk-art masterpieces. In the past, this spine-tingling display hasn't always pleased everyone. Planted here since at least the 19th century and probably way before that, the crosses were bulldozed by the Soviets, but each night people crept past soldiers and barbed wire to plant more, risking their lives or freedom to express their national and spiritual fervour. The sound of the thousands of crosses tinkling in the breeze is wonderfully unearthly.

🐾 SEE IT ! *The Hill of Crosses is the biggest drawcard of the city of Šiauliai and lies 10km north of town. Trains and buses run between Šiauliai and the capital Vilnius in three to four hours.*

Top, a dancer at Cartagena's Independence festivities. Right, a sculpture by Colombian artist Fernando Botero in Plaza Santa Domingo; and a view of Cartagena's cathedral.

Cartagena Old Town

389

COLOMBIA // Having pierced the rind of *Las Murallas* (the city walls), an explosion of tangy citrus colours confronts you in Cartagena's Old Town, on the Caribbean coast of Colombia. The Caribbean has long had a pirate problem, as the hill fortress of Castillo San Felipe de Barajas attests, but Cartagena's sturdy walls are a direct legacy of the visit, in 1586, of one Francis Drake, who invaded the city on behalf of Elizabeth I and stripped it of pretty much everything he could make off with. In the aftermath of the Englishman's attack and occupation, the city concluded that it needed better defences. Once you're in the walled town, the best way to explore the historical districts of El Centro and San Diego is simply to meander its vibrant streets, inhaling the sights and smells, tasting local street treats and mingling with the vivacious locals.

☛ SEE IT ! *Cartagena is 1000km north of Bogotá – roughly an hour's flight. If you're looking for an alternative experience, check out the Volcán del Totumo, a mud volcano about 45km northeast of Cartagena on the road to Barranquila, where you can enjoy a therapeutic splat bath.*

390

Tsarskoe Selo

RUSSIA // Constructed over nearly 50 years by three design-savvy ladies and their favourite architects, Catherine's Palace has 32 rooms (and counting) with enough gold and glitz to make your eyes glaze. Destroyed by the Nazis and ignored by the Soviets, the Rococo palace is slowly being restored to former glories. Observe the parquet floor in the Great Hall, an 800 sq metre ballroom covered in baroque or-namentation. Imagine receiving guests in the Enlightenment-inspired Arabesque Room, or feasting in the White State Dining Room. Gawk at the Amber Study, constructed from 450kg of the precious gemstone. You'll ogle room after room of extravagance – irresistible, but exces-sive. Although an Empress may not see it that way.

☛ SEE IT ! *Catherine's Palace is located at Tsarskoe Selo, near the village of Pushkin, 25km south of St Petersburg.*

390

391

391

Mt Rushmore

FOUR STONY FELLOWS

South Dakota, USA // Mt Rushmore casts an enchantment. How else to explain the rock-hewn mugs of George Washington, Abe Lincoln, Thomas Jefferson and Teddy Roosevelt drawing three-million visitors a year to a remote patch of South Dakota? The spell starts with the twisting drive in, dashed by tunnels that open to gape-worthy views of the site. At the monument itself, a half-mile trail skirts the base and brings you within presidential nostril-viewing range. Conceived in 1927 as a way to draw tourists to the state, the undertaking still amaz-es when you think that 400 men managed to carve 60ft faces into a mountain, blasting away almost a half-a-million tons of granite over 14 years. Early morning is best for viewing the stony fellows, when crowds are few and sunlight is just reaching over the horizon.

☛ SEE IT ! *Mt Rushmore stares out from the hills 23 miles southwest of Rapid City, which holds the closest airport.*

392

Butrint

WINDOW INTO THE ANCIENT WORLD

ALBANIA // Ancient Greeks and Romans both left their mark on Butrint, a fortified trading city and subsequent Byzantine ecclesiastical centre that is now an atmospheric ruins complex at the heart of a tiny national park. The remains of an acropolis, a 3rd-century BC theatre (secluded in the forest) and mosaicked public baths are just some of the crumbling gems to blow the dust off here. Pretty Lake Butrinti is a tranquil backdrop.

☛ SEE IT ! *The ruins lie 18km south of Saranda. Views from the Butrint museum courtyard give an idea of the city's layout.*

393

Burgess Shale

DINOSAUR LOVER'S DELIGHT

CANADA // Is this the best dinosaur dig in the world? Hard as it is to believe, the area that makes up the Rockies once lay at the bottom of a vast sea, and the peaks around Mt Burgess in Yoho National Park are littered with the fossilised remains of 120 species of weird and wonderful marine creatures from the earth's early history. Discovered in 1909 and now collectively known as Burgess Shale, they're a paleontologist's dream.

☛ SEE IT ! *Guided hikes can be picked up in the nearby town of Field in British Columbia, less than an hour from Banff.*

394

Loch Lomond

CELTIC CRACKER

SCOTLAND // Caught in a fault between the Highlands and Lowlands, 24 mile-long Loch Lomond (the UK's biggest puddle) is punctuated by more than 30 islands. There are cycling trails all around its historic shores (Rob Roy lived here) and Loch Lomond and the Trossachs National Park is a hiker's heaven. The West Highland Way traces the eastern shore; weary walkers have claimed that some islands float (away from them).

☛ SEE IT ! *Combine a walk or cycle with a boat trip. Stay at the Drovers Inn at the loch's northern end – it has a haunted room.*

394

Blue Hole

395

BELIZE // As every mountaineer *must* ascend Everest, so too are scuba divers drawn to the depths of Belize's Blue Hole. Declared by Jacques Cousteau (who charted its depth of 124m in 1971) as among the world's top scuba sites, the massive underwater cave is unique for both its physical depth and the deep-blue colour for which it is named. The shallow areas by the reef ringing the hole are for acclimation only, and here you'll come face to face with the colourful reef fish, massive groupers and sea turtles. As you descend vertically into the hole's dark depths, you'll pass ancient, storeys-high stalactites hanging from the ceiling of the underwater cave. From the bottom of the hole the light from above is but a pinprick, towards which you'll climb slowly and with the greatest of care.

SEE IT ! *The trip to Blue Hole is two hours each way. Placencia-based Splash Dive is among the most reputable operators in Belize.*

Thiksey Monastery

396

MONASTIC KINGDOM

INDIA // So big is glorious Thiksey Gompa that it looks more like a village than a monastery. Covering a large rocky outcrop with layered white Tibetan-style buildings spectacularly ringed by arid mountains, it incorporates shops, a school, a restaurant and hotel. As a place to stay, it can come as quite a surprise that many rooms here are unexpectedly plush, with geyser-heated water. More than 40 monks gather to chant morning prayers; a fascinating ceremony that's so popular visitors can often outnumber worshippers. A 14m-high Buddha lords over the main gompa's prayer chamber, simultaneously peaceful and vaguely menacing. A museum hidden away beneath the monastery restaurant displays Tantric artefacts, including a wine-vessel made from a human skull.

SEE IT ! *Thiksey is near Leh in the north Indian state of Ladakh. Only two road routes link Ladakh to the rest of India; from about October to May the sole way in is by air.*

397

397

National Palace Museum

THE DRAGON'S (ART) HOARD

TAIWAN // Imagine the finest Chinese art – Ming Dynasty porcelain, ancient scrolls and paintings dating to the days of Confucius, intricate jade pieces and work from the Middle Kingdom's provinces and its dynastic history. Imagine no more, for the experience awaits at Taipei's National Palace Museum. Much of this art was taken, literally, from Chinese museums and private collections by Chiang Kai Shek's nationalist troops during the last days of the civil war. Although the presence of these purloined treasures in Taiwan is a bone of contention between the two parties, nearly all agree that the art wound up in far saner hands during the worst years of the Cultural Revolution, when so much was destroyed. The museum is a must-visit for lovers of Chinese culture and history.

☞ SEE IT ! *The museum is accessible from anywhere in Taipei. Finish with tea and dim-sum in the Sanxitang Tea Room.*

398

Hadrian's Wall
Wonderwall

↓

ENGLAND // Walking the Hadrian's Wall Path, an 80-mile-long trail running coast-to-coast across northern England, from Wallsend in the east to Bowness-on-Solway in the west, you'll appreciate how desperate the Romans were to keep the Scots at arm's length. Built between AD 122 and 128, and named after the emperor who ordered its construction, Hadrian's Wall was an epic feat of engineering, even by Roman standards. After each Roman mile, a guarded gateway was built into the structure.

☛ SEE IT ! *Places to see surviving sections, without walking its length, include Housesteads in Hexham.*

399

Galle Fort

CAPTIVATING COLONIAL-ERA SEA FORT

SRI LANKA // Nowhere in Sri Lanka bears better witness to its rich colonial heritage than Galle Fort, built by the Portuguese in 1588 and fortified by the Dutch in the 1600s. Fusing European and South Asian sensibilities, a spice-heavy air and a blend of towering bastions and veranda-wrapped villas, Galle's green spaces invite impromptu cricket games, while cobblestoned streets are a hub of arts, shopping, hotels and restaurants: proof that its charms are not just historical.

☛ SEE IT ! *Galle is three hours from Colombo by train or bus, and six hours from Kandy by train. For the best sunset views, stroll along the seawall from the lighthouse at dusk.*

400–
500

401

400

Great Zimbabwe

MEDIEVAL MARVEL

ZIMBABWE // Clamber over ancient boulders and ruins, explore narrow crevices and ponder over its significance at the greatest medieval city in sub-Saharan Africa, Great Zimbabwe. Dating back to the 11th century, the World Heritage-listed site is best visited at sunrise or sunset when the light is superb and gives an other-worldly atmosphere to one of the country's most impressive sights.

☛ SEE IT ! *Catch a Kombi van taxi from the town of Masvingo to the Great Zimbabwe Hotel; it's a 1km walk to the main gate.*

401

Swayambhunath

INTOXICATING ECLECTIC TEMPLE

NEPAL // A journey to the sacred Buddhist shrine of Swayambhunath is one of the definitive experiences of Kathmandu. Mobbed by primates and soaring above the city on a lofty hilltop, the 'Monkey Temple' is a fascinating, chaotic jumble of Buddhist and Hindu iconography. However, several parts of the site, if not the all-seeing eyes of the white stupa itself, were damaged during the earthquake that struck Kathmandu Valley in 2015.

☛ SEE IT ! *Reach Swayambhunath by taxi, bicycle or as an easy stroll from Kathmandu. Restoration work is underway.*

402

Tuol Sleng & the Killing Fields

A WALK ON HUMANITY'S DARK SIDE

CAMBODIA // Nothing prepares you for Tuol Sleng Genocide Museum, the original Khmer Rouge security prison. It remains a festering wound for Cambodians who survived the 'prison without walls' that was 'Democratic' Kampuchea from 1975-79. Some 17,000 prisoners passed through its gates and were later executed at Choeung Ek. Driving out towards the killing fields, it is hard to make sense of the violence unleashed in this indolent land.

☛ SEE IT ! *Tuol Sleng is in central Phnom Penh, Cambodia's capital. It can be reached by bus or taxi.*

403

Standing Stones of Callanish

SILENT STONE SENTINELS

SCOTLAND // Forget Stonehenge (p78). A proper stone circle should rise dramatically from a windswept heath, not be fenced in. At Callanish, a circle of crude stone pillars rings a centuries-ravaged tomb like petrified mourners at a Highland funeral. On this barren Isle of Lewis moor, you can get among the stones and feel a tangible link to the ancient past, even if you snort at the idea of mystical powers attached to rings of rocks.

☛ SEE IT ! *There are B&Bs in tiny Callanish village, and more stone circles a short hike southeast at Callanish II and Callanish III.*

404

Avebury Stone Circle

HUB OF IMPENETRABLE ANCIENT SLABS

ENGLAND // There are more famous rocks down the road, but these are more fun. Stonehenge (p78) is iconic, but you can't get at its stones; at Avebury, there are three neolithic circles (including the largest in Europe) and you can wander among them. The menhirs, erected from around 2850 BC, encompass a lovely village and sit in a landscape of other ancient, mysterious monuments. What it was all for? Nobody knows.

☛ SEE IT ! *Avebury is six miles west of Marlborough on the A4361. The nearest train stations are Pewsey and Swindon.*

403

405
Caracol

BELIZE // It's no surprise that the most breathtaking view in Belize is found from atop the country's tallest building. But you'll have to be committed to see it, since Belize's highest building is in Caracol, a city abandoned over a thousand years ago and surrounded by nigh-impenetrable jungle. At the height of its power, Caracol was home to 150,000 souls, twice that of present-day Belize City. It was a rival to nearby Tika and many were the Mayan roads that led here.

Today, Caracol lies vacant, daring adventurers to brave the one bone-jarring road leading between it and civilisation. It's a road worth taking, as what's been excavated is awe-inspiring. The site contains accessible temples and hidden tombs, beautifully restored plazas and ball-courts and, of course, a chance to climb to the top of the 141ft Caana (sky place) pyramid, still modern Belize's tallest building.

☛ SEE IT ! *Most arrive on tours, but a 4WD vehicle can make it from San Ignaciao in two hours. Bandits have been reported, so take care.*

406
Malbork Castle

POLAND // Here is the castle of your childhood daydreams, where righteous knights launched crusades against ungodly pagans, collected tolls from passing ships and traded in precious gemstones. Marienburg was built in the 13th century by the Teutonic Knights, a fierce German military order. The castle was eventually seized by the Polish king, but not before the knights had expanded it to become the biggest in Europe.

Nowadays, Malbork Castle is the perfect place to embrace your inner medieval warrior, fending off attackers and rescuing damsels and dudes as you see fit. Explore the castle's grand vaulted halls, discover its hidden passageways, pay your respects in its many chapels, and venture into the notorious Witold Cell, or prison. More fodder for the imagination: housed in an isolated castle tower, the Gdanisko is a cosy closet with an unceremonious hole, revealing a steep drop to the great outdoors. That's right, the castle loo.

☛ SEE IT ! *Malbork Castle dominates the town of the same name (Marinburg in German), which is 30km southeast of Gdańsk.*

408 La Boca district

Buenos Aires, ARGENTINA // From the sheer artistry of the *fútbol* on display at La Bombonera and the ripple of tension that's palpable on the terraces (especially if River Plate have crossed the city for the Superclasico derby), through to the colour of Benito Quinquela Martín's cobblestone Caminito and the intensity of the tango dancers – Boca is all about passion. By far the most well known of Buenos Aires' 48 barrios – not least because of its internationally famous football team, Boca Juniors, among whose alumni is Argentina's one-time messiah Diego Maradona – la Boca is lively, even by BA's standards. Grab a cold Quilmes in an Italian tavern or visit the third deck at Fundación Proa for views over the Riachuelo River, which gives the suburb its name (la Boca means 'the mouth').

☛ SEE IT ! *La Boca is a real neighbourhood, home to real people and real problems (especially beyond Caminito). Travel by taxi and don't flash cash or dwell in the shadows.*

407 Temple of the Tooth

SRI LANKA // The crowning jewel of Kandy town's offerings, the golden-roofed Temple of the Sacred Tooth plays host to Sri Lanka's most important Buddhist relic – one of the Buddha's canine teeth.

The site attracts many devotees, who bring fragrant flowers as gifts. The veneration provoked by this curio is profound and deeply sincere, and captivating to witness. You won't get a chance to see the object of all the fuss, though: the tooth sits on a solid gold lotus flower, housed in a casket within a two-storey shrine and framed on either side by enormous elephant tusks. The shrine is open to visit during *puja* (prayers), which take place three times a day against a stirring beat of pounding drums and chanting.

The temple complex covers a large area beyond the main shrine, within which lie the Audience Hall and the Royal Palace, where you can visit a mesmerising hall of dozens of Buddha statues.

☛ SEE IT ! *Kandy is 3½ hours from Colombo by bus. When visiting the temple, wear clothes that cover your legs and shoulders, and remove your shoes.*

408

409

409

Heydar Aliyev Cultural Centre

AZERBAIJAN'S ARCHITECTURAL ICON

AZERBAIJAN // The cornerstone of modernising post-Soviet Baku, this Zaha Hadid-designed architectural masterpiece is like a 21st-century incarnation of the Sydney Opera House. Designed to express the optimism of a nation, the soaring pinnacle of the snow-white structure is seemingly held up by the sky. It hosts exhibitions, events and a museum recounting Azeri history and the role of the building's namesake, the revered president of Azerbaijan from 1993 to 2003.

☛ SEE IT ! *It's free to enter the building on the edge of central Baku, but the museum and exhibitions command a small fee.*

410

Kashgar's Grand Bazaar

SEDUCTIVE SPICE TEMPLE

CHINA // Close to the border of Kyrgyzstan, there's a souk-like atmosphere about Kashgar's main bazaar – particularly on Sundays when business cranks up a notch. Step carefully through the packed entrance and allow your senses to guide you through; the pungent smell of cumin, the sight of scorpions in a jar, the sound of *muqam* music from tinny radios, the taste of hot *samsas* (baked mutton dumplings) and the feel of soft sheepskin caps are seductive and overwhelming.

☛ SEE IT ! *Kashgar is in Xīnjiāng, northwest China. It's a conservative Muslim area and women should cover their arms and legs.*

411

Bardo National Museum

NORTH AFRICA'S MAJESTIC MOSAICS

TUNISIA // Home to a magnificent collection of Roman mosaics, the Bardo is Tunisia's most important museum. Inside, a vibrant vision of ancient North African life is presented in detail, thanks to the well-preserved haul of mosaic art. Ponder the glories of the Roman Empire while viewing the famous Virgil mosaic. After the ancient art, view the incredible stash of priceless artefacts raised by underwater archaeologists from a Roman shipwreck off the Tunisian coast.

☛ SEE IT ! *The Bardo, 4km northwest of central Tunis, can be reached by tram. Take tram Line 4 and get off at the Bardo stop.*

413

412

Salzwelten

AUSTRIA // A trip into Halstatt's Salzbergwerk might feel a bit whizz-bang Disneyland, but who can say no when you get transported into the depths of this 3500-year-old salt mine on 60m-long miners' slides? At its heart is an otherworldly subterranean salt lake, where a multimedia show pays homage to the 'white gold' history and mysterious 'salt man' found here. It might sound contrived, but people love it and, even if you don't, your kids certainly will.

☛ SEE IT ! *Car access to Halstatt is limited; trains run from Bad Ischl and Bad Aussee. Funicular is the best way to reach the mine.*

413

Khao Sok National Park

WHERE TIGERS STILL ROAM

THAILAND // There are few spots in Thailand still habitable for large mammals, but ancient and vast Khao Sok, where you'll find dramatic limestone terrain and cascading waterfalls, is one such place. During the wetter months you may be able to spy bears, boars, gaur, tapirs, gibbons, deer, wild elephants and perhaps even a tiger among the juicy thickets. A network of dirt trails snakes through the quiet park on Thailand's peninsula: perfect stalking ground for fauna.

☛ SEE IT ! *Khao Sok is an hour from Surat Thani. Animal viewings are more likely in the wet season, from June to October.*

414

Mansudae Grand Monument

EPICENTRE OF THE KIM CULT

Pyongyang, NORTH KOREA // An audience with these larger-than-life bronze renditions of Kim Il-sung and Kim Jong-il offers a fascinating insight into North Korea's Kim cult. Be aware of the respect foreigners are expected to accord these statues: bow as your tour leader instigates the floral tribute to be placed at the statue's feet. Photographers will be instructed never to photograph one part of the monument – all pictures should be of the entire statue to avoid offence.

☛ SEE IT ! *Don't underestimate the seriousness attached to a visit to this site in the capital; act respectfully.*

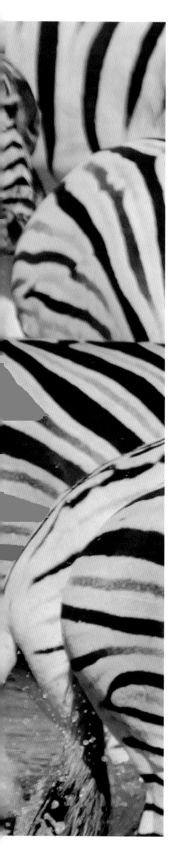

Etosha National Park

415

BIG GAME? A STROLL IN THE PARK

NAMIBIA // Etosha is Safari 101. It is nature for novices, animal-spotting-made-easy – because here, the wondrous wealth of wildlife comes to you. The park is dominated by a vast saline pan the size of Holland, which glitters brilliant-white under the Namibian sun, providing a striking backdrop to photographs and strange heat-haze hallucinations. However, what makes it so special for safari-goers, both new and experienced, is the profusion of waterholes that fleck the pan's southern edge. In such a parched place, water is liquid gold; and where there is gold, thirsty animals will follow.

Self-drive safaris are the norm in Etosha, which has an excellent network of well-maintained roads; all you have to do is park up by one of these precious ponds and wait for the elephants, lions, rhinos, zebra, oryx and other 100-odd mammal species to pop by. The only challenge is making it there without getting stuck in a giraffe-jam en route. The action doesn't stop after dark either. The rest camps within the park have floodlit waterholes, where you can sit with a bottle of Windhoek lager as large numbers of game likewise enjoy a night-time drink.

🐾 SEE IT ! *Etosha is a six-hour drive from Windhoek. Visit from May-October, when animals are at waterholes and grass is low.*

416

Port Arthur

AUSTRALIA // Those who landed at Port Arthur in the 19th century may
have felt that they had arrived at a prelapserian paradise; pristine seas
fringed a shore where their new home stood among the Huon pines.
But it would have been a short-lived sensation, for this was a state-of-
the-art prison, run by the British on Tasmania, Australia's island state.

Port Arthur was no ordinary prison. This is where – in the eyes of
the British Crown – the worst of the worst were sent. It pioneered new
techniques of control and incarceration, such as silence and solitary
confinement. Many prisoners were driven mad by the system so an asy-
lum was also constructed here. Today, the complex consists of several
beautifully preserved buildings, including the Model Prison itself, which is
eerily fascinating, and the Government Cottage.

☛ SEE IT ! *Port Arthur is an hour's drive from Hobart. Along the
way on Arthur Hwy, stop at the Tasmanian Devil Conservation Park.*

417

Jungfraujoch

SWITZERLAND // If you haven't heard of Jungfraujoch, you need
to get on board. At a mere 3454m it might be more than 1000m
squatter than the Matterhorn and Mont Blanc, but it's a once-in-a-
lifetime trip that you need to experience first-hand. There's a reason
why two million people a year visit Europe's highest train station. The
icy wilderness of swirling glaciers and 4000m turrets that unfolds at
the top is staggeringly beautiful. Within the sci-fi Sphinx meteorolog-
ical station, where trains disgorge passengers, there are restaurants,
viewpoints and an Ice Palace gallery of otherworldly ice sculptures.
But it's the tantalising journey that's the icing on the cake: the last
stage of the train ride burrows into the heart of the Eiger through a
tunnel that took 3000 men 16 years to drill.

☛ SEE IT ! *Jungfraujoch is in the Swiss Alps. From the Bern resort
town of Interlaken, the rail journey is 2½ hours each way.*

418 Phu Quoc Island

DESERT-ISLAND DREAM

VIETNAM // Fringed with white-sand beaches that look a bit more South Pacific than Southeast Asia, and with large tracts still cloaked in dense tropical jungle, Phu Quoc has become a pin-up boy for Vietnam's once undervalued coastline. Still, this is no Ko Tao (p68) or Ko Phi Phi (p279): despite development (including an international airport and improved roads), much of the island is still protected and Phu Quoc National Park covers close to 70 percent of this teardrop isle, an area of 31,422 hectares. Becoming bronzed and happy here is classic island escapism. Dive the reefs, kayak in the bays, eat up the back-road miles on a motorbike, or just live the life of a lotus eater, lounging on the beach and chowing down on fresh seafood.

☛ SEE IT ! *Phu Quoc is in Vietnam's Mekong Delta. Peak travel season is November to May, and most diving stops from May to October when seas are rough.*

419 Melk Abbey

MONASTIC GOLDEN BOY

AUSTRIA // Baroque gone barmy is the best way to describe Stift Melk, Austria's most famous abbey. In the 11th century it was a castle, then donated to Benedictine monks who converted it into a fortified abbey. After that Melk was claimed by fire, and then baroque got hold of it. Regiments of smiling cherubs, gilt twirls and polished faux marble set the scene. The monastery church dominates the complex with its twin spires and high octagonal dome. The high-altar scene, depicting St Peter and St Paul (the church's two patron saints), and ceiling paintings are theatrical. Besides the church, highlights include the *Bibliothek* (library) and the *Marmorsaal* (Marble Hall); both have amazing trompe l'oeil–painted tiers on the ceiling. Check out the imperial rooms, now housing a museum, where Napoleon once stayed.

☛ SEE IT ! *Melk is one of the most popular destinations in Austria, less than 1½ hours from Vienna by train.*

422

420

Nazca Lines

A BEAUTIFUL MYSTERY

PERU // One of the great archaeological mysteries, the Nazca Lines comprise more than 800 straight lines, 300 geometric figures, and 70 animal and plant drawings spread over 500 sq km of arid, rock-strewn plain in Peru's Pampa Colorada. Figures include a huge lizard, a monkey with an extravagantly curled tail, and a condor. Some say these mystical beasts look better in photos, but we can vouch for witnessing this stunning spectacle with your own eyes.

☛ SEE IT ! *Dozens of companies offer flights over the lines from Maria Reiche Neuman Airport near Nazca. The ride can be bumpy.*

421

Cementerio de la Recoleta

CELEBRITY CEMETERY

ARGENTINA // Evita Peron's tomb is the star attraction here, but the cemetery itself is often regarded as Buenos Aires' number-one sight (though we ranked it after La Boca on p267) . You can wander for hours in this amazing city of the dead, where countless 'streets' are lined with impressive statues and marble sarcophagi. Peeking into the crypts you'll see dusty coffins of past presidents, military heroes, influential politicians and the just plain rich and famous who've made it past the gates.

☛ SEE IT ! *Recoleta is a suburb of mansions and grand monuments. Time your visit to coincide with one of the free tours in English.*

422

Altun Ha

THE PLACE BEHIND THE BEER

BELIZE // If you've spent time in Belize you'll be familiar with the Temple of Masonry Altars, as their stylised facade is the symbol of the national beer. But drinking Belikin is no substitute for visiting the temple itself at Altun Ha. A trading centre during the Classical Maya period, what's left today is merely the ceremonial plaza containing two grand temples and smaller excavated structures, a reminder of the empire that ran Central America long before Columbus was born.

☛ SEE IT ! *A regular stop for tour operators, Altun Ha is close enough to the coast to be a day-trip from Caye Caulker or Ambergris.*

423 Khongoryn Els

SPECTACULAR DUNE COUNTRY

MONGOLIA // About twice as high and four times as long as the Sahara's famous Erg Chebbi dunes, the Khongoryn Els range in Mongolia's Gobi Desert is home to some of the largest and most spectacular sand dunes in the world. They stand proud at up to 300m high, so getting to the top is an exhausting slog that can take up to an hour, but the views of the desert from the sandy summit are wonderful. Before you lies an undulating blanket of pillow-soft mounds, which intensifies in colour from mellow yellow to burnished gold as the day goes on. Locally they are known as Duut Mankhan – the Singing Dunes, a nod to the lilting sound they make when the sand is moved by the wind or as it collapses in small avalanches. Magically, as if from nowhere, locals will appear, leading camels to whisk you away.

🐾 SEE IT ! *Khongoryn Els is in southern Mongolia's Gurvan Saikhan National Park. A mini naadam (traditional games festival) featuring horse racing, archery and wrestling is held annually on 15 August.*

423

424

424 425 426

Titanic Belfast

ONE HULL OF A MUSEUM

NORTHERN IRELAND // That this museum sits on the shipyard where the Titanic was built is the tip of the iceberg: the complex – Northern Ireland's most popular tourist attraction – is a multimedia extravaganza immersing the visitor in minutiae covering the doomed ship's history via rides, talking holograms, film footage, computer 'fly-throughs' – even projected odours and dropped temperatures. It doesn't feel macabre, celebrating instead the achievements of shipbuilders.

🖝 SEE IT ! *The museum building, supposed to represent a prow, is located on Queen's Island, an easy stroll from Belfast city centre.*

Zwinger

BAROQUE CHARMER

Dresden, GERMANY // Confronted by ravishing Zwinger, you can't help but envy those 18th-century Saxons who had the run of this baroque beauty as a party palace. Ornate portals lead into a fountain-studded courtyard, framed by buildings festooned with evocative sculpture. Today it houses several museums, including a precious *Gemälde-galerie Alte Meister* (Old Masters Gallery) displaying such art-world darlings as Botticelli, Titian, Rubens, Vermeer and Dürer.

🖝 SEE IT ! *Dresden is a two-hour train ride from Berlin. Virtually flattened in WWII, the town has made a remarkable comeback.*

Skeleton Coast

OFF-THE-CHART NATURE

NAMIBIA // This remote shore is as infamous as it is famous. Countless ships met their end on this foggy coast, and the desert that backs it killed most who reached land. Yet travel here today, past sculpted dunes, rusting shipwrecks and bleached whale skeletons, and you'll be captivated by its scale and majesty. Sharks patrol the depths, sea lions dominate the shallows, jackals patrol the beaches and desert-adapted lions, rhinos and elephants roam the river valleys.

🖝 SEE IT ! *The south is reached by coastal salt road from Swakopmund; the north by light aircraft or 4WD (via the Kaokoveld).*

427

Iona

SCOTLAND'S SPIRITUAL HEART

SCOTLAND // Few destinations in the world can match Iona for atmosphere. Best known as the resting place of the early kings of Scotland, today it's a place of pilgrimage and spiritual retreat as well as a major honey-pot for visitors touring the Highlands and Islands. Iona reveals itself slowly, being reached by a narrow 38-mile road from the ferry terminal at Craignure on Mull and then a five-minute ferry ride from Fionnphort. The sense of reaching somewhere very special, very slowly, is unmistakable.

Iona's attractions go well beyond some weather-worn gravestones of Celtic nobles: as well as Iona Abbey and a heritage centre, the island is the jumping-off point for boat trips to Staffa, and there are walking paths that take you away from the crowds to superb vantage points over neighbouring islands.

☛ SEE IT ! *Day trips from Oban involve a beautiful crossing from the mainland to Mull and onward transport to Iona.*

428

Stirling Castle

CASTLE TO RIVAL EDINBURGH

SCOTLAND // Castles are as synonymous with Scotland as bagpipes, and behind Edinburgh Castle none makes more of a song and dance than its near-twin – Stirling's walloping great keep. Many find Stirling's fortress more atmospheric – the location, architecture, historical significance and commanding views combine to make it a rollicking great adventure. The stone behemoth that stands today dates from the 14th to the 16th century, when Stewart monarchs ruled the roost. The highlight is the fabulous Royal Palace, which has been restored to look brand-spanking new. The result is a sumptuous riot of colours – boy, those Stewart's knew how to live! Tapestries, vaults, a statue of Robert the Bruce, and stirring rampart views from the castle's dominating bird's-eye vantage point complete the kingdom-come-hither allure.

☛ SEE IT ! *Head north from either Edinburgh or Glasgow and you can be in Stirling within an hour. Visit late afternoon to have the castle to yourself and leave time to explore Stirling's Old Town.*

429

Zócalo

MEXICO CITY'S BEATING HEART

MEXICO // Mexico City is cosmopolitan, bustling and huge, and the Zócalo is its beating heart. This vast square is flanked with power: the presidential palace, the Catedral Metropolitana, government offices, luxury shops and hotels. The enormous space at its centre is often full of life, with costumed dancers putting on displays that reference Aztec rituals. There are events here too – concerts, protests and an ice-skating rink – while during the Day of the Dead festivities the square is a mass of dressed-up humanity.

☛ SEE IT ! *Accommodation is plentiful nearby. Get here via Zócalo metro station.*

430

Nyungwe Forest National Park

CHIMPS IN DEEP FOREST

RWANDA // The vast rainforests of the African interior are largely off-limits, so this park is special. Nyungwe Forest, one of Africa's oldest, provides refuge for 13 species of primate (including habituated chimps and colobus monkeys), rich birdlife and a biodiversity seldom found elsewhere, making this an important conservation area. Whether hiking through this equatorial forest in search of our evolutionary kin, or just a waterfall, your inner Tarzan will be nurtured in Nyungwe.

☛ SEE IT ! *Visit Nyungwe in your own vehicle, rented (with driver) from Kigali. Bring wet-weather gear as it rains often.*

430

Above, a Batwa woman in Nyungwe village makes clay pottery. Right, a dancer in traditional costume in Mexico City's Zócalo.

429

433

431

St Fagans National History Museum

HISTORY BROUGHT TO LIFE

WALES // St Fagans provides a microcosm of life in Wales, a lesson in Welshness like no other. Boring history class this is not, however. In this living museum of more than 40 original buildings, you can peek inside still-smoky-scented 16th-century farmhouses, time-travel through miners' cottages and marvel at an ancient church that was moved here stone by stone. The whole display is anchored by a medieval castle worthy of its eclectic dominion.

☛ SEE IT ! *St Fagans is five miles west of Cardiff. Events include farmers markets, gardening sessions and craft demonstrations.*

432

Eisriesenwelt

ICE KINGDOM UNDER THE MOUNTAIN

AUSTRIA // If the Austrian tourist board told us that Eisriesenwelt inspired *Ice Age* the movie or Narnia's eternal winter, we'd believe them. Billed as the world's largest accessible ice caves, this glittering ice empire spans 30,000 sq m and 42km in length, with narrow passages burrowing deep into the heart of the mountains. A tour through its chambers of blue ice and cavernous, twinkling *Eispalast* (ice palace) is so startling it could freeze you in your tracks.

☛ SEE IT ! *The nearest town is Werfen, an easy day trip from Salzburg. Bring warm clothing and sturdy footwear year-round.*

433

Pafos Archaeological Site

ANCIENT GREEK CITY

CYPRUS // Sprawling Pafos Archaeological Site will fire the imagination of your inner Indiana Jones. It's a tantalising work in progress, as what you see is only a modest part of the 4th-century-BC ancient city and it is widely believed there are many treasures still to be discovered here. What a delicious thought. Besides playing explorer for the day, take time to enjoy the mesmerising collection of intricate mosaics and the stories they whisper of ancient Greek myths.

☛ SEE IT ! *The site is in the southerly resort of Pafos; there's a large free car park near the entrance west of Kato Pafos.*

434

437

434

Lavena
Coastal Walk

AMBLE IN PARADISE

FIJI // The most celebrated of Fiji's lush
walking trails, this 5km coastal walk has
all the eye-popping components of the
perfect wander in paradise. It follows the
rainforest edge along stunning white-sand
Lavena beach, passes peaceful villages,
crosses a rickety suspension bridge and
traverses an ancient valley. Just as the heat
begins to feel unbearable, the finale: a
gushing waterfall to dip in. It's like something
straight out of *Jurassic Park*.

🐾 SEE IT ! *Lavena is on Taveuni, joined
to the main island via flights that can be
cancelled at the hint of bad weather.*

435

Brandenburg
Gate

IMMORTAL PORTAL

Berlin, GERMANY // Intended as a monument
to peace when built in the late 18th century,
the Brandenburg Gate has since been hi-
jacked by several committed non-pacifists,
including Napoleon and the Nazis. During the
Cold War it shut for 28 years, epitomising the
division of Berlin, but in 1989 the gate burst
open when a wave of change swept through
its arches. A powerful symbol of freedom,
friendship and togetherness since – this is
the best rendezvous place in the city.

🐾 SEE IT ! *The gate's south wing houses a
tourist information centre, so this is a good
place to start a tour of the city.*

436

Amboseli
National Park

ELEPHANTS BELOW KILIMANJARO

KENYA // There's no better place to watch
elephants than Amboseli. Part of its appeal
lies in the setting: Africa's highest mountain,
Kilimanjaro (p210), is the backdrop for every
photo you'll take here, while, at dawn or dusk,
the clouds part and the elephants come out
to play. Better still, Amboseli has been spared
the worst of Kenya's poaching crisis and the
big-tusked beasts are remarkably tolerant of
humans. A full suite of predators, prey and
370 bird species round out the experience.

🐾 SEE IT ! *Rent a vehicle (with driver) from
Nairobi or Mombasa. Avoid the March to
May rainy season when wildlife disperses.*

438

437

Ifugao (Banaue) Rice Terraces

PHILIPPINES // Ancient, yet still in use. Rudimentary, yet sublime. The Ifugao rice terraces are impressive for many reasons. These mud-walled organic shelves, introduced by the Chinese 2000 years ago and built by the once-headhunting Ifugao, might not sound much but cast your eyes upon their chiselled beauty and be converted. The way they undulate for miles is hypnotic. But it's their positioning, carved into sharply sloping mountains, which is pure magic.

☛ SEE IT ! *Banaue is accessible from Manila by bus (nine hours). Best viewing is June to July and February to March.*

438

Carpathian National Nature Park

UKRAINE // The Carpathians are rural Ukraine at its best. The country's largest national park is 503 sq km of forest-clad mountains and sweeping alpine meadows that feel a continent away from the flatness of the steppe. Strike out in search of the atmospheric abandoned astronomical observatory, lead a charge up easily accessible Mt Hoverla (2061m), Ukraine's highest mountain, and hit the slopes for an unusual alternative to Europe's western resorts.

☛ SEE IT ! *Yaremche is a good base to find a hiking guide (advisable); Bukovel is Ukraine's glitziest ski resort.*

439

Segovia's Acueducto

SPAIN // That such a stunning monument to Roman grandeur has survived in the heart of a modern city is a miracle. Totally incongruous, Segovia's aqueduct rises from the streetscape like an Escher-esque mirage, repeating on and on ad infinitum. Erected here by the Romans in the 1st century AD, its 163 arches and neck-craning high point 28m above town will bowl you over. For a different perspective, climb the stairs next to the aqueduct from behind the tourist office.

☛ SEE IT ! *The fast train to Segovia whizzes northwest from the capital Madrid in less than 30 minutes.*

BEST
BEACHES

↓

Explore Colombia's
Caribbean coast at
Tayrona National
Park, where sandy
bays back onto
steamy jungle.

 page 128

↓

Bora Bora's ver-
sion of paradise
features thatched
bungalows on stilts
over azure water,
crystalline arcs of
sand, great diving,
and cocktail hour.

 page 112

↓

How about a beach
with a light-show?
Puerto Rico's Bio-
luminescent Bays
witness night-time
displays of phos-
phorescence.

 page 229

Ipanema beach

440

BRAZIL // Nothing quite compares to the experience of kicking off your Havaianas and strolling along Rio de Janeiro's most famous stretch of sand. Curving around from the base of the Dois Irmãos (Two Brothers Mountain) at the western tip of the beach, Ipanema is the city's great backyard, free and open to all, with amusements of all kinds: from jogging along the tiled promenade to sitting back, *agua de coco* (coconut water) in hand, and watching the foot-volley players work up a sweat.

Divided by a series of *postos* (lifeguard towers), each segment of the 2km beach is typically favoured by a different tribe: Posto 9 marks Garota de Ipanema, where Rio's most lithe bodies tend to migrate. The area is also known as the Cemitério dos Elefantes because of the handful of old leftists, hippies and artists who hang out there. In front of Rua Farme de Amoedo, the beach is known as Praia Farme, and is the stomping ground for gay society. Posto 8 is mostly the domain of favela kids. Wherever you roll out your towel, there's no denying that the birthplace of the string bikini is still as sexy as ever.

☛ SEE IT ! *Go early on weekends to stake out a prime people-watching spot on the sand; chairs and sun umbrellas can be hired at local barraca (beach stalls).*

441

Matmata

TUNISIA // *Star Wars* fans may come just for a filmic pilgrimage but this wacky village of underground pit houses is more than just the stage for Luke Skywalker's home. Due to the furnace heat, the Berbers who live here have long sought shelter from the sun by carving ingenious dwellings below the surface that famously resemble bomb craters. Today, many of the houses can be visited and also function as simple hotels. The most well-known dwelling is the Sidi Driss Hotel, which was used for interior shots of the Lars family homestead in *Star Wars* and is still littered with bits of the set left in place after filming finished. Roaming the lunarscape surface, which is pockmarked by troglodyte trenches, then spending the night cocooned in your very own cave is the closest you'll come on earth to the experience of sleeping in outer space, Luke Skywalker or not.

☛ SEE IT ! *Matmata has regular bus services from Tunis (eight hours) and frequent minibuses from the city of Gabès (45 minutes).*

441

442

442

Everglades National Park

USA // There is no wilderness in America quite like the Everglades. Called the 'River of Grass' by its initial Native American inhabitants, this is not just a wetland, or a swamp, or a lake, or a river, or a prairie, or a grassland – it is all of the above, twisted together into a series of soft horizons, long vistas and sunsets that stretch across your field of vision. You get to share the view with panthers, manatees and abundant alligators. The best way to explore this waterlogged wonderland is by kayak along the mangrove channels or, for a touch of backwoods chic, on a fan-powered airboat. There's more here than weeds and water; the Everglades spill out on the coral-fringed beaches of southern Florida, so you can finish with a relaxing bake on the sand.

☛ SEE IT ! *The three entrances to Everglades – Ernest Coe, Shark Valley and Gulf Coast – are all accessible from Miami by hire car.*

444

443

Sea of Galilee

BEACHES & BIBLE STORIES

ISRAEL // Why visit the Sea of Galilee? Oh, no reason. You might want to walk on the same shores as Jesus and the apostles maybe, but other than that... Israel's largest freshwater lake has more Bible references than a Billy Graham tour, and it's also a stunningly peaceful place to relax in the Mediterranean sunshine, due to its beaches, hiking trails, nature reserves and natural mineral springs. You probably won't be able to recreate Jesus' miracle of walking on the water (though you might stand a chance nearby in the Dead Sea), but you can follow the so-called Jesus Trail, lunching at Tabgha (where fishes and loaves fed the five thousand), searching for divine inspiration at Capernaum, then recharging in the hot springs at Tiberias.

☛ SEE IT ! *A 50km drive inland from Haifa to Tiberias will deposit you on the lakeshore; bring a bike or hire car, or hike the Jesus Trail.*

444

Ostrog Monastery

MONTENEGRO'S MIRACLE MONASTERY

MONTENEGRO // There's something special about churches in caves; as if everyone secretly longs to be a hermit. The spectacular complex at Ostrog Manastir was pressed into a rocky cliff face by gravity-defying monks in the 17th century, and it has grown into the most important pilgrimage destination in Montenegro, attracting up to a million visitors a year. You won't get a silent spiritual retreat here, but you will get a potent sense of shared belief, a tangible feeling of history, and a couple of items for your chintzy souvenir collection. Fill your bottle with sacred spring water at the Holy Trinity Church, before you hike up to 'Sveti Vasilije's miracle' – the magnificent upper monastery, spread across two natural caverns high above the Zeta Valley.

☛ SEE IT ! *Podgorica to Nikšić buses pass the turn-off to Ostrog; walk or take a cab to the monastery and stay overnight in summer.*

445

Kinderdijk Windmills

NETHERLANDS // For every backpacker seeking coffeeshop enlightenment in Rotterdam, there's an enthusiastic cyclist looking for the master painter's vision of the Netherlands: serene canals, fields of flowers and windmills. Indeed, Kinderdijk was considered so quintessentially Dutch that Unesco added it to the World Heritage list. There's nowhere better to recharge than these gently shifting marshlands, where the swish of sails and the chirp of birds is all that breaks the silence. If you venture past the first couple of mills, you can leave the day trippers behind and enjoy the stark beauty of Kinderdijk, with the windmills rising above the marshes and waterways like sentinels.

☛ SEE IT ! *Kinderdijk is 15km east of Rotterdam; come on Saturday in July and August to see most of the windmills in operation.*

446

445

446

Church of Sveti Jovan Bigorksi

MACEDONIA // There's no shortage of intriguingly titled churches in the Ultimate Travelist: Sveti is the Balkan word for saint, and Sveti Jovan Bigorksi is the most picture perfect of the many monasteries across the Macedonian countryside. Founded in 1020 during the Byzantine Empire, this basilica nestles against a backdrop of forested hills, the trees of which provided the wood for the church's famous iconostasis, a wonder of the Orthodox world. This colossal frieze depicting biblical scenes is adorned with more than 700 human and animal figures engaged in an astonishing array of activities, carved by local craftsmen Makarije Frčkovski and the brothers Filipovski between 1829 and 1835. Upon finishing, the carvers allegedly flung their tools into the Radika River – ensuring that the secret of their artistic genius would be washed away forever.

☛ SEE IT ! *Sveti Jovan Bigorksi is secreted away in Mavrovo National Park between Debar and Gostivar; you'll need your own transport.*

448

447 448 449

Hal Saflieni Hypogeum

MALTA // The limestone beneath Malta is such that ancient carvers managed to hollow out a whole underground city with only stone tools. But the Hal Saflieni Hypogeum was a city for the dead – more than 7000 bodies are believed to have been interred here, piled in halls, chambers and passageways. These tombs were discovered by accident by workmen digging foundations in 1902, and visiting feels likes stepping into a mysterious world, hidden below Paola's modern streets.

☛ SEE IT ! *Visits are by tour only; tickets must be pre-booked from the Hypogeum or the National Museum of Archaeology.*

Taipei 101

TAIWAN // Towering above the city like the gigantic bamboo shoot it was designed to resemble, Taipei 101 is impossible to miss. At just 508m high, it has had to drop its claim to be the 'world's tallest building', but when you see the vertigo-inducing view from the 89th-floor observatory, that won't matter. What marks Taipei 101 out from other towers is how much taller it is than surrounding buildings; think Saruman's Tower in *Lord of the Rings* and you won't be far off the mark.

☛ SEE IT ! *Taipei 101 rises above the heart of downtown; a pressure-controlled lift zips up to the observation deck in 40 seconds.*

Si Phan Don

LAOS // Si Phan Don (Four Thousand Islands) is where Laos truly becomes the land of the lotus eaters: an archipelago of islands where the pendulum of time swings at half speed and life drifts by as lazily as the murky waters of the Mekong River. Some islands are backpacker playgrounds, but others are rocky hummocks marooned by waterfalls or spits of sand dotted with fishing villages. Here you'll find inner and outer peace swinging in hammocks and watching the river flow by.

☛ SEE IT ! *There are said to be 4000 islands, but Don Det and Don Khon have the pick of the accommodation and activities.*

450

Church on the Spilled Blood
Church or ice-cream sundae?

↓

RUSSIA // Much more than a copycat St Basil's, St Petersburg's Church on the Spilled Blood was founded in bloodshed, raised by tsars, dressed in gold and crowned by some of the most outrageous church towers ever humanly conceived.

Its picturesque setting, in a genteel neighbourhood on the Griboedov Canal, belies the violence that marked its foundation. On this site in 1881, Emperor Alexander II was assassinated by radicals, setting back the reform of power in Russia by decades.

☞ SEE IT ! *The Church is an amble along the canal from Nevsky Prospekt metro stop.*

451 Archipiélago de San Blas

PANAMA'S SECRET ISLANDS

PANAMA // Tumbling off the Caribbean coast of Panama like scattered gems, the San Blas islands are the tropical home of the Kuna people, who follow a life of alluring simplicity as they fish the rich waters of the Caribbean. A slow stream of travellers have started following their lead, finding a mostly untouched vision of the Caribbean on the islands that run west from Cartí almost all the way to the Colombian border. In other words, it's ideal for people who prefer not to share their island paradise with a crowd.

Part of the Comarca de Kuna Yala, this is the place to find out what the Caribbean was like before the beach bars, plantations and empire builders. You'll find languorous islands where the ghosts of pirates and tribal chieftains drift among the palms. There's plenty to see below the water, of course – the pristine reefs swarm with tropical fish.

☛ SEE IT ! *Cartí town is the entrance to the archipelago. Boats hop between the islands; Hostel Mamallena in Panama City offers advice.*

452 Kyevo-Pecherska Lavra

MYSTERY, MUMMIES, MAGIC

UKRAINE // You want icons? You want shining golden domes? You want mummified monks? You got them. Set in lush, green grounds beside the Dnipro River in Kiev, the Lavra is the definitive Eastern Orthodox monastery, a tight cluster of golden domes and soaring arches graced with mosaics of the saints. Founded by tunnelling monks – who now spend the centuries in the catacombs below the lower church – this baroque beauty is a living vision of imperial Russia.

Like other Russian – and former Russian – treasure houses, the Lavra hides genuine treasure, in this case a magnificent hoard of Scythian gold, gathered from the tombs of the ancient horsemen of the steppes. The real surprise, though, lies in the basement, where the monastery's founders lie desiccated but preserved in elegant coffins in winding passages that bring to mind the private vault of the family Dracula. Mobs of pilgrims fingering rosaries and kissing the mummies and icons only add to the atmosphere.

☛ SEE IT ! *The Lavra is accessible by metro from downtown Kiev; disembark at Dnipro or Arsenalna and walk south through the park.*

454

453

Horton Plains & World's End

WHERE THE WORLD (WELL, SRI LANKA) ENDS

SRI LANKA // Horton Plains is a beautiful, silent, strange world, lorded over by two of Sri Lanka's highest mountains, Kirigalpotta (2395m) and Totapola (2359m). In fact, the famous 'plains' are actually a plateau soaring 2000m above the surrounding countryside, coming to a sudden halt at World's End, where the landscape plunges dramatically to the forested lowlands. Come for otherworldly landscapes, eerie cloud-forests and giddying views over toy-town tea plantations.

🐛 SEE IT ! *Haputale is the portal to Horton Plains and most people come by chartered taxi, though a hill railway climbs to Ohiya.*

454

Mt Roraima

ENTER THE LOST WORLD

VENEZUELA/BRAZIL/GUYANA // If there were a lost world, it would be here, on the looming tabletop mountains of Venezuela. A soaring slab of limestone marking the boundary between three countries, Mt Roraima is Precambrian in nature and Precambrian in atmosphere, an alien world inhabited by flora and fauna found nowhere else. The best approach is on foot, via a challenging trek from Paraitepui village, or via house-air-balloon, according to the Disney film *Up*.

🐛 SEE IT ! *Trekking trails to Mt Roraima start at Paraitepui, a two-hour drive from Santa Elena; local guides can arrange.*

455

Nizwa Fort

OMAN'S MOST FORMIDABLE FORT

OMAN // The Omani desert bristles with forts, but Nizwa Fort is the real deal. What marks it out is not its many battlements and bastions, but its maze of chambers, corridors and staircases that offer a tantalising glimpse of life in the days of sultans and djinns. Robbed of a living garden by nature, the desert-dwellers of Nizwa painted one on the wooden ceilings of the fortress chambers; sit back and imagine yourself sipping sherbet in your finest pair of curly-toed slippers.

🐛 SEE IT ! *Nizwa sprawls around a series of streambeds about 140km west of Muscat; the fort looms dramatically over downtown.*

456

Bucovina Monasteries
Wall-painting wow!

↓

ROMANIA // Not content with covering the interiors of their monasteries in mesmerising frescoes, the monks of southern Bucovina extended their creative talents to the outside walls as well. That any of this remains after 500 years of Romanian winters, Hapsburg squabbling and Communist neglect is akin to a miracle. To wander around these time capsules is to step back into ancient Byzantium, when the miracles of the saints were communicated to the illiterate masses in vivid pigment.

☛ SEE IT ! *The monasteries lie off the tourist circuit: book a car or a tour to visit those around Suceava.*

457 458 459

L'Anse aux Meadows

SO THE VIKINGS DID DISCOVER AMERICA?

CANADA // Who hasn't, in secret, longed to be a Viking? On this barren moor at the northern tip of Newfoundland, you can at least see how they lived. The most compelling evidence of the Viking discovery of the Americas, L'Anse aux Meadows is a crude cluster of earth houses built by Norse explorers in AD 1000. Three restored versions are inhabited by dress-up Vikings who act out Viking life. It could be tacky, but with the desolate setting, it ends up rather stirring.

☛ SEE IT ! *L'Anse aux Meadows is 51km from St Anthony; hire a car or rent a taxi and drive north until you run out of road.*

Black Forest

GERMANY'S FAIRY-TALE FOREST

GERMANY // Let's dispel some myths. The Schwarzwald (Black Forest) isn't black, it's green. The name comes from the dense, brooding forest canopy – and when you see it, you'll understand the inspiration for fairy-tales such as *Hansel and Gretel* and *Little Red Riding Hood*. In this wooded wonderland, you can walk and cycle in unspoilt nature or explore postcard-pretty villages comprising houses that resemble giant versions of the cuckoo clocks the Black Forest is famous for.

☛ SEE IT ! *Freudenstadt is a great base; roam to pretty Freiburg, cuckoo-clock capital Triberg and charming St Blasien.*

Mt Fuji

JAPAN'S MUST-SEE MOUNTAIN

JAPAN // Seeing Mt Fuji in the flesh is like stepping into a Japanese woodcut. This volcano was the muse for Katsushika Hokusai, the print-maker who created enduring images of imperial Japan. Climbing to the barren crater is a Japanese rite of passage, but you'll have to share the experience, and the sense of reward that comes from reaching the rim, with a crowd. Many are content to contemplate the mountain from the Fuji-goko lakes or the cherry orchards of Fujiyoshida.

☛ SEE IT ! *Trekking season is July to August. Start at one of four '5th stations': Gotemba, Fujinomiya, Subashiri or Kawaguchiko.*

460

The Mighty Volcano (Piton de la Fournaise)

MORDOR IN THE INDIAN OCEAN

Réunion Island, FRANCE // The French island of Réunion owes a lot to the volcano known as Piton de la Fournaise (literally, 'peak of the furnace'). For one thing, a significant proportion of the island spewed from its summit as molten magma. Despite the paradisial island setting, this is one of the world's most active volcanoes, with more than 100 catalogued eruptions since 1640. Even if you don't get treated to the full fountaining magma lightshow, there's plenty of sulphur and brimstone to go round, particularly if you trek across the tortured lava on the volcano's flanks. If you've seen the depiction of Mordor in Peter Jackson's *Lord of the Rings*, you'll have some idea of what to expect...

☛ SEE IT ! *The village of Bourg-Murat is the gateway; to get personal with the Piton, trek to the Dolomieu, the most active cone.*

460

461

461

Mt Kenya

HIT GLACIAL EQUATORIAL HIGHS

KENYA // Sometimes it's better to be second. When Mt Kenya was the highest point in Africa it was a rather boring affair, with predictably gentle slopes and a simple conical summit. But glaciation devastated that drab exterior, leaving an enthralling variety of valleys and jagged peaks. Multiday treks through this ever-changing environment are challenging and rewarding, with the summit of Point Lenana (4985m) being most trekkers' aim. Spend a day on the Summit Circuit that circumnavigates the main peaks at an average elevation of 4500m. A highlight is looking up the vertical Diamond Couloir to the Gates of Mist between the two highest summits, Nelion (5188m) and Batian (5199m). It may lack Kilimanjaro's street cred, but Kili hogs the crowds due to its 'tallest' status, leaving Mt Kenya as a hugely enjoyable climb.

☛ SEE IT ! *Mt Kenya is less than 200km from Nairobi. Climb in dry season: mid-January to late February and late August to September.*

462

Kalon Minaret

MIGHTY MOSQUE, MIGHTY MINARET

UZBEKISTAN // Few spots capture the imagination like the Kalon (Kalyan) Minaret, which towers above Arslan Khan's great mosque at Bukhara like an intricately inlaid candlestick. Wrapped in delicate bands of ornamentation, the minaret was once the tallest building in central Asia, and its grandeur even swayed the heart of Genghis Khan, who spared it during his devastating rampage across the steppes. The awe-inspiring vistas over the umber-coloured city of Bukhara from the top are now off-limits, but no matter – the views towards the minaret are just as impressive.

Among other firsts, this was the first building in Central Asia to use the distinctive blue tiles that were later scattered across the empire by Timur. Today, standing in the shadow of the Kalon mosque's towering blue-tiled facade feels like standing in the shadow of history.

🖝 SEE IT ! *The Kalon Minaret is at the heart of old Bukhara; combine with a trip to the astonishing 'Ark' fortress, Bukhara's oldest building.*

463

Trakai Castle

LIVE LIKE A KNIGHT IN LITHUANIA

LITHUANIA // There are certain rules for a fairy-tale castle. It must be brooding and ancient. It must have towers complete with roofs like witches' hats. And it absolutely must have a moat. The island castle at Trakai in Lithuania ticks all the boxes. The approach to this impenetrable-looking 14th-century fortress follows a wooden causeway that hops from island to island as it crosses Lake Galvė (you can almost hear the clip-clop of horses' hooves).

Appropriately, the castle was besieged by everyone from the Teutonic Knights to the Muscovites before falling into forlorn ruin during WWI and WWII. The castle has been impressively restored today, and its halls and chambers echo with the ghosts of its long and convoluted history. To see Trakai Castle at its most picturesque, visit in winter when the lake freezes all the way to the peninsula, from where the journey back to town takes the visitor past museums and the remains of the even older Peninsula Castle.

🖝 SEE IT ! *A series of causeways zigzags out to the castle from the northern tip of the peninsula; from here, you can stroll back to town.*

464

465

El-Jem

TUNISIA // What did the Romans ever do for us? Well, at El-Jem, they built one of the wonders of North Africa. In its 3rd-century heyday, the great amphitheatre at El-Jem could accommodate about 35,000 spectators, who bayed for blood as gladiators pitted muscle and metal against wild animals and each other for the pleasure of the Roman emperor. This was the third largest amphitheatre in the Roman world, and it survives largely intact, a stone exclamation mark to the legacy of Rome.

Unlike the Colosseum in Rome, on which it was almost certainly modelled, the theatre at El-Jem soars above the surrounding city, which is characterised by low-rise, flat-roofed Arabic houses. You can still imagine the adrenaline that must have surged as wild beasts were released onto the floor in the central arena. In case any of this looks familiar, it should do – the amphitheatre had cameos in both *Gladiator* and *Life of Brian*.

🐾 SEE IT ! *The amphitheatre dominates the centre of the Tunisian town of El-Jem (El-Djem), an easy day-trip from Sousse or Sfax.*

Schilthorn

SWITZERLAND // Only in Switzerland would they put a revolving restaurant on top of a 2970m mountain. Reached by an epic cable-car ride from Stechelberg or Birg, or an arduous hike from Gimmelwald, Schilthorn is an engineering marvel, surrounded by the natural engineering of colliding continents. The 360-degree, 200-peak panorama is best appreciated from the Skyline view platform or the uniquely Swiss Piz Gloria revolving restaurant. On a clear day, you can take in an epic sweep from Titlis round to Mont Blanc and across to the Black Forest in Germany.

Yet some visitors seem more preoccupied with practising their delivery of the line, 'The name's Bond, James Bond', because a few scenes from *On Her Majesty's Secret Service* were shot here in 1968–69. We say forget the spies and concentrate on the views.

🐾 SEE IT ! *Cable cars run from Stechelberg, via Gimmelwald, Mürren and Birg; or you can hike it in five hours from Gimmelwald.*

Griffith Observatory

466

USA // More than just a monument, the Griffith Observatory is a Los Angeles icon. Plonked on the slopes of Mt Hollywood, this gorgeous art deco institution was a film location waiting to happen. Indeed, it features in dozens of Hollywood movies, from *Rebel Without a Cause* to *Transformers* and *The Terminator*. The sci-fi connection is actually tied to science fact – the observatory has been scanning the stars for evidence of life beyond earth since before WWII.

Today, this essential stop-off on the movie-location tour of LA boasts the world's most advanced star projector, which uses lasers to project a tour of the cosmos on to the aluminium interior of the observatory dome. Visitors can get a first-hand glimpse of outer space through the Zeist Telescope in the east dome, and get hands-on with a science-lab's worth of astronomical paraphernalia. On this trip to space at least, you get to be more than just a spectator.

Don't forget to look down as well as up. The views over downtown Los Angeles at sunset are the stuff that dreams, and movies, are made of.

☛ SEE IT ! *Hike through Griffith Park to the Observatory from Fern Dell or the Greek Theater, or ride the bus from Vermont/Sunset Metro Red Line station.*

467

Tower of London

ENGLAND'S CROWNING GLORY

ENGLAND // If you manage to keep your head during the queuing for tickets, you can witness the spot where two of Henry VIII's wives lost theirs. Raised by William the Conqueror to enforce his rule over the unruly English, the Tower of London is not one castle but a succession, built on top of and in and out of one another. An astonishing number of pivotal events in English history took place inside its walls – Sir Walter Raleigh was imprisoned here, and the princes Edward V and Richard of Shrewsbury were bumped off by Uncle Richard in the Bloody Tower. Then there's the Royal Armoury, with King Henry VIII's (probably exaggerated) codpiece, and the Crown Jewels, an astonishing collection of frippery with enough diamonds to buy several quite large countries. More recently, artists Paul Cummins and Tom Piper filled its moat with ceramic poppies to commemorate WWI.

☛ SEE IT ! *The tower dominates the north bank of the Thames near Tower Bridge; take a free guided tour led by the cheery Beefeaters.*

468

Trinity College

UNIVERSITY GREENS

Dublin, IRELAND // If it were possible to acquire intelligence by osmosis, then Trinity College would be a great place to hang out, as its list of alumni includes Jonathan Swift, Edmund Burke, Oliver Goldsmith, Oscar Wilde and Samuel Beckett. The gorgeous Georgian buildings and 16-hectares of greens and grounds that sprawl around the prestigious Dublin university still combine to create one of the city's loveliest areas for strolling, even if there's no cerebral kickback. Trinity, granted a charter by Elizabeth I in 1592, is home to the world famous *Book of Kells*, an illustrated manuscript produced in the 8th or 9th century. Other interesting antiquities here include a rare copy of the Proclamation of the Irish Republic, read by Pádraig Pearse at the start of the Easter Rising, and the 600-year-old harp of Brian Ború.

☛ SEE IT ! *It's free to meander through the university's expansive grounds, which are open daily between 8am and 10pm.*

469
Capital Castles

SMALL NATION, BIG CASTLE COLLECTION

LUXEMBOURG // For such a tiny nation, Luxembourg has more than its fair share of fortifications. The crude Bock Casemates fortress, raised by Count Siegfried in AD 983, was superseded over the centuries by a string of other forts and castles, each tasked with protecting the fabulous wealth of the Duchy. Today, wandering Capital Castles is a tour though the ages, and an atmospheric reminder that there's more to Luxembourg than tax scandals and Eurocrats.

☛ SEE IT ! *Luxembourg city only covers 50 sq km, so it's easy to get from castle to castle; start at Bock Casemates on Rue Sigefroi.*

470
Camp Nou

FOOTBALL'S CATALAN HOME

SPAIN // There's a hint of the Roman amphitheatre about Futbol Club Barcelona's Camp Nou stadium, particularly when tens of thousands of home fans start up a chant. It is an epic arena to take in a game, not least because the supporters own the place, literally, thanks to an association of 170,000 paying members. Football fans unable to see a match can get a taste of the excitement at the museum, packed with memorabilia, and take a tour of the stadium.

☛ SEE IT ! *Camp Nou is within walking distance of several metro stops; buy tickets for matches in advance from FC Barcelona.*

471
Panama Canal

SHORT CUT FROM THE ATLANTIC TO THE PACIFIC

PANAMA // The argument between Panama and Suez about who has the best canal will probably never be won, but Panama has the upper hand when it comes to atmosphere. Stretching 80km from Panama City on the Pacific coast to Colón on the Atlantic coast, the Canal provides passage for nearly 14,000 ocean-going vessels each year; seeing a massive transporter nudge its way through the narrow canal with vast tracts of virgin jungle on both sides is a humbling sight.

☛ SEE IT ! *The only way to really see the Canal is by boat; cruises run from Panama City through the locks to Miraflores lake.*

473

472

Bay Islands

HONDURAS // Mainland Honduras may have dropped off the bucket list thanks to soaring crime rates but, out in the bay, the islands of Roatán, Utila and Guanaja are as idyllic as ever. In times past, these palm-flecked Caribbean isles hosted everyone from Christopher Columbus to a bloodthirsty gaggle of French, English and Dutch pirates. Today, you're more likely to encounter backpackers enjoying the blissed-out vibe and some of Central America's best scuba diving.

☛ SEE IT ! *Fly there from La Ceiba on the mainland, which has ferries to Roatán and Utila (head to Trujillo for a boat to Guanaja).*

473

Monet's Garden

MONET'S CORNUCOPIA OF COLOUR

Giverny, FRANCE // No matter your impression of Impressionism, you'll be moved by the loveliness of Monet's personal gardens. You'll recognise settings from some of the painter's famous works as you stroll the sweet-smelling blooms. In spring, daffodils, tulips, rhododendrons, wisteria and irises appear, followed by poppies and lilies; by June, nasturtiums, roses and sweet peas flower; and in September, the gardens are a riot of dahlias, sunflowers and hollyhocks.

☛ SEE IT ! *Tiny Giverny is easy to navigate on foot; the Fondation Claude Monet opens to the garden from, aptly, Rue Claude Monet.*

474

Grouse Mountain

VIEW VANCOUVER LIKE EAGLES DO

CANADA // This mountaintop playground offers sweeping views of downtown Vancouver shimmering in the water below. In summer, the Skyride gondola gives access to everything from lumberjack shows to hiking trails and a grizzly bear refuge. It's touristy, but with this much fun on offer, who's complaining? For the best view, ride the elevator up the 20-storey turbine tower to the Eye of the Wind's panoramic viewing pod; that'll get your camera itching for action.

☛ SEE IT ! *The Skyride cable car takes just eight minutes from Vancouver; buses zip from downtown to the lower Skyride station.*

477

475

Graceland

Memphis, USA // The last residence and resting place of Elvis Aaron Presley, Graceland rivals Jerusalem as a pilgrimage destination. A stream of devotees files through its music-note gates to gaze on The King's astonishing collection of sequinned jumpsuits, Hawaiian kitsch and gold records. Amid the sentimental displays and excess chintz are moments of genuine emotion, particularly at Elvis' graveside, where tears flow as freely as the rock'n'roll hits on the in-house radio station.

☛ SEE IT ! *There's more to Memphis than Graceland; make time for a blues show on Beale Street, where BB King cut his teeth.*

476

To Sua Ocean Trench

SAMOA // A sapphire in a sea of emeralds, To Sua Ocean Trench is mesmerising. There are actually two sinkhole-like depressions, dressed in tropical greenery and linked by an aquamarine pool that flows via a hidden channel from the sea. After clambering 20-odd metres down a wooden ladder, swim under a broad arch of rock into the hidden second pool, serenaded by droplets hitting the water surface while enjoying a serene sense of being removed from the world.

☛ SEE IT ! *To Sua is tucked away on Upolo's southeast coast; look for the faded sign on the Main South Coast Road, near Lotofaga.*

477

Plaza Mayor

CUBA // The sleepy heart of Trinidad, Plaza Mayor is an enchanting collection of civic buildings and palm trees that oozes colonial charm. Anywhere else, this elegant square would be crammed with traffic, but in Trinidad, more sedate rhythms play, though you may spot the odd vintage American jalopy ferrying just-married couples. Take a seat on a park bench and watch the city go by; you might even get invited to dance at the energetic socials that fill the square after dark.

☛ SEE IT ! *In this heart of colonial Trinidad you can stroll at leisure: at first light for photo ops, or at sunset to test your dancing shoes.*

Flanders Fields

478

BELGIUM/FRANCE // Even after a century, it's hard to conceive the tragic events that put Flanders Fields on the map. During four blood-soaked years along the Western Front, entire cities of young men perished amid the mud, barbed wire and trenches.

These days, the sites of such notorious engagements as the Second Battle of Ypres and the Battle of Passchendaele stand as poignant reminders of the ultimate price of war and the tragic, hopeless loss of almost a whole generation.

There's no single place called Flanders Fields – the name actually comes from a haunting poem by Canadian physician and soldier John McCrae – but the war cemeteries and memorials that straddle the French–Belgian border around the city of Ypres still stand as silent witnesses to the unimaginable events that took place here. In addition to statues and arches, and endless avenues of neat white crosses, abundant red poppies bloom across the countryside every summer like the ghosts of the fallen.

It's humbling stuff that may leave you reaching for a strong Belgian beer – thankfully readily available – by the end of the day.

SEE IT ! Ypres is the gateway to the Western Front, and its Menin Gate is engraved with the names of 54,896 of the fallen.

479

479 Pol-e Khaju

THE SHAH'S BRIDGE

IRAN // Arguably the finest of Esfahan's bridges, this arched marvel was constructed by Shah Abbas II circa 1650 to span the Zayandeh River, but it was always as much of a meeting place as it was a bearer of traffic. As well as linking the Islamic and Zoroastrian quarters of the city, and acting as a weir to manage the flow of the Zayandeh, the bridge served as a public meeting house for the great and the good, as well as a personal retreat for the Shah to enable him to look out over his pleasure gardens.

As you wander the terraced arcades today, you can still see original paintings and tiles, and the remains of stone seats built for Shah Abbas II to sit on and admire the views. In the centre, the pavilion built exclusively for his pleasure is now open to all and it's a fine spot to contemplate the passage of centuries.

☛ SEE IT ! *The Pol-e Khaju stands in the heart of old Esfahan; at night, the illuminated arches are brilliantly reflected in the river.*

480 Sanduny Baths

MOSCOW'S BEAUTIFUL BANYA

RUSSIA // It has been said that some of the most secretive deals in Moscow are struck during baths in the elegant Sanduny Banya, the oldest and most luxurious public bathhouse in the Russian capital. The stately Gothic Room falls somewhere between steam-room and English gentlemen's club, and the surreal effect is only compounded by the cup-shaped felt hats that are worn by patrons in order to protect their hair from being frazzled. Then there is the aristocratic main shower room, which has more than just a hint of Roman baths about it.

Visiting Sanduny is a costly experience, especially if you rent the essential items – a sheet to wrap yourself in, that enigmatic felt hat and a pair of slippers – but perhaps there are few experiences so quintessentially Russian as being lashed with birch twigs by strangers in a hot room, then sitting down in a felt bonnet to a cup of hot tea from a porcelain cup and saucer.

☛ SEE IT ! *The Sanduny Banya sits discreetly at Neglinnaya ulitsa 14, north of the Moscow Architectural Institute.*

481

Cañón del Colca
Truly grand canyon

↓

PERU // It's not just Colca's depth that makes it so fantastical, it's the shifts in its mood. There are more scenery changes along its 100km passage than there are in most European countries; from the steppe of Sibayo, through the ancient farm terraces of Yanque and Chivay, into the steep-sided canyon proper beyond Cabanaconde.

The world's second-deepest canyon is twice as deep as the Grand Canyon. And it is blessed with history and culture; you may bump into descendants of the Cabana and the Collagua people, who've called this wonder home for centuries.

☞ SEE IT ! *Start at Chivray, 160km from Arequipa.*

482 483 484

Spiš Castle

SPOOKY, SLOVAKIAN & SPECTACULAR

SLOVAKIA // You want drama? Scale? History? Spiš Castle has them all by the cartload. Heralding from as early as the 13th century, this vast complex of roofless halls and sundered battlements is one of Europe's largest castles, spread across the hillside above the village of Spišské Podhradie. With its black, empty windows and ruined towers, it casts an eerie spell when viewed from a distance; once inside, the views across the surrounding landscape are even more spectacular.

☞ SEE IT ! *Spiš Castle is 1km east of Spišské Podhradie, an uphill hike above the spur rail station; audio tours bring the past into focus.*

Aletsch Glacier

THE DEFINITIVE RIVER OF ICE

SWITZERLAND // This nation has glaciers like other countries have motorways, but even here, the Aletsch is special. The longest, most voluminous glacier in the Alps is a 23km-long swirl of crevassed ice that slices past thundering falls, jagged rock spires and pine forests from Jungfrau in the Bernese Oberland to the edge of the Rhône. This river of ice is a year-round winter playground; seek the best views at the Konkordia and Hollandia huts, run by the Swiss Alpine Club.

☞ SEE IT ! *Start your journey to the Aletsch Glacier at Jungfraujoch railway station, served by train from Interlaken.*

Mt Ararat

A SUITABLE RESTING PLACE FOR AN ARK

TURKEY // The twin peaks of Mt Ararat have figured in legends since time began. Ottomans and Armenians idolised its mysterious, snowcapped summits, and Christians have looked to Ararat as the last resting place of Noah's Ark. Today, climbers strain for the summit, while less ambitious travellers content themselves with the arid landscapes on the lower slopes. For the definitive Ararat view, head for the ancient monastery of Khor Virap on the Armenian plains.

☞ SEE IT ! *To climb Ararat, arrange a guide and obtain a permit in Turkey; ascents start at Doğubayazıt, close to the Iranian border.*

485

485
Stingray City

Grand Cayman, CAYMAN ISLANDS // Like an ocean version of an aquarium petting tank, Stingray City offers the chance to get within touching distance of southern stingrays on their own turf. In water this shallow, you don't even have to dive to enjoy one of the Caribbean's great wildlife encounters. The origin of this experience was a happy accident; fishermen used to clean their catch on this sandbank and rays began to associate the sounds of boat engines with food.

🐟 SEE IT ! *Dive boats and catamaran trips to Stingray City leave from Seven Mile Beach to tour Grand Cayman's idyllic North Sound.*

486
Foteviken Viking Reserve

SWEDEN // If you mourn the passing of big hairy men in longboats, find solace here, a fascinating reconstruction of a late-Viking Age village, complete with working villagers, who live as the Vikings did, eschewing most modern conveniences and adhering to old traditions, laws and religions, even after the last tourist has left for the day. For visitors, it's a chance to visualise a lifestyle lost in legend; the residents of Foteviken are just reconnecting with their Viking roots.

🐟 SEE IT ! *The Reserve is on the edge of Höllviken, south of Malmö; Viking Week in late June has a market and warrior training.*

487
Wawel Castle

Krakow, POLAND // The political and cultural centre of Poland until the late 16th century, Wawel Castle is a potent symbol of national identity. It was home to the kings of Poland and a succession of rampaging armies, each of which paused for a spot of remodelling before being ejected by the next invading empire. Today, the castle looks as if the last king just rode out of the gates, thanks to decades of restoration, which continued even during the turmoil of WWI and WWII.

🐟 SEE IT ! *The castle is tucked into a bend on the Vistula River in Old Krakow; entry is via a complex time-limited ticket system.*

488

📷

A portrait of a priest at the church of Abreha we Atsbeha, a well-known Tigray church, 18km west of Wukro.

488

Rock-Hewn Churches of Tigray

ETHIOPIA // Tigray's churches reek of mystery and adventure, and several require visitors to have nerves of steel. Carved into mountaintops and sheer cliffs, they were virtually unknown to the outside world until the mid-1960s. Some think these remote locations were used to avoid Muslim raiders, others believe the lofty perches close the distance to God. Either way, their confines are covered in frescoes that date back over a millennia. Outside is one hell of a view.

☛ SEE IT ! *Mekele is a good base, linked by air to Addis Ababa. Visit October to February.*

489

Isla Mujeres

MEXICO // Cancún has the bright lights and bling, but those in the know prefer the blissful Isla Mujeres (Island of Women), a brushstroke of sand in a sea of turquoise out in the bay. Sure, the island has its share of tacky gift shops, but folks still get around by golf cart, and the crushed-coral beaches are even better than at Cozumel and Holbox. As for the turquoise-blue water of Isla Mujeres, you really have to see it for yourself (preferably with scuba tanks or a mask and snorkel).

☛ SEE IT ! *Ferries run to Isla Mujeres from Puerto Juárez or Gran Puerto near Cancún.*

490

Fingal's Cave

SCOTLAND // It sounds like something from *The Hobbit* and has inspired Pink Floyd and Mendelssohn. Even the boat trip to Fingal's Cave is an adventure: you may see eagles and whales before the island of Staffa comes into view. The cave, reached by a path cut into the rock, is cathedral-like, its interior marked with hexagonal basalt pillars. Perhaps they were created by volcanic activity, perhaps by the same hero who built the Giant's Causeway (p109). Either way, it's a magical trip.

☛ SEE IT ! *View Fingal's Cave on a boat tour from the Isle of Mull or Oban.*

491

Leaning Tower of Pisa

ITALY // Although we aspire to it, most people find perfection quite dull. If the Torre di Pisa hadn't been built on dodgy foundations in 1173, and had stayed pointing skywards, then it might have been just another vanilla campanile – albeit an exquisite one. Give it a tipsy lilt, however, and *voila*! A unique attraction that people travel from around the world to see, climb and pose in front of, pretending to prop it up in playful photos.

☛ SEE IT ! *Queues can be long – book early and have picnic in the grassy Piazza dei Miracoli (Square of Miracles).*

492

Orheiul Vechi

MOLDOVA // Carved into a limestone cliff in a rocky curve in the Răut River, the Orheiul Vechi monastery complex is Moldova's most haunting and picturesque sight. Orthodox monks hollowed out this warren of caverns in the 13th century, and the surrounding hillsides are dotted with historical relics, from Tatar mosques to time-scarred fortresses. Stay in the monastery HQ, as guests of the monks who reoccupied the complex in 1996.

☛ SEE IT ! *Buses run from Chişinău to Orhei on to Trebujeni (Orheiul Vechi's local name); stay in the monastery, or nearby in Butuceni.*

493

Musée Océanographique de Monaco

MONACO // If you lose in Monaco's casinos, you can plot a watery fate for those croupiers at the Musée Océanographique, where sharks patrol a turquoise lagoon and a giant octopus writhes across the ceiling. As fascinating as the displays is the building, a baroque revival palace that seems to grow from a cliff-face. The Oceanographic Institute has been pioneering sea exploration since 1910; Jacques Cousteau was a director.

☛ SEE IT ! *The Musée rises handsomely on Avenue Saint-Martin, east of Fontvieille Marina; see it from the harbour on a cruise.*

494 Oslo Opera House

ICE-COOL DESIGN ICON

NORWAY // The jewel in the Norwegian capital's design crown, the Oslo Opera House is that rarest of things – a piece of modern architecture that actually resembles the source that allegedly inspired it, in this case a shimmering glacier carving into the Oslofjord. The effect is made still more convincing by vast slabs of Italian marble that slide, ice-like, into the waters of the bay.

As well as attracting hordes of opera and ballet fans, the building has become one of Oslo's favourite places simply to sit and admire the view. Although impressive at any time, the opera house is probably at its most magical during the winter months when snow provides it with a gleaming coat and the surrounding harbour fills with sparkling sheets of ice. Before you venture inside the building, be sure to take a wander on the roof, which was designed to act as a living public space. The design obviously works, because locals love to sprawl out across it on sunny days to soak up the rays.

SEE IT ! *To explore the building's eye-catching interior, you'll have to join a guided tour or book a ticket for a performance.*

495 Kolmanskop

THE DIAMOND MINING TOWN ABANDONED TO THE DESERT

NAMIBIA // Nature will out in the end. At least that's the feeling you get at the deserted mining town of Kolmanskop. After a diamond was discovered in this southern Namibian spot in 1908, a settlement rapidly sprang up to service the hopeful prospectors. Built in Germanic style, Kolmanskop soon had a wealth of facilities, including a school, a hospital, a theatre, even a casino and skittle alley.

In just a few decades, however, the diamond field was exhausted; the town was finally abandoned in 1954. Now, the planet is slowly reclaiming its territory. Houses are sunken into dunes, and surges of apricot sand have snuck in through doorways and glassless windows, coating floorboards, swallowing furniture and banking up in paint-peeled corners. It's a granulated ghost town, left to be consumed by the rapacious Namib Desert. It's also creepy, made more so because you need permission to visit: Kolmanskop is within the vast Sperrgebiet 'prohibited area', off-limits since that first sparkler was found.

☛ **SEE IT !** *Kolmanskop is near the southern port of Lüderitz. It can only be visited on a pre-booked guided tour; tours run daily.*

496

Mutrah Souq

MAGICAL MUSLIM MARKETPLACE

OMAN // Never mind the gleaming shopping malls; Mutrah Souq is Muscat's favourite shopping spot, an Arabic bazaar that has been mobbed by traders since at least the 16th century. In its cool interior, the scent of frankincense wafts along narrow passageways lined with vendors touting the virtues of their wares, as they have since the days when Oman ruled the waves of the Indian Ocean. Locals call it the *Al Dhalam* (darkness) Souq because only rare shafts of natural light penetrate into its atmospheric alleyways.

In a region increasingly swapping tradition for the theme-park, megamall version, the Mutrah Souq offers a nostalgic glimpse of the old Arabia that people come to the Gulf hoping to see. To experience the souq at its best, just sit and sip a cup of Arabic coffee and watch locals come and go in their distinctive, embroidered *kumma* hats.

🡆 SEE IT ! *The entrance to the Mutrah Souq is right on the Corniche in Muscat, where dhows would once have unloaded their cargos.*

496

497

497

Rock of Cashel

ROCK OF AGES

IRELAND // One of the Emerald Isle's most spectacular archaeological sites, the 'Rock' rises from a grassy plain on the edge of the town of Cashel and bristles with ancient fortifications – the word 'cashel' is an anglicised version of the Irish word *caiseal*, which means 'fortress'. Sturdy walls circle an enclosure that contains a complete round tower, a 13th-century Gothic cathedral and the finest 12th-century Romanesque chapel in Ireland.

It was actually the Eóghanachta clan from across the Irish Sea in Wales who set the ball rolling on Cashel in the 4th century, forging their fiefdom on top of this grassy hummock, before ceding it to the O'Brien clan, who gifted the Rock to the church in order to keep it from falling back into Eóghanachta hands. Hordes gather here daily to connect with Ireland's history, both real and imagined, but the Rock still exudes a glorious, bleak magic that you'll remember far more readily than you will the crowds.

🡆 SEE IT ! *The Rock is a five-minute stroll from the centre of Cashel; follow Bishop's Walk from the gardens of the Cashel Palace Hotel.*

Erdene Zuu Khiid

Mongolian magic

↓

MONGOLIA // The oldest surviving Buddhist monastery in Mongolia, Erdene Zuu (Hundred Treasures) was founded in 1586 and much of what can be seen today dates back centuries, preserved through Communist purges by local Buddhists. It was only in 1990 that the monastery returned to active service, when religious freedom was restored in Mongolia. An English-speaking guide can tell the full story of its salvation. As you leave the suburbs of Kharkhorin, the *khiid* (monastery) appears as a line of white-washed stupas, backed by soaring steppes skies.

🕿 SEE IT ! *The khiid is a 2km walk from Kharkhorin.*

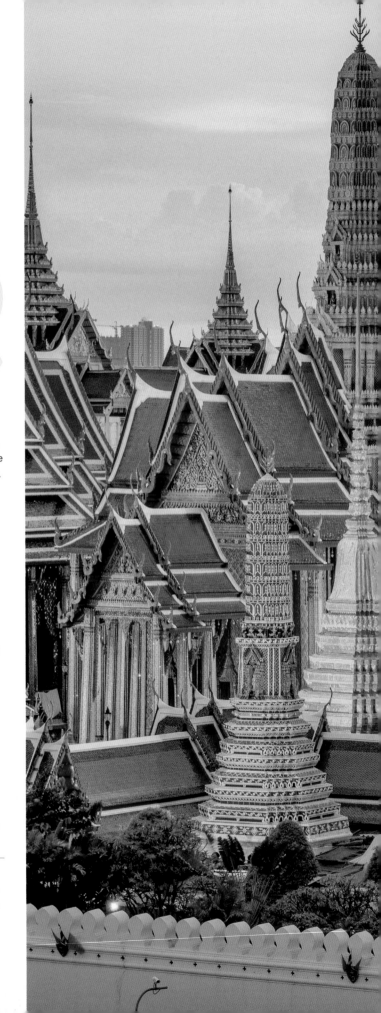

Grand Palace

499

HIGH WATTAGE PALACE!

THAILAND // Bangkok groans under the weight of gold at its shimmering wats and temples, but the Grand Palace, and the adjacent royal monastery at Wat Phra Kaew, raise the bar even higher. This vast, fairy-tale compound is the zenith of Thai architecture, dripping with gold trim, Buddha statues and mirrored mosaics. Such lavish ornamentation should not be entirely surprising – this was, after all, the former residence of the kings of Thailand – but combined with the stunning symmetry of the palace and wat, the effect is almost supernatural.

The buildings of the palace that are open to visitors today tell a wistful tale of dynasties and empires. The architects behind the royal digs were inspired by the grand houses of Europe, blending Italian Renaissance flourishes with traditional Thai motifs, yet the kings who inhabited this extravagant structure never surrendered to colonial powers, leaving the palace voluntarily when the Thai people voted to abolish the absolute monarchy in 1932.

For views of towering *chedis* (stupas) and *mon dòps* (ceremonial towers) rising over the rooftops of old Bangkok like a crystal garden, the palace is best approached from across the churning Chao Phraya river.

☛ SEE IT ! *The Palace is just south of Banglamphu; ride the Chao Phraya ferry to Tha Tien pier, and you can also visit Wat Po.*

500

Independence National Historic Park

Where the US began

↓

USA // You can't visit Philadelphia without paying homage to America's creation legend in this shady city park, dotted with buildings where the seeds of Revolutionary War were planted and the US government came into being. Many a patriot has become teary at the threshold of Independence Hall, where the Declaration of Independence was signed, or when gazing on the Liberty Bell. Costumed actors wander around, hoping to inspire a chorus of 'Oh say can you see...'

☛ **SEE IT !** *Ride the SEPTA subway train to 5th Street Station to begin your journey into American history.*

Index

A

Abu Dhabi
Sheikh Zayed Grand Mosque 225
Albania
Butrint 257
Algeria
Timgad 194
ancient cities
Ayuthaya (Thailand) 115
Baalbek (Lebanon) 246
Beit She'an (Israel) 228
Butrint (Albania) 257
Caracol (Belize) 266
Carthage (Tunisia) 171
Ephesus (Turkey) 129
Fatehpur Sikri (India) 239
Forbidden City (China) 99
Great Zimbabwe (Zimbabwe) 264
Karnak (Egypt) 155
Kilwa Kisiwani (Tanzania) 207
Lalibela (Ethiopia) 90
Machu Picchu (Peru) 16-17
Pafos Archaeological Site (Cyprus) 279
Persepolis (Iran) 240
Petra (Jordan) 30-31
Polonnaruwa (Sri Lanka) 250
Pompeii (Italy) 62
Sigiriya Rock (Sri Lanka) 156
Skara Brae (Scotland) 127
Tikal (Guatemala) 32-33
Timgad (Algeria) 194
ancient monuments
Acropolis (Greece) 48
Altun Ha (Belize) 274
Brú na Bóinne (Ireland) 174
Calakmul (Mexico) 221
Chichén Itzá (Mexico) 93
Choquequirao (Peru) 129
Colosseum (Italy) 22
Copán (Honduras) 252
Isla del Sol (Bolivia) 249
Luxor Temple (Egypt) 180
Nazca Lines (Peru) 274
Palenque (Mexico) 84-85
Pyramids of Giza (Egypt) 48
Pyramids of Teotihuacán (Mexico) 101
Stonehenge (England) 78
Tulum (Mexico) 131
Valley of the Kings (Egypt) 95
Wat Phou (Laos) 159
Antarctica
Ross Ice Shelf 206
Shackleton's Hut 143
architecture
Aya Sofya (Turkey) 26-27
Blue Mosque (Turkey) 135
Burj Khalifa (Dubai) 185
Chichén Itzá (Mexico) 93
Duomo Santa Maria di Fiore (Italy) 82
Empire State Building 112
Heydar Aliyev Centre (Azerbaijan) 268
Kizhi Pogost (Russia) 203
Lalibela (Ethiopia) 90
Mezquita, Cordoba (Spain) 89
Museum of Old & New Art (Australia) 40-41
Naqsh-e Jahan (Iran) 72
Oslo Opera House (Norway) 310

Pantheon (Italy) 71
Portmeirion (Wales) 166
Real Alcázar (Spain) 179
Reichstag (Germany) 172
Sagrada Familia (Spain) 35
Sydney Opera House (Australia) 74
Taj Mahal (India) 18
Temppeliaukio Kirkko (Finland) 220
Argentina
Cementerio de la Recoleta 274
Cerro Fitz Roy 118
Glaciar Perito Moreno 193
Iguazú Falls 23
La Boca district 267
Parque Nacional Nahuel Huapi 169
artists
Dalí, Salvador 241
Monet, Claude 300
Picasso, Pablo 247
Van Gogh, Vincent 156
Australia
12 Apostles 28-29
Blue Mountains National Park 163
Cradle Mountain 54
Great Barrier Reef 14-15
Kakadu National Park 74
Museum of Old & New Art 40-41
Ningaloo Marine Park 193
Port Arthur 272
Sydney Opera House 74
Uluru 55
Austria
Eisriesenwelt 279
Grossglockner Road 234
Melk Abbey 273
MuseumsQuartier 40, 232
Salzwelten 269
Azerbaijan
Heydar Aliyev Cultural Centre 268

B

Bangladesh
Old Dhaka 208
beaches
Anakena Beach (Chile) 116
Anse Vata (New Caledonia) 207
Bioluminescent Bays (Puerto Rico) 229
Bora Bora (French Polynesia) 112
D-Day Beaches (France) 233
Dead Sea (Jordan/Israel/Palestine) 210
Ipanema Beach (Brazil) 282-283
Ko Phi-Phi (Thailand) 202
Phu Quoc Island (Vietnam) 273
Tayrona National Park (Colombia) 128
Belgium
Brussels' Grand Place 148
Flanders Fields 302-303
Grand Place 51
Belize
Actun Tunichil Muknal Cave 136
Altun Ha 274
Blue Hole 258
Caracol 266
Glover's Reef 245
Bhutan
Punakha Dzong 244
bird-watching
Asa Wright Nature Centre (Trinidad & Tobago) 195

Danube Delta (Romania) 242
Bolivia
Isla del Sol 249
Salar de Uyuni 44-45
Bosnia-Herzegovina
Stari Most 114
Botswana
Central Kalahari Game Reserve 228
Chobe National Park 144, 145
Okavango Delta 107
Brazil
Cristo Redentor 146
Iguazú Falls 23
Ipanema Beach 282-283
Meeting of the Waters 245
Mt Roraima 290
Pantanal 125
Pão de Açúcar 88
Parque Nacional Dos Lençóis Maranhenses 250
Pelourinho 235
bridges
Acueducto, Segovia (Spain) 281
Charles Bridge, Prague (Czech Republic) 56-57
Golden Gate Bridge (USA) 108
Pol-e Khaju (Iran) 304
Pont du Gard (France) 179
Stari Most (Bosnia-Herzegovina) 114
Buddhist sites
Bagan (Myanmar) 46-47
Bodhnath Stupa (Nepal) 159
Borobudur (Indonesia) 182-183
Daibutsu (of Nara) (Japan) 125
Erdene Zuu Khiid (Mongolia) 313
Grand Buddha, Lèshān (China) 136
Jokhang Temple (Tibet) 230
Kinkaku-ji (Japan) 149
Lake Manasarovar (Tibet) 234
Shwedagon Paya (Myanmar) 100
Swayambhunath (Nepal) 264
Temple of the Tooth (Sri Lanka) 267
Tian Tan Buddha (China) 229
Wat Pho (Thailand) 226
Bulgaria
Rila Monastery 177

C

Cambodia
Angkor Wat 10-13
Tuol Sleng & the Killing Fields 264
Canada
Athabasca Glacier 194
Bay of Fundy 224
Burgess Shale 257
Glacier Skywalk 235
Grouse Mountain 300
Haida Gwaii 137
L'Anse aux Meadows 292
Moraine Lake 144
Niagara Falls 110
Québec City 171
canyons & gorges
Blyde River Canyon (South Africa) 240
Cañón del Colca (Peru) 305
Copper Canyon (Mexico) 118
Gorges du Verdon (France) 151
Grand Canyon (USA) 21-22
Tiger Leaping Gorge (China) 73
castles

Caernarfon Castle (Wales) 222
Château de Chenonceau (France) 191
Edinburgh Castle 74
Himeji Castle (Japan) 238
Karlštejn Castle (Czech Republic) 242
Luxembourg 299
Malbork Castle (Poland) 266
Prague Castle (Czech Republic) 148
Schloss Neuschwanstein (Germany) 141
Sintra (Portugal) 132
Spiš Castle (Slovakia) 306
Stirling Castle (Scotland) 277
Tower of London (England) 298
Trakai Castle (Lithuania) 294
Wawel Castle (Poland) 307

caves
Actun Tunichil Muknal Cave (Belize) 136
Eisriesenwelt (Austria) 279
Fingal's Cave (Scotland) 309
Grotte De Lascaux (France) 230
Mògāo Caves (China) 159
Phong Nha-Ke Bang National Park (Vietnam) 146
Postojna Cave (Slovenia) 177
Waitomo Caves (New Zealand) 202

Cayman Islands
Stingray City 307

cemeteries & mausoleums
Cementerio de la Recoleta (Argentina) 274
Cimetière Du Père Lachaise (France) 102
Flanders Fields (Belgium/France) 303
Hal Saflieni Hypogeum (Malta) 287
Taj Mahal (India) 18-19

Chile
Anakena Beach 116
Torres del Paine 60
Valle de la Luna 192

China
798 Art District 233
Bund 177
Confucius Temple 118
Forbidden City 99
Grand Buddha, Lèshān 136
Great Wall of China 18
Kashgar's Grand Bazaar 268
Lóngjī Rice Terraces 193
Mògāo Caves 159
Summer Palace 170
Terracotta Warriors 142
The Peak, Hong Kong 116
Tian Tan Buddha 229
Tiger Leaping Gorge 73

churches & cathedrals
Aya Sofya (Turkey) 26-27
Canterbury Cathedral (England) 171
Cathedral of Santiago de Compostela (Spain) 251
Churches of Tigray (Ethiopia) 309
Church of Sveti Jovan Bigorksi (Macedonia) 286
Church of the Holy Sepulchre (Israel) 188
Church on the Spilled Blood (Russia) 288
Cologne Cathedral (Germany) 211
Dome of the Rock (Israel) 98
Duomo Santa Maria di Fiore (Italy) 82
Lalibela (Ethiopia) 90
Melk Abbey (Austria) 273
Mezquita, Cordoba (Spain) 89
Milan's Duomo (Italy) 185
Notre Dame (France) 73
Pantheon (Italy) 71

Sagrada Familia (Spain) 35
St Davids Cathedral (Wales) 209
St Paul's Cathedral (England) 117
St Peter's Basilica (Italy) 97
Temppeliaukio Kirkko (Finland) 220
Tintern Abbey (Wales) 247
York Minster (England) 156

coastal scenery
12 Apostles (Australia) 28
Ao Phang-Nga (Thailand) 240
Bay of Fundy (Canada) 224
Bay of Islands (New Zealand) 124
Big Sur (USA) 103
Cape Cod National Seashore (USA) 225
Cinque Terre (Italy) 181
Cliffs of Moher (Ireland) 249
Halong Bay (Vietnam) 80-81
Skeleton Coast (Namibia) 276

Colombia
Cartagena Old Town 254-255
Museo Del Oro 232
Tayrona National Park 128

Costa Rica
Bosque Nuboso Monteverde 184
Parque Nacional Corcovado 110
Parque Nacional Manuel Antonio 184
Parque Nacional Tortuguero 214
Volcán Arenal 195

Croatia
Diocletian's Palace 248
Dubrovnik 43
Plitvice Lakes National Park 122

Cuba
Habana Vieja 63
Malecón 174
Valle de Viñales 140

Cyprus
Pafos Archaeological Site 279

Czech Republic
Charles Bridge, Prague 56-57
Karlštejn Castle 242
Old Town Square, Prague 64
Prague Castle 148
Sedlec Ossuary 238

deserts
Central Kalahari (Botswana) 228
Erg Chebbi Dunes (Morocco) 164
Khongoryn Els (Mongolia) 275
Parque Nacional Dos Lençóis Maranhenses (Brazil)
250
Sossusvlei (Namibia) 168
Valle de la Luna (Chile) 192
Wadi Rum (Jordan) 180

diving
Bacuit Archipelago (Philippines) 167
Bay Islands (Honduras) 300
Blue Hole (Belize) 258
Bora Bora (French Polynesia) 112
Great Barrier Reef (Australia) 14-15
Jellyfish Lake (Palau) 169
Ko Phi-Phi (Thailand) 202
Ko Tao (Thailand) 83
Pulau Sipadan (Malaysia) 209
Rainbow Reef (Fiji) 205
Silfra (Iceland) 186
Stingray City (Cayman Islands) 307

Underwater Sculpture Park (Grenada) 208
Dubai
Burj Khalifa 185

Ecuador
Galapagos Islands 39
Parque Nacional Cotopaxi 211

Egypt
Abu Simbel 102
Egyptian Museum 151
Karnak 155
Luxor Temple 180
Mt Sinai 88
Pyramids of Giza 48
Valley of the Kings 95

El Salvador
Ruta de las Flores 249

England
Avebury Stone Circle 265
British Museum 34
Canterbury Cathedral 171
Eden Project 203
Hadrian's Wall 261
Lake District National Park 59
Natural History Museum 181
Roman Baths, Bath 144
Stonehenge 78
St Paul's Cathedral 117
Tate Modern 71
Tower of London 298
York Minster 156

Estonia
Tallinn Old Town 114

Ethiopia
Churches of Tigray 309
Lalibela 90

Fiji
Lavena Coastal Walk 280
Rainbow Reef 205

Finland
Temppeliaukio Kirkko 220

fjords
Bay of Kotor (Montenegro) 67
Borgarfjörður Eystri (Iceland) 168
Fiordland (New Zealand) 36-37
Geirangerfjord (Norway) 128
Ilulissat Kangerlua (Greenland) 86-87
Seyðisfjörður (Iceland) 168

football
Camp Nou (Spain) 299
La Boca district (Argentina) 267

forests
Białowieża Forest (Poland) 233
Black Forest (Germany) 292
Bosque Nuboso Monteverde (Costa Rica) 184
Redwood National Park (USA) 92
Yakushima (Japan) 199

fortresses
Aït Benhaddou (Morocco) 238
Amber Fort (India) 152
Cape Coast (Ghana) 148
Carcassonne (France) 133
Dubrovnik (Croatia) 43
Elmina (Ghana) 148
Galle Fort (Sri Lanka) 261

Jaisalmer (India) 68-69
Kalemegdan (Serbia) 244
La Citadelle la Ferrière (Haiti) 187
Lahore Fort (Pakistan) 236
Nizwa Fort (Oman) 290
Rock of Cashel (Ireland) 312
France
Aiguille du Midi 118
Carcassonne 133
Château de Chenonceau 191
Château de Versailles 50
Cimetière du Père Lachaise 102
D-Day Beaches 233
Eiffel Tower 61
Flanders Fields 302-303
Gorges du Verdon 151
Grotte de Lascaux 230
Louvre 60
Monet's Garden 300
Mont Blanc 154
Mont St-Michel 162
Notre Dame 73
Pont du Gard 179
The Mighty Volcano 293
French Polynesia
Bora Bora 112
Mo'orea 236

G

Georgia
Davit Gareja 188
Tbilisi Old Town 158
geothermal areas
Blue Lagoon (Iceland) 101
Geysir (Iceland) 241
Rotorua (New Zealand) 77
Whakarewarewa (New Zealand) 199
Yakushima (Japan) 199
Yellowstone National Park (USA) 77
Germany
Berlin Wall 78
Black Forest 292
Brandenburg Gate 280
Cologne Cathedral 211
Reichstag 172
Schloss Neuschwanstein 141
Zwinger 276
Ghana
Cape Coast & Elmina 148
glaciers & icebergs
Aletsch Glacier (Switzerland) 306
Athabasca Glacier (Canada) 194
Fox Glacier & Franz Josef Glacier (New Zealand) 95
Glaciar Perito Moreno (Argentina) 193
Icehotel (Sweden) 143
Ilulissat Kangerlua (Greenland) 86-87
Jökulsárlón (Iceland) 76
Ross Ice Shelf (Antarctica) 206
Shackleton's Hut (Antarctica) 143
Vatnajökull National Park (Iceland) 134
Greece
Acropolis 48
Meteora 117
Rhodes Old Town 188
Santorini 38
Greenland
Ilulissat Kangerlua 86-87
Grenada

Underwater Sculpture Park 208
Guatemala
Lago de Atitlán 175
Tikal 32-33
Guyana
Mt Roraima 290

Haiti
La Citadelle la Ferrière 187
hiking & trekking
Abel Tasman National Park (New Zealand) 58
Ben Nevis (Scotland) 222
Borgarfjörður Eystri (Iceland) 168
Cerro Fitz Roy (Argentina) 118
Everest Base Camp (Nepal) 99
Fiordland National Park (New Zealand) 36
Gros Piton (St Lucia) 218
Kilimanjaro (Tanzania) 210
Lake District National Park (England) 59
Lavena Coastal Walk (Fiji) 280
Mont Blanc (France) 154
Mt Kenya (Kenya) 293
Mt Kinabalu (Malayasia) 145
Snowdonia (Wales) 152
Torres del Paine (Chile) 60
Yakushima (Japan) 199
Hindu sites
Dashashwamedh Ghat (India) 108
Meenakshi Amman Temple (India) 157
Mt Kailash (Tibet) 204
Temples of Angkor (Cambodia) 10
Virupaksha Temple (India) 173
Wat Phou (Laos) 159
Honduras
Bay Islands 300
Copán 252
hot springs, baths & spas
Blue Lagoon (Iceland) 101
Budapest's Thermal Baths 113
Pamukkale (Turkey) 248
Sanduny Baths (Russia) 304
Hungary
Budapest's Thermal Baths 113
Memento Park 199

I

Iceland
Blue Lagoon 101
Borgarfjörður Eystri 168
Geysir 241
Gullfoss 150
Jökulsárlón 76
Seyðisfjörður 168
Silfra 186
Snæfellsnes 237
Vatnajökull National Park 134
India
Amber Fort 152
Dashashwamedh Ghat 108
Fatehpur Sikri 239
Golden Temple 227
Jaisalmer 68-69
Meenakshi Amman Temple 157
Old Delhi 181
Taj Mahal 18-19
Thiksey Monastery 259
Virupaksha Temple 173

Indonesia
Borobudur 182-183
Gunung Leuser National Park 175
Komodo National Park 251
Iran
Naqsh-e Jahan 72
Persepolis 240
Pol-e Khaju 304
Ireland
Brú na Bóinne 174
Cliffs of Moher 249
Rock of Cashel 312
Trinity College 298
islands
Archipiélago de San Blas (Panama) 289
Bacuit Archipelago (Philippines) 167
Bay Islands (Honduras) 300
Bay of Islands (New Zealand) 124
Bazaruto Archipelago (Mozambique) 122
Bora Bora (French Polynesia) 112
Capri (Italy) 215
Galapagos Islands (Ecuador) 39
Glover's Reef (Belize) 245
Halong Bay (Vietnam) 80-81
Iona (Scotland) 277
Isla del Sol (Bolivia) 249
Isla de Ometepe (Nicaragua) 225
Isla Mujeres (Mexico) 309
Island of Gorée (Senegal) 162
Isle of Skye 79
Ko Phi-Phi (Thailand) 202
Ko Tao (Thailand) 83
Mont St-Michel (France) 162
Mo'orea (French Polynesia) 236
Mozambique Island (Mozambique) 164
Phu Quoc Island (Vietnam) 273
Reed islands (Peru) 224
Si Phan Don (Laos) 287
Stewart Island (New Zealand) 121
Israel
Beit She'an 228
Church of the Holy Sepulchre 188
Dead Sea 210
Dome of the Rock 98
Makhtesh Ramon 229
Sea of Galilee 285
Italy
Capri 215
Cinque Terre 181
Colosseum 22
Duomo Santa Maria di Fiore 82
Leaning Tower of Pisa 309
Milan's Duomo 185
Mt Etna 138
Pantheon 71
Piazza del Campo 176
Piazza San Marco 48
Pompeii 62
San Gimignano 165
St Peter's Basilica 97
Uffizi 99
Vatican Museums 116

J

Japan
Arashiyama's Bamboo Grove 91
Daibutsu (Great Buddha) of Nara 125
Gion District 136

Himeji Castle 238
Hiroshima Peace Memorial Park 70
Itsukushima-Jinja Gate 190
Kinkaku-ji 149
Kōya-san 138
Mt Fuji 292
Naoshima 186
Shibuya Crossing 140
Tōshō-gū Shrine 248
Tsukiji Market 131
Yakushima 199

Jordan
Dead Sea 210
Petra 30-31
Wadi Rum 180

K

Kenya
Amboseli National Park 280
Masai Mara National Reserve 93
Mt Kenya 293

L

lakes, rivers & canals
Danube Delta (Romania) 242
Dashashwamedh Ghat (India) 108
Inle Lake (Myanmar) 145
Jökulsárlón (Iceland) 76
Lago de Atitlán (Guatemala) 175
Lake Baikal (Russia) 61
Lake Bled (Slovenia) 91
Lake District National Park (England) 59
Lake Geneva (Switzerland) 216
Lake Malawi (Tanzania) 241
Lake Manasarovar (Tibet) 234
Lake Wanaka (New Zealand) 101
Loch Lomond (Scotland) 257
Lower Zambezi (Zambia) 219
Meeting of the Waters (Brazil) 245
Moraine Lake (Canada) 144
Okavango Delta (Botswana) 107
Panama Canal (Panama) 299
Prinsengracht Canal (Netherlands) 122
Salar de Uyuni (Bolivia) 44-45
Sea of Galilee (Israel) 285
Xochimilco (Mexico) 154

Laos
Si Phan Don 287
Wat Phou 159

Lebanon
Baalbek 246

Lithuania
Hill of Crosses 253
Trakai Castle 294

Luxembourg
Capital Castles 299

M

Macedonia
Church of Sveti Jovan Bigorksi 286

Madagascar
Parc National d'Andringitra 215

Malaysia
Petronas Towers 220
Pulau Sipadan 209
Mt Kinabalu 145

Mali
Djenné Mosque 185

Malta
Hal Saflieni Hypogeum 287

markets & bazaars
Chatuchak Market (Thailand) 214
Kashgar's Grand Bazaar (China) 268
Mutrah Souq (Oman) 312
Tsukiji Market (Japan) 131

memorials
Auschwitz-Birkenau (Poland) 109
Flanders Fields (Belgium/France) 302-303
Hill of Crosses (Lithuania) 253
Hiroshima Peace Memorial Park (Japan) 70
Kigali Memorial Centre (Rwanda) 230
Lincoln Memorial (USA) 190
National September 11 Museum & Memorial (USA) 192
Taj Mahal (India) 18
Tuol Sleng Genocide Museum & the Killing Fields (Cambodia) 264

Mexico
Calakmul 221
Chichén Itzá 93
Copper Canyon 118
Isla Mujeres 309
Palenque 84-85
Pyramids of Teotihuacán 101
Tulum 131
Xochimilco 154
Zócalo 51
Zócalo, Mexico City 278

Moldova
Orheiul Vechi 309

Monaco
Casino de Monte Carlo 30, 235
Musée Océanographique de Monaco 309

monasteries & missions
Bucovina Monasteries (Romania) 291
Davit Gareja (Georgia) 188
Erdene Zuu Khiid (Mongolia) 313
Jesuit missions of Trinidad and Jesus (Paraguay) 250
Kōya-san (Japan) 138
Kyevo-Pecherska Lavra (Ukraine) 289
Meteora (Greece) 117
Mosteiro Dos Jerónimos (Portugal) 247
Orheiul Vechi (Moldova) 309
Ostrog Monastery (Montenegro) 285
Potala Palace (Tibet) 111
Punakha Dzong (Bhutan) 244
Rila Monastery (Bulgaria) 177
Sedlec Ossuary (Czech Republic) 238
Thiksey Monastery (India) 259

Mongolia
Erdene Zuu Khiid 313
Khongoryn Els 275

Montenegro
Bay of Kotor 67
Ostrog Monastery 285

monuments
Brandenburg Gate (Germany) 280
Eiffel Tower (France) 61
Leaning Tower of Pisa (Italy) 309
National Mall (USA) 146
Statue of Liberty (USA) 134

Morocco
Aït Benhaddou 238
Djemaa El-Fna 51
Erg Chebbi Dunes 164
Fès el-Bali 28
Majorelle Garden 228

mosques
Aya Sofya (Turkey) 26-27
Blue Mosque (Turkey) 135
Djenné Mosque (Mali) 185
Dome of the Rock (Israel) 98
Kalon Minaret (Uzbekistan) 294
Mezquita, Cordoba (Spain) 89
Sheikh Zayed Grand Mosque (Abu Dhabi) 225

mountains
Aiguille du Midi (France) 118
Ben Nevis (Scotland) 222
Cradle Mountain (Australia) 54
Eiger (Switzerland) 138
Everest Base Camp (Nepal) 99
Glencoe (Scotland) 154
Kilimanjaro (Tanzania) 210
Matterhorn (Switzerland) 103
Mt Ararat (Turkey) 306
Mt Kailash (Tibet) 204
Mt Kenya (Kenya) 293
Mt Kinabalu (Malaysia) 145
Mt McKinley/Denali (USA) 194
Mt Roraima (Venezuela/ Brazil/Guyana) 290
Mt Rushmore (USA) 256
Mt Sinai (Egypt) 88
Pão de Açúcar (Brazil) 88
Schilthorn (Switzerland) 295
Table Mountain (South Africa) 64
Tajik National Park (Tajikistan) 186

movie & TV locations
Dubrovnik (Croatia) 43
Griffith Observatory (USA) 297
Matmata (Tunisia) 30, 284
Monte Carlo 30
Portmeirion (Wales) 30

Mozambique
Bazaruto Archipelago 122
Mozambique Island 164

museums & galleries
798 Art District (China) 233
Anne Frank Huis (Netherlands) 74
Art Institute of Chicago (USA) 217
Bardo National Museum (Tunisia) 268
British Museum (England) 34
Egyptian Museum (Egypt) 151
Graceland (USA) 301
Hermitage 66
Heydar Aliyev Cultural Centre (Azerbaijan) 268
Kelvingrove Art Gallery & Museum (Scotland) 252
Louisiana Museum of Modern Art (USA) 219
Louvre (France) 60
Metropolitan Museum of Art (USA) 94
Museo Del Oro (Colombia) 232
Museo del Prado (Spain) 174
Museo Guggenheim (Spain) 223
Museum of Old & New Art (Australia) 40-41
MuseumsQuartier (Austria) 40, 232
Museu Picasso (Spain) 247
Naoshima (Japan) 186
National Museum of Anthropology 126
National Palace Museum (Taiwan) 260
Natural History Museum (England) 181
Rijksmuseum (Netherlands) 178
St Fagans National History Museum (Wales) 279
Tate Modern (England) 71
Teatre-Museu Dalí (Spain) 241
Te Papa Tongarewa (New Zealand) 206
Titanic Belfast (Northern Ireland) 276

Tuol Sleng Genocide Museum & the Killing Fields
(Cambodia) 264
　Uffizi 99
　Underwater Sculpture Park (Grenada) 208
　Van Gogh Museum (Netherlands) 156
　Vatican Museums (Vatican City) 116
　Vigelandsparken (Norway) 170
　Wieliczka Salt Mine (Poland) 169
Myanmar
　Bagan 46-47
　Inle Lake 145
　Shwedagon Paya 100

N

Namibia
　Etosha National Park 270-271
　Kolmanskop 311
　Skeleton Coast 276
　Sossusvlei 168
national parks
　Abel Tasman (New Zealand) 58
　Amboseli (Kenya) 280
　Blue Mountains (Australia) 163
　Brecon Beacons (Wales) 244
　Bwindi Impenetrable (Uganda) 186
　Carpathian National Nature Park (Ukraine) 281
　Chitwan (Nepal) 222
　Chobe (Botswana) 144, 145
　Death Valley (USA) 200-201
　Etosha (Namibia) 270-271
　Everglades (USA) 284
　Fiordland (New Zealand) 36-37
　Grand Canyon (USA) 21
　Gunung Leuser (Indonesia) 175
　Kakadu (Australia) 74
　Khao Sok (Thailand) 269
　Komodo (Indonesia) 251
　Lake District (England) 59
　Lower Zambezi (Zambia) 219
　Murchison Falls (Uganda) 221
　Nyungwe Forest (Rwanda) 278
　Andringitra (Madagascar) 215
　Corcovado (Costa Rica) 110
　Cotopaxi (Ecuador) 211
　Lençóis Maranhenses (Brazil) 250
　Manuel Antonio (Costa Rica) 184
　Nahuel Huapi (Argentina) 169
　Tortuguero (Costa Rica) 214
　Viñale (Cuba) 140
　Phong Nha-Ke Bang (Vietnam) 146
　Picos de Europa (Spain) 196
　Plitvice Lakes (Croatia) 122
　Redwood (USA) 92
　Rocky Mountain (USA) 151
　Serengeti (Tanzania) 65
　Snowdonia (Wales) 152
　South Luangwa (Zambia) 191
　Tajik (Tajikistan) 186
　Tayrona (Colombia) 128
　Vatnajökull (Iceland) 134
　Volcanoes (Rwanda) 153
　Yellowstone (USA) 77
　Yosemite (USA) 42
Nepal
　Bodhnath Stupa 159
　Chitwan National Park 222
　Durbar Square 122
　Everest Base Camp 99

　Swayambhunath 264
Netherlands
　Anne Frank Huis 74
　Kinderdijk Windmills 286
　Prinsengracht Canal 122
　Rijksmuseum 178
　Van Gogh Museum 156
New Caledonia
　Anse Vata 207
New Zealand
　Abel Tasman National Park 58
　Bay of Islands 124
　Fiordland National Park 36-37
　Franz Josef & Fox Glacier 95
　Lake Wanaka 101
　Rotorua 77
　Stewart Island 121
　Te Papa Tongarewa 206
　Waitomo Caves 202
　Whakarewarewa 199
Nicaragua
　Isla de Ometepe 225
Northern Ireland
　Giant's Causeway 109
　Titanic Belfast 276
North Korea
　DMZ 158
　Mansudae Grand Monument 269
Norway
　Bryggen 120
　Geirangerfjord 128
　Oslo Opera House 310
　Pulpit Rock 224
　Vigelandsparken 170

O

'Old Town' districts
　Bairro of Ribeira (Portugal) 137
　Bryggen (Norway) 120
　Cartagena Old Town (Colombia) 254-55
　Gamla Stan (Sweden) 104
　Gion District, Kyoto (Japan) 136
　Habana Vieja (Cuba) 63
　Hanoi (Vietnam) 52-53
　Hoi An Old Town (Vietnam) 96
　La Boca district (Argentina) 267
　Lisbon's Alfama (Portugal) 231
　Old Delhi (India) 181
　Old Dhaka (Bangladesh) 208
　Pelourinho (Brazil) 235
　Québec City (Canada) 171
　Rhodes Old Town (Greece) 188
　Royal Mile (Scotland) 146
　Tallinn Old Town (Estonia) 114
　Tbilisi Old Town (Georgia) 158
Oman
　Mutrah Souq 312
　Nizwa Fort 290
　Ras al-Jinz 207

P

Pakistan
　Lahore Fort 236
palaces
　Alhambra (Spain) 25
　Amber Fort (India) 152
　Changdeokgung Palace (South Korea) 158
　Château de Chenonceau (France) 191

　Château de Versailles (France) 50
　Diocletian's Palace (Croatia) 248
　Grand Palace (Thailand) 314-315
　İshak Paşa Palace (Turkey) 236
　Real Alcázar (Spain) 179
　Summer Palace (China) 170
　Topkapi Palace (Turkey) 114
　Tsarskoe Selo (Russia) 256
　Zwinger (Germany) 276
Palau
　Jellyfish Lake 169
Palestine
　Dead Sea 210
Panama
　Archipiélago de San Blas 289
　Panama Canal 299
Paraguay
　Jesuit missions of Trinidad and Jesus 250
parks & gardens
　Eden Project (England) 203
　Gardens by the Bay (Singapore) 155
　Independence National Historic Park (USA) 316
　Majorelle Garden (Morocco) 228
　Monet's Garden (France) 300
Peru
　Cañón del Colca 305
　Choquequirao 129
　Machu Picchu 16-17
　Nazca Lines 274
　Reed islands 224
Philippines
　Bacuit Archipelago 167
　Ifugao (Banaue) Rice Terraces 281
piazzas & squares
　Djemaa El-Fna (Morocco) 51
　Durbar Square (Nepal) 122
　Grand Place (Brussels) 148
　Naqsh-e Jahan (Iran) 72
　Old Town Square, Prague (Czech Republic) 64
　Piazza del Campo (Italy) 176
　Piazza San Marco (Italy) 48
　Plaza Mayor (Trinidad & Tobago) 51, 301
　Red Square (Russia) 98
　Registan (Uzbekistan) 189
　Rynek Główny (Poland) 159
　Times Square (USA) 166
　Zócalo, Mexico City (Mexico) 278
pilgrimage sites
　Cathedral, Santiago de Compostela (Spain) 251
　Dashashwamedh Ghat (India) 108
　Lake Manasarovar (Tibet) 234
　Mont St-Michel (France) 162
Poland
　Auschwitz-Birkenau 109
　Białowieża Forest 233
　Malbork Castle 266
　Rynek Główny 159
　Wawel Castle 307
　Wieliczka Salt Mine 169
　Wolf's Lair 253
Portugal
　Bairro of Ribeira 137
　Lisbon's Alfama 231
　Mosteiro Dos Jerónimos 247
　Sintra 132
prisons
　Alcatraz (USA) 175
　Auschwitz-Birkenau (Poland) 109

Robben Island (South Africa) 168
Tuol Sleng Genocide Museum & the Killing Fields (Cambodia) 264

promenades
Bund (China) 177
Malecón (Cuba) 174

Puerto Rico
Bioluminescent Bays 229

reefs
Glover's Reef (Belize) 245
Great Barrier Reef (Australia) 14-15
Ningaloo Marine Park (Australia) 193
Rainbow Reef (Fiji) 205

rice terraces
Ifugao (Banaue) (Philippines) 281
Lóngjī (China) 193

rock-climbing
Ben Nevis (Scotland) 222
Cerro Fitz Roy (Argentina) 118
Eiger (Switzerland) 138
Matterhorn (Switzerland) 103
Mont Blanc (France) 154
Yosemite National Park (USA) 42

rock formations
12 Apostles (Australia) 28-29
Aiguille du Midi (France) 118
Cappadocia (Turkey) 83
Drakensburg Amphitheatre (South Africa) 211
Giant's Causeway 109
Makhtesh Ramon (Israel) 229
Monument Valley (USA) 97
Pulpit Rock (Norway) 224
Sigiriya Rock (Sri Lanka) 156
Uluru (Australia) 55
Yosemite National Park (USA) 42

Roman civilisation
Acueducto, Segovia (Spain) 281
Baalbek (Lebanon) 246
Bardo National Museum (Tunisia) 268
Beit She'an (Israel) 228
Colosseum (Italy) 22
Diocletian's Palace (Croatia) 248
El-Jem (Tunisia) 295
Hadrian's Wall (England) 261
Pantheon (Italy) 71
Pompeii (Italy) 62
Roman Baths, Bath (England) 144
Timgad (Algeria) 194

Romania
Bucovina Monasteries 291
Danube Delta 242

Russia
Church on the Spilled Blood 288
Hermitage 66
Kizhi Pogost 203
Lake Baikal 61
Red Square 98
Sanduny Baths 304
Tsarskoe Selo 256

Rwanda
Kigali Memorial Centre 230
Nyungwe Forest National Park 278
Volcanoes National Park 153

salt lakes & mines

Salar de Uyuni (Bolivia) 44-45
Salzwelten (Austria) 269
Wieliczka Salt Mine (Poland) 169

Samoa
To Sua Ocean Trench 301

scenic journeys
Blue Ridge Parkway (USA) 243
Grossglockner Road (Austria) 234
Jungfraujoch (Switzerland) 272
Ruta de las Flores (El Salvador) 249

Scotland
Ben Nevis 222
Edinburgh Castle 74
Fingal's Cave 309
Glencoe 154
Iona 277
Isle of Skye 79
Kelvingrove Art Gallery & Museum 252
Loch Lomond 257
Royal Mile 146
Skara Brae 127
Standing Stones of Callanish 265
Stirling Castle 277

Senegal
Island of Gorée 162

Serbia
Kalemegdan 244

ships
Titanic Belfast (Northern Ireland) 276
Vasamuseet (Sweden) 166

Singapore
Gardens by the Bay 155
Singapore Zoo 179

Slovakia
Spiš Castle 306

Slovenia
Lake Bled 91
Postojna Cave 177

South Africa
Blyde River Canyon 240
Drakensberg Amphitheatre 211
iSimangaliso Wetland Park 155
Kruger National Park 130
Robben Island 168
Table Mountain 64

South Korea
Changdeokgung Palace 158
DMZ 158
N Seoul Tower 234

Spain
Acueducto, Segovia 281
Alhambra 25
Camp Nou 299
Cathedral, Santiago de Compostela 251
Mezquita, Cordoba 89
Museo del Prado 174
Museo Guggenheim 223
Museu Picasso 247
Picos de Europa National Park 196-197
Real Alcázar 179
Sagrada Familia 35
Teatre-Museu Dalí 241

Sri Lanka
Galle Fort 261
Horton Plains & World's End 290
Polonnaruwa 250
Sigiriya Rock 156
Temple of the Tooth 267

statues
Cristo Redentor (Brazil) 146
Daibutsu of Nara (Japan) 125
Grand Buddha, Lèshān (China) 136
Mansudae Grand Monument (North Korea) 269
Memento Park (Hungary) 199
Mt Rushmore (USA) 256
Tian Tan Buddha (China) 229
Wat Pho (Thailand) 226

St Lucia
Gros Piton 218

stone circles
Avebury Stone Circle (England) 265
Standing Stones of Callanish (Scotland) 265
Stonehenge (England) 78

Sweden
Foteviken Viking Reserve 307
Gamla Stan 104
Icehotel 143
Vasamuseet 166

Switzerland
Aletsch Glacier 306
Eiger 138
Jungfraujoch 272
Lake Geneva 216
Matterhorn 103
Schilthorn 295

Taiwan
National Palace Museum 260
Taipei 101 287

Tajikistan
Tajik National Park 186

Tanzania
Kilimanjaro 210
Kilwa Kisiwani 207
Lake Malawi 241
Ngorongoro Crater 70
Selous Game Reserve 195
Serengeti National Park 65

temples & shrines
Abu Simbel (Egypt) 102
Altun Ha (Belize) 274
Angkor Wat (Cambodia) 10-13
Bagan (Myanmar) 13, 47
Borobudur (Indonesia) 182-183
Confucius Temple (China) 118
Golden Temple (India) 227
Itsukushima-Jinja Gate (Japan) 190
Jokhang Temple (Tibet) 230
Kinkaku-ji (Japan) 149
Luxor Temple (Egypt) 180
Meenakshi Amman Temple (India) 157
Shwedagon Paya (Myanmar) 100
Swayambhunath (Nepal) 264
Temple of the Tooth (Sri Lanka) 267
Tōshō-gū Shrine (Japan) 248
Virupaksha Temple (India) 173
Wat Pho (Thailand) 226
Wat Phou (Laos) 159

Thailand
Ao Phang-Nga 240
Ayuthaya 115
Chatuchak Weekend Market 214
Grand Palace 314-315
Khao Sok National Park 269
Ko Phi-Phi 202

Ko Tao 83
Wat Pho 47, 226
Tibet
Jokhang Temple 230
Lake Manasarovar 234
Mt Kailash 204
Potala Palace 111
Trinidad & Tobago
Asa Wright Nature Centre 195
Plaza Mayor 51, 301
Tunisia
Bardo National Museum 268
Carthage 171
El-Jem 295
Matmata 284
Turkey
Aya Sofya 26-27
Blue Mosque 135
Cappadocia 83
Ephesus 129
Gallipoli Cemeteries 187
İshak Paşa Palace 236
Mt Ararat 306
Pamukkale 248
Topkapi Palace 114

u

Uganda
Bwindi Impenetrable National Park 186
Murchison Falls 221
Ukraine
Carpathian National Nature Park 281
Chernobyl 139
Kyevo-Pecherska Lavra 289
USA
Alcatraz 175
Art Institute of Chicago 217
Big Sur 103
Blue Ridge Parkway 243
Cape Cod National Seashore 225
Death Valley National Park 200-201
Ellis Island 134
Empire State Building 112
Everglades National Park 284
Golden Gate Bridge 108
Graceland 301
Grand Canyon 20-21
Griffith Observatory 296-297
Independence National Historic Park 316
Lincoln Memorial 190
Louisiana Museum of Modern Art 219
Metropolitan Museum of Art 94
Monument Valley 97
Mt McKinley (Denali) 194
Mt Rushmore 256
National Mall 146
National September 11 Memorial 18
National September 11 Museum & Memorial 192
Redwood National Park 92
Rocky Mountain National Park 151
Statue of Liberty 134
Times Square 166
Walt Disney World 139
Yellowstone National Park 77
Yosemite National Park 42
Uzbekistan
Kalon Minaret 294
Registan 189

V

Venezuela
Angel Falls 198
Mt Roraima 290
Vietnam
Cu Chi Tunnels 216
Halong Bay 80-81
Hanoi 52-53
Hoi An Old Town 96
Phong Nha-Ke Bang National Park 146
Phu Quoc Island 273
viewpoints & lookouts
Burj Khalifa (Dubai) 185
Cristo Redentor (Brazil) 146
Eiffel Tower (France) 61
Empire State Building (USA) 112
Glacier Skywalk (Canada) 235
Griffith Observatory (USA) 296-297
Grouse Mountain (Canada) 300
Jungfraujoch (Switzerland) 272
N Seoul Tower (South Korea) 234
Petronas Towers (Malaysia) 220
Pulpit Rock (Norway) 224
Schilthorn (Switzerland) 295
Taipei 101 (Taiwan) 287
The Peak, Hong Kong (China) 116
volcanoes
Isla de Ometepe (Nicaragua) 225
Mt Etna (Italy) 138
Mt Fuji (Japan) 292
Ngorongoro Crater (Tanzania) 70
Parque Nacional Cotopaxi (Ecuador) 211
Snæfellsnes (Iceland) 237
The Mighty Volcano-Piton de la Fournaise (Reunion Island, France) 293
Volcán Arenal (Costa Rica) 195

W

Wales
Brecon Beacons 244
Caernarfon Castle 222
Portmeirion 166
Snowdonia 152
St Davids Cathedral 209
St Fagans National History Museum 279
Tintern Abbey 247
waterfalls
Angel Falls (Venezuela) 198
Gullfoss (Iceland) 150
Iguazú Falls (Brazil/Argentina) 23
Murchison Falls (Uganda) 221
Niagara Falls (Canada) 110
Victoria Falls (Zambia/Zimbabwe) 48
wildlife-watching
Amboseli National Park (Kenya) 280
Asa Wright Nature Centre (Trinidad & Tobago) 195
Bazaruto Archipelago (Mozambique) 122
Białowieża Forest (Poland) 233
Bioluminescent Bays (Puerto Rico) 229
Bwindi Impenetrable National Park (Uganda) 186
Chitwan National Park (Nepal) 222
Chobe National Park (Botswana) 144, 145
Etosha National Park (Namibia) 270
Galapagos Islands (Ecuador) 39
Great Barrier Reef (Australia) 14-15
Gunung Leuser National Park (Indonesia) 175
iSimangaliso Wetland Park (South Africa) 155

Jellyfish Lake (Palau) 169
Khao Sok National Park (Thailand) 269
Komodo National Park (Indonesia) 251
Kruger National Park (South Africa) 130
Lower Zambezi National Park (Zambia) 219
Masai Mara National Reserve (Kenya) 93
Murchison Falls (Uganda) 221
Ngorongoro Crater (Tanzania) 70
Ningaloo Marine Park (Australia) 193
Nyungwe Forest National Park (Rwanda) 278
Okavango Delta (Botswana) 107
Pantanal (Brazil) 125
Parque Nacional Corcovado (Costa Rica) 110
Parque Nacional Tortuguero (Costa Rica) 214
Ras al-Jinz (Oman) 207
Rocky Mountain National Park (USA) 151
Selous Game Reserve (Tanzania) 195
Serengeti National Park (Tanzania) 65
Singapore Zoo (Singapore) 179
Socotra Island (Yemen) 208
South Luangwa National Park (Zambia) 191
Stewart Island (New Zealand) 121
Volcanoes National Park (Rwanda) 153
WWI
Flanders Fields (Belgium/France) 302-303
Gallipoli Cemeteries 187
WWII
Anne Frank Huis (Netherlands) 74
Auschwitz-Birkenau (Poland) 109
D-Day Beaches (France) 233
Hiroshima Peace Memorial Park (Japan) 70
Wolf's Lair (Poland) 253

Y

Yemen
Socotra Island 208

Z

Zambia
Lower Zambezi National Park 219
South Luangwa National Park 191
Victoria Falls 48
Zimbabwe
Great Zimbabwe 264
Victoria Falls 48
zoos & aquariums
Musée Océanographique de Monaco (Monaco) 309
Singapore Zoo (Singapore) 179

Image credits

p11 Mark Read; p12 Mark Read; p13 (L) Mark Read; p13 (R) Mark Read; p14 Andrew Watson/Getty Images; p16 Philip Lee Harvey; p17 Philip Lee Harvey; p19 Pete Seaward; p19 Pete Seaward; p19 Pete Seaward; p20 John & Lisa Merrill/Getty Images; p22 Justin Foulkes; p23 Matt Munro; p24 Pete Seaward; p26 Mark Read; p27 Matt Munro; p29 DrRave/Getty Images; p30 (L) Tom Mackie; p30 (R) Mark Read; p31 Tom Mackie; p32 Justin Foulkes; p34 Matt Munro; p35 Matt Munro; p36 Philip Lee Harvey; p37 Pete Seaward; p38 Justin Foulkes; p39 Jürgen Ritterbach/4Corners; p40 Mona/Remi Chauvin Image courtesy of Mona; p42 Mark Read; p42 Mark Read; p43 Mark Read; p44 Onfokus/Getty Images; p46 Matt Munro; p47 Matt Munro; p49 Mark Read; p50 Pete Seaward; p51 (T) Gary Yeowell/Getty Images; p51 (B) Michael Heffernan; p52Matt Munro; p53 Jordan Banks/4Corners; p54 Rob Blakers/Getty Images; p55 Paul Sinclair/Getty Images; p56 Mark Read; p58 Christian Kober/Getty Images; p59 Justin Foulkes; p60 (L) Michele Falzone/Getty Images; p60 (R)Pawel Libera/Getty Images; p61 (L) Philip Lee Harvey; p61 (R) Julian Elliott Photography/Getty Images; p62 (L) Buena Vista Images/Getty Images; p62 (R) Guido Cozzi/Corbis;p63 Mark Williamson Stock Photography/Getty Images; p64(L) Jon Cunningham/Getty Images; p64 (R) Henk Badenhorst/Getty Images; p65 Joseph Van Os/Getty Images; p66 Amos Chapple/Getty Images; p67 (T) Alan Copson/Getty Images; p67 (B) o-che/Getty Images; p68 Michele Falzone/Getty Images; p69 Juergen Ritterbach/Getty Images; p70 Ariadne Van Zandbergen/Getty Images; p70 Benoist Sébire/Getty Images; p71 Justin Foulkes; p71 shomos uddin/Getty Images; p72 Izzet Keribar/Getty Images; p73 Matt Munro; p75 Pete Seaward; p76 Dave Moorhouse/Getty Images; p77 Matt Munro; p77 Matt Munro; p78 (L) Image Source/Getty Images; p78 (R) Philip Kramer/Getty Images; p79 James Ross/Getty Images; p80 Matt Munro; p82 Justin Foulkes; p83 (L) Matt Munro; p83 (R) Mark Read; p85 Justin Foulkes; p86 Grant Dixon/Getty Images; p88 Philipp Chistyakov/Getty; p89 Matteo Colombo/Getty Images; p90 Philip Lee Harvey; p91 LesleyGooding/Getty Images; p91 MistikaS/Getty Images; p92 Chad Ehlers/Getty Images; p93 (R) Oliver J Davis Photography/Getty Images; p93 (R) narvikk/Getty Images; p94 David Zimmerman/Getty Images; p95 (L) Bo Tornvig/Getty Images; p95 (R) Rory McDonald/Getty Images; p96 Ian Trower/Getty Images; p97 (L) Ash-Photography/ www.flickr.com/photos/ashleeigh/Getty Images; p97 (R) Lola L. Falantes/Getty Images; p98 (L) Daniel Zelazo/Getty Images; p98 (R) Les and Dave Jacobs/Getty Images; p99 Whitworth Images/Getty Images; p100 Luigi Vaccarella/SIME/4Corners; p101 Tuul and Bruno Morandi/Getty Images; p102 Bruno De Hogues/Getty Images; p103 (L) Susanne Kremer/4Corners; p103 (R) Jorg Greuel/Getty Images; p104 Marco Brivio/Getty Images; p107 Buena Vista Images/Getty Images; p108 Hakbong Kwon/Alamy; p109 joe daniel price/Getty Images; p110 Hiroyuki Matsumoto/Getty Images; p111 CHRIS LEWINGTON/Alamy; p112 (L) Daniel Schoenen/Corbis; p112 (R) Image Source/Getty Images; p113 Will Sanders; p114 Matt Munro; p115 Nicholas Reuss/Getty Images; p116 Justin Foulkes/Getty; p117 (L) Jon Bower at Apexphotos/Getty Images; p117 (R) Jaana Eleftheriou/Getty Images; p119 Glenn Van Der Knijff/Getty Images; p120 Justin Foulkes; p121 Life on white/Alamy; p123 Mark Read; p124 Mark Read; p125 (L) ZUMA Press, Inc /Alamy; p125 (R) Mint Images - Frans Lanting/Getty Images; p126 Christian Kober/Getty Images; p127 Bernard van Dierendonck/Getty Images; p128 (L) JS/Corbis; p128 (R) Justin Foulkes; p129 Danita Delimont/Getty Images; p130 Gallo Images-Heinrich van den Berg/Getty Images; p131 Peter Adams/Getty Images; p132 Shaun Egan/Getty Images; p133 MONTICO Lionel/Hemis.fr/Getty Images; p134 (T) Merten Snijders/Getty Images; p134 (B) Danita Delimont/Getty Images; p135 Matt Munro; p136 Andrew Rich/Getty Images; p137 G&M Therin-Weise/Getty Images; p138 Jorg Greuel/Getty Images; p139 (L) Akash Banerjee Photography/Getty Images; p139 (R) AF archive/Alamy; p140 Lottie Davies; p140 Mark Read; p141 Andrew Montgomery; p142 Grant Faint/Getty Images; p143 (T) Painting by Sir Wally Herbert – Robert Harding Picture Library Ltd/Alamy; p143 (B) Lars Thulin/Getty Images; p144 Basic Elements Photography/Getty Images; p145 Mint Images/Art Wolfe/Getty Images; p147 Michael Heffernan; p148 Jorg Greuel/Getty Images; p149 Allan Baxter/Corbis; p150 Frans Lemmens/Getty Images; p151 Adrian Assalve/Getty Images; p152 (T) Matt Munro; p152 (B) Guy Edwardes/Getty Images; p153 Danita Delimont/Getty Images; p154 (L) Chris Hepburn/Getty Images; p154 (R) Mike Kemp Images/Getty Images; p155 John Harper/Getty Images; p156 A Photo By Bhagiraj Sivagnanasundaram/Getty Images; p157 Niels van Gijn/Getty Images; p158 Keren Su/Getty Images; p159 Heather Elton/Design Pics/Getty Images; p162 LEMAIRE Stephane/hemis.fr/Getty Images; p163 Peter Walton Photography/Getty Images; p164 Sune Wendelboe/Getty Images; p165 Ken Scicluna/Getty Images; p166 keith morris/Alamy; p167 Michael Runkel/Getty Images; p168 Gigja Einarsdottir/Getty Images; p169 Ethan Daniels/Getty Images; p170 (L) Paul Thompson/Getty Images; p170 (R) Matteo Colombo/Getty Images; p171 De Agostini/S.Vannini/Getty Images; p172 Thomas Kurmeier/Getty Images; p173 imageBROKER/Alamy; p174 Mark Read; p175 Anup Shah/Getty Images; p176 Giovanni Simeone/SIME/4Corners; p177 Religious Images/UIG/Getty Images; p178 Mark Read; p179 Image Source/Getty Images; p180 Tom Mackie; p181 Justin Foulkes; p182 Filippo Maria Bianchi/Getty Images; p184 Mint Images - Frans Lanting/Getty Images; p185 Timothy Allen/Getty Images; p187 (L) Doug Allan/Getty Images; p187 (R) John Miles/Getty Images; p187 (B) Nature Picture Library/Alamy; p188 Guy Corbishley/Getty Images; p189 SEUX Paule/hemis.fr/Getty Images; p190 (L) Image Source/Getty Images; p190 (R) DAJ/Getty Images; p191 Danita Delimont/Getty Images; p192 Walter Bibikow/Getty Images; p193 Keren Su/Getty Images; p194 Daniel A. Leifheit/Getty Images; p195 Judy Bellah/Getty Images; p196 Matt Munro; p196 Matt Munro; p197 Matt Munro; p198 Rowan Castle/Getty Images; p199 Richard I'Anson/Getty Images; p201 Mark Read; p202 (L) Chris McLennan/Alamy; p202 (R) Catherine Sutherland; p203 (L) Holger Leue/Getty Images; p203 (R) Fergus Kennedy/Getty Images; p204 Feng Wei Photography/Getty Images; p205 Casey Mahaney/Getty; p206 (L) Courtesy of Te Papa Museum; p206 (R) Hulton-Deutsch Collection/Corbis; p207 Paul Joynson Hicks/Getty Images; p208 Pacific Press/Getty Images; p209 (L) Leemage/Getty Images; p209 (R) Reinhard Dirscherl/Getty Images; p210 (L) Simon Tonge/Getty Images; p210 (R) Andrew Peacock/Getty Images; p211 Allan Baxter/Getty Images; p214 Oliver Strewe/Getty Images; p215 (L) Arnt Haug/Getty Images; p215 (R) Robert Harding World Imagery/Alamy; p216 Steve Raymer/Corbis; p217 Dan Welldon; p218 Justin Foulkes; p219 Bjarke Ørsted courtesy of Louisiana Museum of Modern Art; p220 Stephen Saks Photography/Alamy; p221 Balan Madhavan/Getty Images; p222 VisitBritain/Britain on View/Getty Images; p223 © FMGB Guggenheim Bilbao Museoa, London 2015, Mark Mawson/Getty Images; p224 BarrettÊ&ÊMacKay/Getty; p225 Betty Wiley/Getty Images; p226 Matt Munro; p227 Matt Munro; p228 Maremagnum/Getty Images; p229 Charlie Kwan/Getty Images; p230 Buena Vista Images/Getty Images; p231 Jose Manuel Azcona/Getty; p232 (T) Alfredo Maiquez/Getty Images; p232 (B) Yadid Levy/Getty Images; p233 Slow Images/Getty Images; p234 Moritz Attenberger/Look-foto/Corbis; p235 Gonzalo Azumendi/Getty; p236 David Hiser/Getty Images; p237 David Noton; p238 Visions Of Our Land/Getty Images; p239 epics.ca/Getty Images; p240 Heinrich van den Berg/Getty Images; p241 Bernard van Dierendonck/LOOK-foto/Getty; p242 (L) Profimedia.CZ a.s./Alamy; p242 (R) Stelian Porojnicu/Alamy; p243 Jim McKinley/Getty Images; p244 Jonathan Gregson; p245 National Geographic Image Collection/Alamy; p246 Slow Images/Getty Images; p247 Pictorial Press Ltd/Alamy; p248 Julian Ward/Getty Images; p249 Michael Taylor/Getty Images; p250 Zé Martinusso/Getty; p251 Barry Kusuma/Getty Images; p251 Matt Munro; p252 Jose Cabezas/Getty Images; p252 AFP/Getty; p253 Simon Butterworth/Getty Images; p253 Paul Biris/Getty Images; p254 (T) AlfredoMaiquez/Getty Images; p254 (B) Jane Sweeney/Getty Images; p255 Enzo Figueres/Getty Images; p256 (R) Katie Garrod/Getty Images; p256 (L) Richard Cummins/Getty Images; p257 Alan Majchrowicz/Getty Images; p258 Greg Johnston/Getty Images; p259 Hugh Sitton/Corbis; p260 Craig Ferguson/Getty Images; p261 Age Fotostock/Alamy; p261 Clearview/Alamy; p264 Paul Biris/Getty Images; p265 Lizzie Shepherd/Getty Images; p266 Keren Su/Getty Images; p266 Manfred Mehlig/Corbis; p267 ESCUDERO Patrick/hemis.fr/Getty Images; p268 Jane Sweeney/Getty Images; p269 Alex Hare/Getty Images; p270 Johann van Heerden/Getty Images; p272 (L) Sean Savery Photography/Getty Images; p272 (R) Danita Delimont/Getty Images; p273 (L) Bruno De Hogues/Getty Images; p273 (R) Danita Delimont/Getty Images; p274 Andrew Hounslea/Getty Images; p275 Jenny Jones/Getty Images; p276 Andrew Michael/Getty Images; p277 (L) Stephen Dorey/Getty Images; p277 (R) Sean Caffrey/Getty Images; p278 (B) Chris Cheadle/Getty Images; p278 (T) Peter Stuckings/Getty Images; p279 Paul Biris/Getty Images; p280 (L) Ulana Switucha/Alamy; p280 (R) Anthony Asael/Corbis; p281 Sergiy Trofimov Photography/Getty Images; p282 Michael Heffernan; p283 Ingo Rösler/Getty; p284 (L) Luis Castaneda Inc./Getty Images; p284 (R) Cultura Travel/Philip Lee Harvey/Getty Images; p285 Martin Lehmann/Alamy; p286 (L) frans lemmens/Alamy; p286 (R) Danita Delimont/Getty; p287 Craig Ferguson/Getty Images; p288 ArtMarie/Getty Images; p289 (L) HUGHES Herve/hemis.fr/Getty Images; p289 (R) Tibor Bognar/Alamy; p290 adalbertop photography/Getty Images; p291 ralucahphotography.ro/Getty Images; p292 Stefano Politi Markovina/Getty Images; p293 (T) Philippe Bourseiller/Getty Images; p293 (B) Design Pics/Keith Levit/Getty Images; p294 Keven Osborne/Fox Fotos/Getty Images; p294 De Agostini/C. Sappa/Getty Images; p295 (L) Education Images/UIG/Getty Images; p295 (R) Doug Pearson/Getty Images; p296 Eddie Brady/Getty Images; p298 (L) Raquel Lonas/Getty Images – 'Blood Swept Lands and Seas of Red' – poppies and original concept created by artist Paul Cummins and installation designed by Tom Piper at HM Tower of London, (R) Andrew Montgomery; p299 Khaled Kassem/Alamy; p300 Danita Delimont/Getty Images; p301 Maria Pavlova/Getty Images; p302 Philip Game/Alamy; p304 Andrea Thompson Photography/Getty Images; p305 Cultura Travel/Ben Pipe Photography/Getty Images; p306 Cornelia Doerr/Getty Images; p307 Fotograferen.net/Alamy; p308 Philip Lee Harvey; p310 Ivan Brodey/Getty Images; p311 Andy Nixon/Getty Images; p312 (L) Trish Punch/Getty Images; p312 (R) David South/Alamy; p313 Christophe Boisvieux/Corbis; p314 thebang/Getty Images; p316 Anna Serrano/SIME/4Corners

First Edition
Published in August 2015
by Lonely Planet Global Limited
ABN 36 005 607 983
www.lonelyplanet.com
ISBN 978 1 7436 0747 3
© Lonely Planet 2015
Printed in China
10 9 8 7

Managing Director, Publishing Piers Pickard
Associate Publisher Robin Barton
Art Direction Daniel Di Paolo
Editors Karyn Noble, Ross Taylor, Nick Mee
Cover Illustrations Jacob Rhoades
Cartographers Corey Hutchinson, Wayne Murphy
Pre-press Production Tag Publishing
Print Production Larissa Frost, Nigel Longuet

Thanks to Ryan Evans, Mazzy Prinsep, Barbara di Castro

Written by: Andrew Bain, Anthony Ham, Emily Matchar, James Smart, Jessica Cole, Jessica Lee, Joe Bindloss, Joshua Samuel Brown, Karla Zimmerman, Karyn Noble, Kate Morgan, Lee Slater, Lorna Parkes, Luke Waterson, Mara Vorhees, Matt Phillips, Nick Ray, Nicola Williams, Oliver Smith, Pat Kinsella, Robin Barton, Sarah Baxter, Sarah Reid, Tamara Sheward, Tom Hall, Will Gourlay

All rights reserved. No part of this publication may be reproduced, stored in a retrieval system or transmitted in any form by any means, electronic, mechanical, photocopying, recording or otherwise except brief extracts for the purpose of review, without the written permission of the publisher. Lonely Planet and the Lonely Planet logo are trademarks of Lonely Planet and are registered in the US patent and Trademark Office and in other countries.

Lonely Planet offices

AUSTRALIA
The Malt Store, Level 3, 551 Swanston Street, Carlton Victoria 3053 Phone 03 8379 8000

IRELAND
Unit E, Digital Court, The Digital Hub, Rainsford St, Dublin 8

USA
124 Linden St, Oakland, CA 94607 Phone 510 250 6400

UNITED KINGDOM
240 Blackfriars Road, London SE1 8NW Phone 020 3771 5100

STAY IN TOUCH
lonelyplanet.com/contact

Although the authors and Lonely Planet have taken all reasonable care in preparing this book, we make no warranty about the accuracy or completeness of its content and, to the maximum extent permitted, disclaim all liability from its use.

MIX
Paper from responsible sources
FSC™ C021741
www.fsc.org

Paper in this book is certified against the Forest Stewardship Council™ standards. FSC™ promotes environmentally responsible, socially beneficial and economically viable management of the world's forests.